An Overheated World

Although economic, cultural and demographic changes are part and parcel of the modern world, changes in a number of areas have accelerated in the last quarter-century – a period sometimes spoken of as the global information society, a world of 'liquid modernity' – or of fully fledged global neoliberalism associated with deregulation, flexible accumulation and financialisation.

At a global level, some of the substantial areas where change has accelerated are, apart from the spectacular spread of new information technology, tourism, foreign direct investment, urbanisation, resource extraction through mining, energy use, species extinction, displacement, and international trade. These and other changes are, needless to say, perceived and acted upon differently in different countries and localities, and in order to understand the implications of the present acceleration of history, they have to be explored locally.

This book gives a compelling perspective on the contemporary, 'overheated' world, presenting ethnographic material from many countries and weaving the local and particular together with large-scale global acceleration. This book was first published as a special issue of *History and Anthropology*.

Thomas Hylland Eriksen is a Professor of Social Anthropology at the University of Oslo and was PI of the ERC AdvGR project 'Overheating' (2012–2017).

An Overheated World
An Anthropological History of the Early Twenty-first Century

Edited by
Thomas Hylland Eriksen

LONDON AND NEW YORK

First published 2018
by Routledge
2 Park Square, Milton Park, Abingdon, Oxon, OX14 4RN, UK

and by Routledge
711 Third Avenue, New York, NY 10017, USA

Routledge is an imprint of the Taylor & Francis Group, an informa business

Chapters 1–8 © 2018 Taylor & Francis
Chapter 9 © Chris Hann, originally published as Open Access

All rights reserved. No part of this book may be reprinted or reproduced or utilised in any form or by any electronic, mechanical, or other means, now known or hereafter invented, including photocopying and recording, or in any information storage or retrieval system, without permission in writing from the publishers.

Trademark notice: Product or corporate names may be trademarks or registered trademarks, and are used only for identification and explanation without intent to infringe.

British Library Cataloguing in Publication Data
A catalogue record for this book is available from the British Library

ISBN 13: 978-1-138-74222-2

Typeset in MyriadPro
by diacriTech, Chennai

Publisher's Note
The publisher accepts responsibility for any inconsistencies that may have arisen during the conversion of this book from journal articles to book chapters, namely the possible inclusion of journal terminology.

Disclaimer
Every effort has been made to contact copyright holders for their permission to reprint material in this book. The publishers would be grateful to hear from any copyright holder who is not here acknowledged and will undertake to rectify any errors or omissions in future editions of this book.

Contents

Citation Information   vii
Notes on Contributors   ix

1   Overheating: the world since 1991   1
      Thomas Hylland Eriksen

2   Building a city: Korean capitalists and navy nostalgia in "overheated" Subic Bay   20
      Elisabeth Schober

3   Mining, expectations and turbulent times: locating accelerated change in rural Sierra Leone   36
      Robert J. Pijpers

4   Temporalities, time and the everyday: new technology as a marker of change in an Estonian mine   53
      Eeva Keskülä

5   The refugee crisis: destabilizing and restabilizing European borders   68
      Synnøve K. N. Bendixsen

6   From coal to Ukip: the struggle over identity in post-industrial Doncaster   87
      Cathrine Thorleifsson

7   Dreams of growth and fear of water crisis: the ambivalence of "progress" in the Majes-Siguas Irrigation Project, Peru   101
      Astrid B. Stensrud

8   Creating and dissolving social groups from New Guinea to New York: on the overheating of bounded corporate entities in contemporary global capitalism   117
      Adam Leaver and Keir Martin

CONTENTS

9   Overheated Underdogs: Civilizational Analysis and Migration on the Danube-Tisza Interfluve   134
Chris Hann

Index   149

Citation Information

The chapters in this book were originally published in *History and Anthropology*, volume 27, issue 5 (December 2016). When citing this material, please use the original page numbering for each article, as follows:

Chapter 1
Overheating: the world since 1991
Thomas Hylland Eriksen
History and Anthropology, volume 27, issue 5 (December 2016) pp. 469–487

Chapter 2
Building a city: Korean capitalists and navy nostalgia in "overheated" Subic Bay
Elisabeth Schober
History and Anthropology, volume 27, issue 5 (December 2016) pp. 488–503

Chapter 3
Mining, expectations and turbulent times: locating accelerated change in rural Sierra Leone
Robert J. Pijpers
History and Anthropology, volume 27, issue 5 (December 2016) pp. 504–520

Chapter 4
Temporalities, time and the everyday: new technology as a marker of change in an Estonian mine
Eeva Keskülä
History and Anthropology, volume 27, issue 5 (December 2016) pp. 521–535

Chapter 5
The refugee crisis: destabilizing and restabilizing European borders
Synnøve K. N. Bendixsen
History and Anthropology, volume 27, issue 5 (December 2016) pp. 536–554

Chapter 6
From coal to Ukip: the struggle over identity in post-industrial Doncaster
Cathrine Thorleifsson
History and Anthropology, volume 27, issue 5 (December 2016) pp. 555–568

CITATION INFORMATION

Chapter 7
Dreams of growth and fear of water crisis: the ambivalence of "progress" in the Majes-Siguas Irrigation Project, Peru
Astrid B. Stensrud
History and Anthropology, volume 27, issue 5 (December 2016) pp. 569–584

Chapter 8
Creating and dissolving social groups from New Guinea to New York: on the overheating of bounded corporate entities in contemporary global capitalism
Adam Leaver and Keir Martin
History and Anthropology, volume 27, issue 5 (December 2016) pp. 585–601

Chapter 9
Overheated Underdogs: Civilizational Analysis and Migration on the Danube-Tisza Interfluve
Chris Hann
History and Anthropology, volume 27, issue 5 (December 2016) pp. 602–616

For any permission-related enquiries please visit:
http://www.tandfonline.com/page/help/permissions

Notes on Contributors

Synnøve K. N. Bendixsen is a postdoctoral fellow at the Department of Social Anthropology, University of Bergen, Norway.

Thomas Hylland Eriksen is an anthropologist and writer based at the Department of Social Anthropology, University of Oslo, Norway.

Chris Hann is Director and Scientific Member at the Max Planck Institute for Social Anthropology, Germany.

Eeva Keskülä is a senior researcher at the School of Humanities, Tallinn University, Estonia.

Adam Leaver is a Professor in Financialization and Business at the Alliance Manchester Business School, UK.

Keir Martin is an Associate Professor at the Department of Social Anthropology, University of Oslo, Norway.

Robert J. Pijpers is a PhD fellow at the Department of Social Anthropology, University of Oslo, Norway.

Elisabeth Schober is an Associate Professor at the Department of Social Anthropology, University of Oslo, Norway.

Astrid B. Stensrud is a postdoctoral fellow at the Sosialantropologisk institutt (SAI), University of Oslo, Norway.

Cathrine Thorleifsson is a researcher at the Department of Social Anthropology, University of Oslo, Norway.

Overheating: the world since 1991

Thomas Hylland Eriksen

ABSTRACT
This special issue, which includes articles on Sierra Leone, Peru, Estonia, Hungary, Norway, the Philippines, Britain and Melanesia, presents some of the salient features of the accelerated post-1991 world. We emphasize the importance of comparison for theoretical development in anthropology and the relevance of contemporary history for anthropological research on globalization. We also demonstrate the importance of taking ethnography seriously in research on globalization. This article outlines the origins and central features of the post-Cold War world, showing the significance of shifting between global, transnational, national and local perspectives in order to understand the processes of change affecting communities in all parts of the world. This article also introduces the overheating approach to globalization [Eriksen, Thomas Hylland. 2016. *Overheating: An Anthropology of Accelerated Change*. London: Pluto], indicating ways in which new forms of connectedness and acceleration can shed new light on phenomena such as neo-liberalism, identity politics and climate change.

The contemporary world is … too full? Too intense? Too fast? Too hot? Too unequal? Too neo-liberal? Too strongly dominated by humans?[1]

All of the above, and more. Ours is a world of high-speed modernity where change hardly needs to be explained by social scientists; what comes across as noteworthy are rather eddies, pockets and billabongs of calm and continuity. Modernity entails in itself change, but for decades, change was synonymous with progress, and the standard hegemonic narrative about the recent past was one of improvement and development. Things seemed to be getting better for some, many or even most humans, and seen from the vantage point of the North Atlantic world, history seemed to move in a direction, whether one of linear, cumulative progress (the mainstream, or bourgeois, view) or one of rupture and revolution leading to higher stages of development (Marxism).

In the last few decades, the belief in progress has been dampened. Modernity and enlightenment did not, in the end, eradicate atavistic ideologies, sectarian violence and fanaticism, but sometimes seemed to encourage them. Wars continued to break out. Inequality and poverty did not go away, but were exacerbated in the era of global neoliberalism. Recurrent crises with global repercussions forced economists to concede, reluctantly, that theirs was not a precise science after all. Although many countries were democratic in name, a growing number of people felt that highly consequential changes were taking place in their lives and immediate surroundings without their having been consulted beforehand. Significantly, the forces of progress turned out to be a double-edged sword. What seemed to have been the salvation of humanity for 200 years, namely inexpensive and accessible energy based on fossil fuels, was about to become our damnation through environmental destruction and climate change. At the same time, accelerated change continued in a number of interrelated domains. It was as if modernity, always committed to change, had shifted to a higher gear and increased the pace of change in the economy, with implications for the environment, mobility and collective identities. These accelerated changes, which form a premise for this special issue, can be captured conceptually by the term *overheating* (Eriksen 2015a, 2016). In physics, speed and heat are two sides of the same coin. As a metaphor, overheating thus refers to the kind of speed that will eventually lead a car engine to grind to a halt, spewing out black smoke in copious quantities, unless the style of driving changes.

It is chiefly in the sense of loss of the faith in linear progress that it is meaningful to talk of the present time as being postmodern. The old recipes for societal improvement, whether socialist, liberal or conservative, have lost their lustre. The political left, historically based on demands for social justice and material improvements, is now confronted with a double challenge in the shape of multiculturalism and climate change, and creating a consistent synthesis of the three is not an easy task. Generally speaking, in complex systems, the unintended consequences are often more conspicuous than the planned outcomes of a course of action (see Tainter 2014 for a historical perspective on societal collapse).

Contradictions of globalization

It is only in the last couple of decades that the term "globalization" has entered into common usage, and it may be argued that capitalism, globally hegemonic since the nineteenth century, is now becoming universal in the sense that scarcely any human group now lives independently of a monetized economy. Traditional forms of land tenure are being replaced by private ownership, subsistence agriculture is being phased out in favour of wagework, TV and Internet replace orally transmitted tales, and since 2007, UN estimates suggest that more than half the world's population lives in urban areas (predicted to rise to 70% by 2050). The state, likewise, enters into people's lives almost everywhere, though to different degrees and in different ways.

It is an interconnected world, but not a smoothly and seamlessly integrated one. Rights, duties, opportunities and constraints continue to be unevenly distributed, and the capitalist world system itself is fundamentally volatile and contradiction-ridden, as indicated by its recurrent crises, which are rarely predicted by experts. One fundamental contradiction consists in the conflicts between the universalizing forces of global modernity and the desire for autonomy in local communities. The drive to standardization, simplification and universalization is usually countered by a defence of local values, practices and relationships. In other words, globalization does not lead to global homogeneity, but highlights a tension, typical of modernity, between the system world and the life world, between the standardized and the unique, the universal and the particular.

AN OVERHEATED WORLD

At a higher level of abstraction, the tension between economic development and environmental sustainability is also a chronic one, and it constitutes the most fundamental double-bind of twenty-first century capitalism. Trade-offs between economic growth and ecology have become an integral element in economies. There is a broad global consensus among policy-makers and researchers that the global climate is changing irreversibly due to human activity (mostly the use of fossil fuels). However, other environmental problems are also extremely serious, ranging from air pollution in cities in the Global South to the depletion of phosphorus (a key ingredient in chemical fertilizer), overfishing and erosion. Yet, the same policy-makers who express concern about environmental problems also advocate continued economic growth, which so far has hinged on the growing utilization of fossil fuels and other non-renewable resources, thereby contradicting another fundamental value and contributing to undermining the conditions for its own continued existence.

This globally interconnected world may be described through its tendency to generate chronic crises, being complex in such a way as to be ungovernable, volatile and replete with unintended consequences – there are double binds, there is an uneven pace of change, and an unstable relationship between universalizing and localizing processes.

The overheating perspective is an attempt to make sense of these transformations. It represents a critical anthropological perspective on the contemporary world, insisting on the primacy of the local and studying global processes as being inherently contradictory. We also hope to make a contribution to a transdisciplinary history of the early twenty-first century with a basis in ethnography. We argue that it would be misleading to start a story about the contemporary world by looking at the big picture – for example, the proportion of the world's population that is below the UN poverty limit; the number of species driven to extinction in the last half-century; the number of Internet users in India and Venezuela – unless these abstract figures are related to locally constructed worlds. It stands to reason that 7% economic growth in, say, Ethiopia does not automatically mean that Ethiopians are on the whole 7% better off than they were last year (whatever *that* means); yet, those who celebrate abstract statistical figures depicting economic growth often fail to look at the fine meshwork behind the numbers. They remain at an abstract level of scale, which is not where life takes place. Similarly, the signing of an international agreement on climate change, which took place in Paris in December 2015, does not automatically lead to practices which mitigate climate change. So while trying to weave the big picture and connecting the dots, the credibility of the anthropological story about globalization depends on its ability to show how global processes interact with local lives, in ways which are both similar and different across the planet.

A hegemonic discourse about globalization can easily be identified. Typically, it tends to privilege flows over structures, rhizomes over roots, reflexivity over doxa, individual over group, flexibility over fixity, rights over duties and freedom over security in its bid to highlight globalization as something qualitatively new and more or less uniform. Anthropologists may respond by speaking about the jargon of "globalbabble" or "globalitarism" (Trouillot 2001), and tend to react against simplistic generalizations by reinserting (and reasserting) the uniqueness of the local, or the glocal.

There is doubtless something qualitatively new about the compass, speed and reach of current transnational networks. Some globalization theorists argue that the shrinking of the world will almost inevitably lead to a new value orientation, some indeed heralding the coming of a new, postmodern kind of person (e.g. Sennett 1998). These writers, who predict the emergence of a new set of uprooted, deterritorialized values and fragmented identities, are often accused of generalizing from their own North Atlantic middle-class habitus, the "class consciousness of frequent travellers" in the words of Calhoun (2002). The sociologist John Urry, who may be seen as a target for this criticism, argued in the following year (2003) that globalization has the potential of stimulating widespread cosmopolitanism – however, he does not say among whom. At the same time, Urry readily admits that the principles of closeness and distance still hold in many contexts, for example, in viewing patterns on television, where a global trend consists in viewers' preferences for locally produced programmes.

The newness of the contemporary world was described by Castells in 1998, in his trilogy *The Information Society*, where – after offering a smorgasbord of new phenomena, from real-time global financial markets to the spread of human rights ideas – he remarks, in a footnote tucked away towards the end of the third and final volume, that what is new and what is not does not really matter; his point is that "this is our world, and therefore we should study it" (Castells 1998, 336). However much I appreciate Castells' analysis, I disagree with his cavalier dismissal of the importance of recent change. It does matter what is new and what is not, if we are going to make sense of the contemporary world. Different parts of societies, cultures and life-worlds change at different speeds and reproduce themselves at different rhythms, and it is necessary to understand the disjunctures between speed and slowness, change and continuity in order to grasp the conflicts arising from accelerated globalization.

This is a story of contemporary neo-liberal global capitalism and the global information society, a story about the world after the bipolar deadlock of the Cold War: the rise of information technologies enabling fast, cheap and ubiquitous global communication in real time, the demise of "the Second World" of state socialism, the hegemony of neo-liberal economics, the rise of China as an economic world power, the heightened political tensions, often violent, around religion (often Islam, but also other religions), the growing concern for the planet's ecological future in the political mainstream, and the development of a sprawling, but vocal "alterglobalization movement" growing out of discontent with the neo-liberal world order – all these recent and current developments indicate that this is indeed a new world, markedly different from that twentieth century which, according to an influential way of reckoning (*pace* Hobsbawm 1994), began with the First World War and the Russian Revolution, and ended with the formal dissolution of the Soviet Union in 1991.

The idea that there was a uniform "Cold War" and similarly, that it was succeeded by a "post-Cold War" world, has been challenged, and rightly so, by several anthropologists in recent years. In *The Other Cold War*, Kwon (2010) shows that the repercussions and lasting effects of the bipolar world of the Cold War are perceptible and consequential in large parts of the Global South (and North), and that decolonization, ensuing violence and the forging of new political alliances even today must be connected to, and complicate the standard picture of, the recent history of the Cold War. In an essay about the intellectual legacies of Cold War thinking and of postcolonialism, Chari and Verdery (2009) argue that it is necessary to "liberate the Cold War from the ghetto of Societ area studies and postcolonial thought from the ghetto of Third World and colonial studies" (Chari and Verdery 2009, 29) in order to develop a comparative global anthropology mindful of the major differences in local circumstances, effects and responses to world history in the late twentieth century, including decolonization and the "postcolonial turn", the Cold War and its aftermath. Like others before them, they advocate a research agenda and an intellectual conversation which includes, as equal partners, voices from outside the hegemonic centres; what is original about their bid is the ambition to relate postsocialist thought directly to postcolonial thought, thereby filling gaps and offering alternative, critical perspectives on the interconnected, contemporary world.

The acceleration of history since 1991

Unlike what some liberal optimists believed as the Berlin wall came down, history did not end, in a pseudo-Hegelian way, as a result. Quite the contrary, it accelerated (Hann 1994), but without a clear direction.

As noted, there once existed a hegemonic narrative about the way in which the modern world had grown. It was a story about enlightenment and inventions, conquest and subsequent decolonization, progress and welfare. The story existed in loyal and critical varieties; it could be narrated in liberal, conservative, socialist or communist versions. More recently, the story of progress lost its lustre, not with a bang, but with a whimper. As of today, there is no story about where we are coming from and where we are going with general appeal in most, or even any, part of the world. Perhaps changes are taking place too fast – it has been said that people belonging to the global middle class today experience seventeen times as much as their great-grandparents, but without an improved apparatus for digesting and understanding their experiences. Or perhaps the side effects of progress have simply become too noticeable. We have at our disposal lucid stories about the transition from hunting and gathering to agriculture and on to the industrial revolution. Naturally, they are contested by feminists, postcolonials, Marxists, poststructuralists and many others, and they are continuously being rewritten, but the template is there. No similar story exists about the emergence of the global information society and where it is headed. Or, rather, if at all considered, future prospects appear to be bleak, based on what the sociologist Furedi (2002) calls "a culture of fear".

As a date for the transition from modernity to postmodernity, I propose 1991, which was a momentous year in the history of the contemporary. First, 1991 was the year in which the Cold War ended in its original form. The two-bloc system that had defined the postwar period was gone. The ideological conflict between capitalism and socialism finally seemed to have been replaced by the triumphant sound of one hand clapping. In the same year, the Indian economy was massively deregulated by Rajiv Gandhi's government. By 1991, it was also clear that apartheid was about to be relegated to the dustbin of history. Mandela had been released from prison the year before, and negotiations between the Nationalist Party and the ANC had begun in earnest. The future of the entire world (notwithstanding a few stubborn outliers like Cuba and North Korea) seemed to consist in a version of global neo-liberalism, that is a virulent and aggressive form of deregulating capitalism where the main role of the state consisted in ensuring the functioning of so-called free markets. However, it soon became clear that neo-liberalism did not deliver the goods. Social inequalities continued to exist, and in some countries, like the USA, they grew enormously. Countries in the Global South did not develop along the predicted lines, that is roughly in the same way as the countries of the Global North.

Commentators as diverse as the economist Joseph Stiglitz (2002), the investor George Soros (2002) and the social philosopher John Gray (1998), former supporters of the neo-liberal paradigm, wrote scathing critiques of the deregulated global economy. At the same time, politicized religion and other forms of identity politics flourished from India to Israel, from Belfast to Brunei, contrary to predictions that education and modernity would weaken such forms of political identity, which were often divisive and reactionary in character. The war in Yugoslavia and the Rwandan genocide, both unfolding in the mid-1990s, were reminders that an identity based on notions of kinship and descent did not belong to the past, but remained crucial for millions, and could erupt in horrible ways at any time. The year 1991 was also at the height of the Salman Rushdie affair. Rushdie's novel *The Satanic Verses* had been published in 1988, denounced as blasphemous by powerful Muslim clerics, and the author had been sentenced to death *in absentia* by Iranian clergy. The affair was a tangible reminder of a new kind of interconnectedness, where local or domestic acts can have instant global ramifications. A couple of years later, the European Union (EU) was formally established, as a successor to the European Economic Community. The ambitious goals of the EU led to the destabilization of borders through the instigation of complex political and economic arrangements with important consequences for its satellite states as well (Green 2013). As a result, the borders of and in Europe became more permeable, negotiable and fuzzy than before.

Around the same time, mobile telephones and Internet began to spread epidemically in the global middle classes, eventually trickling down to the poor as well. A certain kind of flexibility grew: you could soon work anywhere and any time, but these technologies contributed to fragmentation as well; what flexibility was gained with respect to space seemed to be lost regarding time. Life began to stand still at a frightful speed. Your gaze was now fixed at a point roughly one minute ahead. This spelled bad news for the slow, cumulative temporality of growth and development (Eriksen 2001; Morozov 2012).

A similar kind of flexibility began to affect labour and business, and it was not the kind of flexibility that offers alternative paths for action, but one which created insecurity and uncertainty. Companies that used to distinguish between short-term and long-term planning ceased to do so, since everything now seemed to be short term; nobody knew what the world might look like in five or ten years' time. To workers, the most perceptible change is basic insecurity. One of the most widely used new concepts in the post-millennial social sciences (along with the Anthropocene and neo-liberalism) is *the precariat* (Standing 2011), and there are good reasons for its sudden popularity. The precariat consists of the millions of employees whose jobs are short term and temporary, and who, accordingly, have no clue as to whether they will have work next year or even next month. This "new dangerous class", as the economist Guy Standing has it, is as easily found in the British construction sector and in Danish universities as in a Mexican sweatshop or a shipyard in the Philippines. To millions of people, the freedom of neo-liberal deregulation mainly means insecurity and reduced autonomy.

Accelerated growth

The first fact about the contemporary world is accelerated growth. There are more of us, we engage in more activities, many of them machine-assisted, and depend on each other in more ways than ever before. No matter how you go about measuring it, it is impossible not to conclude that connectedness and growth have increased phenomenally. There are more of us than at any earlier time, and each of us has, on an average, more links with the outside world than our parents or grandparents. We have long been accustomed to the steep curves depicting world population growth, but the fastest growth does not take place in the realm of population. It goes without saying that the number of people with access to the Internet has grown at lightning speed since 1990, since hardly anyone was online at that time. But the growth in Internet use continues to accelerate. Only in 2006, it was estimated that less than 2% had access to the Internet in Subsaharan Africa (bar South Africa, which has a different history). By 2016, the percentage is estimated to be between 25% and 30%, largely owing to affordable smartphones rather than a mushrooming of Internet cafes or the spread of laptops among Africans. Or we could look at migration. Around 1990, there were about 200,000 immigrants (including first-generation descendants) in my native Norway. By 2016, the figure exceeds 700,000. Or we could look at urbanization in the Global South. Cities like Nouakchott in Mauretania and Mogadishu in Somalia have grown, since the early 1980s, from a couple of hundred thousand to a couple of million each. The growth has been a 1000% in one generation.

Or we could look at tourism. As early as the 1970s, cultured North European spoke condescendingly of those parts of the Spanish coast that they deemed to have been "spoiled" by mass tourism. In 1979, shortly after the end of Fascism in the country, Spain received about fifteen million tourists a year. In 2015, the number was about sixty million. We are, in other words, talking about a fourfold growth in less than forty years.

The growth in international trade has been no less spectacular than that in tourism or urbanization. The container ship with its associated cranes, railways, standardized metal containers and reconstructed ports, perhaps the symbol *par excellence* of an integrated, standardized, connected world (Levinson 2006), slowly but surely gained importance from its invention in the 1950s until it had become the industry standard a few decades later. The ports of Shanghai and Singapore more than doubled their turnover of goods only between 2003 and 2014. While world GDP is estimated to have grown by 250% since 1980, world trade grew with 600% in the same period, a development made possible not least through the reduced transport costs enabled by the shipping container.

Websites, international organizations, conferences and workshops, mobile phones and TV sets, private cars and text messages: The growth curves point steeply upwards in all these – and many other – areas. In 2005, Facebook did not yet exist; a decade later, the platform had more than a billion users.

Not all change accelerates, and not everything that changes has similarly momentous consequences. Although the growth in tourism has been staggering, it has been slower than the growth in text messages. But although phenomena like text messaging and Facebook, tourism and cable TV have transformed contemporary lives in ways we only partly understand, there are two changes of a material nature which are especially relevant for an understanding of the contemporary world, and which have undisputable consequences for the future: population growth and the growth in energy use.

The growing human population of seven billion travels, produces, consumes, innovates, communicates, fights and reproduces in a multitude of ways, and we are increasingly aware of each other as we do so. The steady acceleration of communication and transportation of the last two centuries has facilitated contact and made isolation difficult, and is weaving the growing global population ever closer together, influencing but not erasing cultural differences, local identities and power disparities. Since we are now seven times as many as we were at the end of the Napoleonic wars, it comes as no surprise that we use more energy today; but the fact is that energy use in the world has grown much faster than the world population. In 1820, each human used on an average 20 GJ a year. Two centuries later, we have reached eighty, largely thanks to the technology that enabled large-scale use of fossil fuels. Consumption is far from evenly distributed, and so those of us who live in rich countries have access to so much machine power that it can be compared to having fifty slaves each.

The quadrupling in energy use is in reality a growth by a factor of twenty-eight, since there are seven times as many of us today as in 1814. The side effects are well known. The visible and directly experienced ones are pollution and environmental degradation. Those effects which are both more difficult to observe and more consequential, are the long-term climate changes and the depletion of (non-renewable) energy sources.

Writing on the cusp of the industrial revolution, Thomas Malthus famously predicted widespread famine and social unrest unless population was kept in check (Malthus 1982 [1798]). His *Essay on the Principle of Population* was still being reviewed when the fossil fuel revolution took off, proving him wrong by enabling an immense growth in productivity. However, some of Malthus' insights may still turn out to be valuable, now that the side effects of the fossil fuel revolution are becoming ever more palpable. It may indeed be argued that if population had not begun to grow exponentially in the nineteenth century, humanity might have evaded the most serious side effects of the fossil fuel revolution. James Lovelock writes, in his *Revenge of Gaia* (2006), that had there just been a billion of us, we could probably have done as we liked. The planet would recover. Similarly, it is possible to imagine, although the scenario is unrealistic, that world population increased sevenfold without the fossil fuel revolution. In that case, the climate crisis would have been avoided, but instead, the great majority of the world would have lived in a state of constant, abject poverty. Instead, we now live in a world where modernity has shifted to a higher gear, where there is full speed ahead in most areas. It is a volatile and ultimately self-destructive situation. Continued growth is impossible, as shown by Grantham (2011; see also Hornborg 2012; Rowan 2014). This is a central conundrum of contemporary modernity making conventional Enlightenment–industrial ideas of progress and development far more difficult to defend now than it was just a generation ago. The loss of a clear script for the future also affects temporalities, leading to a presentism whereby both future and past are dimmed and out of focus, spoken of by Zeitlyn (2015, 383) as "the evacuation of the near past".

The question is what could be a feasible alternative in a world society which seems to have locked itself to a path which is bound to end with collapse. There is no simple, or single, answer to this, the most important question of our time. Indeed, there is not even general agreement about how to phrase the question. Healthy doses of intellectual and political imagination will be necessary to move ahead, and one size does not fit all. As pointed out by the economist Elinor Ostrom, famous for showing how communities are capable of managing resources sustainably, there is no reason to assume that what works in Costa Rica will work in Nepal (Ostrom 1990). Each place is interwoven with every other place, but they also remain distinctive and unique.

Disenchantment and modernity

The topics explored in this special issue are of great concern to humanity at all scales, from the household to the planetary. The contributors also show, drawing on their original ethnographies, the importance of carrying out multiscalar analysis connecting local realities with large-scale processes, as well as analysing social change comparatively. This approach, while not new in anthropology – among our sources of inspiration are Jack Goody (cf. e.g. Goody 2012) and Wolf (1982) – has always had its detractors among those who hold that its strength lies mainly in the synchronous study of delineated communities, not in its potential contributions to global history. Foremost among the disillusioned critics was, perhaps, Claude Lévi-Strauss. On 28 November 2008, the great French thinker marked his hundredth birthday. He had been one of the most important anthropological theorists of the twentieth century, and although he had ceased publishing years ago, his mind had not given in. But his time was nearly over, and he knew it. The book many consider his most important (on kinship) had been published almost sixty years earlier.

On his birthday, Lévi-Strauss received a visit from President Nicolas Sarkozy, France being a country where politicians can still increase their symbolic capital by socializing with intellectuals. During the brief visit by the president, the ageing anthropologist remarked that he scarcely considered himself among the living any more. By saying so, he did not merely refer to his advanced age and weakened capacities, but also to the fact that the world to which he had devoted his life's work was by now all but gone. The small, stateless peoples featured in his life's work had by now been incorporated, with or against their will, into states, markets and monetary systems of production and exchange.

During his brief conversation with the president, Lévi-Strauss also remarked that the world was too full: *Le monde est trop plein*. By this, he clearly referred to the fact that the world was filled by people, their projects and the material products of their activities. The world was *overheated*. There were by now seven billion of us, compared to two billion at the time of the French anthropologist's birth, and quite a few of them seemed to be busy shopping, posting updates on Facebook, migrating, working in mines and factories, learning the ropes of political mobilization or acquiring the rudiments of English.

Lévi-Strauss had bemoaned the disenchantment of the world since the beginning of his career. Already in his travel memoir *Tristes Tropiques*, published in 1955, he complained that

> [n]ow that the Polynesian islands have been smothered in concrete and turned into aircraft carriers solidly anchored in the southern seas, when the whole of Asia is beginning to look like a dingy suburb, when shanty towns are spreading across Africa, when civil and military aircraft blight the primaeval innocence of the American or Melanesian forests even before destroying their virginity, what else can the so-called escapism of travelling do than confront us with the more unfortunate aspects of our history? (Lévi-Strauss 1961 [1955], 43)

adding, with reference to the culturally hybrid and undeniably modern people of the cities in the New World, that they had taken the journey directly from barbarism to decadence without passing through civilization. The yearning for a lost world is evident, but anthropologists have been nostalgic longer than this. Ironically, the very book which would change the course of European social anthropology more than any other, conveyed a similar sentiment of loss and nostalgia. Malinowski's *Argonauts of the Western Pacific*, published just after the First World War, begins with the following prophetic words:

> Ethnology is in the sadly ludicrous, not to say tragic, position, that at the very moment when it begins to put its workshop in order, to forge its proper tools, to start ready for work on its appointed task, the material of its study melts away with hopeless rapidity. Just now, when the methods and aims of scientific field ethnology have taken shape, when men fully trained for the work have begun to travel into savage countries and study their inhabitants – these die away under our very eyes. (Malinowski 1984 [1922], xv)

Disenchantment and disillusion resulting from the presumed loss of radical cultural difference have, in a word, been a theme in anthropology for a hundred years. It is not the only one, and it has often been criticized, but the Romantic quest for unadulterated authenticity still hovers over anthropology as a spectre refusing to go away (Kuper 2005). Clifford Geertz and Marshall Sahlins, the last major standard-bearers of classic cultural relativism, each wrote an essay in the late twentieth century where they essentially concluded that the party was over. In "Goodbye to tristes tropes", Sahlins quotes a man from the New Guinea highlands who explains to the anthropologist what *kastom* (custom) is: "If we did not have *kastom*, we would be just like the white man" (1994, 378). Geertz, for his part, describes a global situation where "cultural difference will doubtless remain – the French will never eat salted butter. But the good old days of widow burning and cannibalism are gone forever" (Geertz 1986, 105).

A historical anthropology of the present

Geertz' ruminations on sati and anthropophagy are witty, but ultimately unproductive, and we must recommend exactly the opposite conclusion from his. Regardless of the moral position you take, faced with the spread – incomplete and patchy, but consequential and important – of one version or another of modernity, it is necessary to acknowledge, once and for all, that mixing, accelerated change, connectedness and the uneven spread of modernity is the air that most of us breathe in the present world. Moreover, we may argue that precisely because the world is now *trop plein*, full of interconnected people and their projects, it is an exciting place in which to carry out comparative research. People are aware of each other in ways that were difficult to imagine only a century ago; they develop some kind of global consciousness and often some kind of global conscience virtually everywhere. Yet, their global outlooks remain firmly anchored in their worlds of experience, which in turn entails that there remain many distinctly local worlds. The new situation creates new forms of comparability. Rather than, or in addition to, comparing kinship systems and modes of subsistence, we may now compare attitudes to climate change, responses to open-pit mining, discourses about Daesh ("IS") and consumer tastes. Local worlds now speak to each other in ways that were either absent or seen as unwelcome distractions to previous generations of anthropologists.

People now reproduce ties which can just as well be transnational as local, and we are connected through an increasingly integrated global economy, the planetary threat of climate change, the hopes and fears of identity politics, consumerism, tourism and media consumption. One thing that it is not, incidentally, is a homogenized world society where everything is becoming the same. Yet, in spite of the differences and inequalities defining the early twenty-first century world, we are slowly learning to take part in the same conversation about humanity and where it is going.

In spite of its superior research methods and sophisticated tools of analysis, anthropology struggles to come properly to terms with the world today. It needs help from historians, sociologists and others. The lack of historical depth and societal breadth in ethnographically based analysis is a shortcoming, and a further problem concerns normativity and relativism. For generations, anthropologists were, as a rule, content describing, comparing and analysing without passing moral judgement. The people they studied were far away and represented separate moral communities. Indeed, the method of cultural relativism requires a suspension of judgement in order to be effective. However, as the world began to shrink as a result of accelerated change in the postwar decades, it became epistemologically and morally difficult to place "the others" on a different moral scale than oneself. The de facto cultural differences also shrank as peoples across the world increasingly began to partake in a complicated, unequal but also seamless global conversation. By the turn of the millennium, tribal peoples were rapidly becoming a relic, although a dwindling number of tribal groups continue to resist some of the central dimensions of modernity, notably capitalism and the state, or they may remain ignored by capitalism and the state (but, perhaps, not for much longer). Indigenous groups have become accustomed to money, traditional peasants' children have started to go to school, Indian villagers have learnt about their human rights, and Chinese villagers have been transformed into urban industrial workers. In such a world, pretending that what anthropologists did was simply to study remote cultures, would not just have been misleading, but downright disingenuous.

This post-1991 world which involves people (and peoples) differently and asymmetrically rapidly began to create a semblance of a global moral community where there had formerly been none, at least seen from the viewpoint of anthropology. Ethnographers travelling far and wide now encountered Amazonian natives keen to find out how they could promote their indigenous rights in international arenas, Australian aborigines poring over old ethnographic accounts in order to relearn their forgotten traditions, Indian women struggling to escape from caste and patriarchy, urban Africans speaking disparagingly about corrupt politicians and Pacific islanders canvassing for climate treaties while simultaneously trying to establish intellectual copyright over their cultural production in order to prevent piracy.

In such a world, the lofty gaze of the classic anthropological aristocrat searching for interesting dimensions of comparison comes across not only as dated, but occasionally even as somewhat tasteless. Professed neutrality can in itself become a political statement in an overheated, interconnected world.

What had happened – apart from the fact that native Melanesians now had money, native Africans mobile phones and native Amazonians rights claims? The significant change was that the world had, almost in its entirety, been transformed into a single – however bumpy, diverse and patchy – moral space, while many anthropologists had made themselves busy looking the other way, often inwards.

In this increasingly interconnected world, cultural relativism can no longer be an excuse for not engaging existentially with the victims of patriarchal violence in India, human rights lawyers in African prisons, minorities demanding not just cultural survival but fair representation in their governments. Were one to refer to "African values" in an assessment of a particular practice, the only credible follow-up question would be *whose African values*"? In this world, there is friction between competing systems of value and morality. There can be no retreat into the rarefied world of radical cultural difference when, all of a sudden, some of the "radically culturally different" ask how they can get a job or a bank loan, so that they can begin to buy smartphones and other things. The suture between the old and the new can be studied by anthropologists, but it must be negotiated by those caught on the frontier, and in this world, the anthropologist, the "peddler of the exotic" in Geertz' words, cannot withdraw or claim professional immunity, since the world of the remote native is now his own.

Strengths and limitations of the ethnographic method

Many insightful social science books have been written on globalization since around 1990. The best among them highlight contradictions and tensions within the global system – Ritzer (2004) contrasts "the grobalization of nothing" with "the glocalization of something", Castells (1996) speaks about "system world" and "life world" (in a manner akin to Niklas Luhmann), Hann and Hart (2011) contrast a human economy with a neoliberal economy, and Barber (1995) makes an analogous contrast with his concepts of "Jihad" and "McWorld", just to mention a handful. In all cases, the local resists the homogenizing and standardizing tendencies of the global, insisting on its right to self-determination, autonomy and reproduction.

The extant literature on globalization which deals with the relationship of the particular to the universal is huge, and the main argument is valid and important; but much of this literature has its limitations. Notably, most academic studies and journalistic accounts of global phenomena tend to iron out the specificities of the local by treating them in a generic and superficial way, even when they speak of the unique and particular of each locality. Most anthropological studies that exist of globalization, on the other hand, tend to limit themselves to one or a few aspects, and to focus too exclusively on precisely that local reality which the more wide-ranging studies neglect. These limitations must be transcended dialectically, by building the confrontation between the universal and the particular into the research design as a premise: for a perspective on the contemporary world to be convincing and comprehensive, it needs the view from the helicopter circling the world just as much as it needs the details that can only be discovered by a myopic scholar scrutinizing a patch of beach with a magnifying glass. The macro and the micro, the universal and the particular must be seen as two sides of the same coin. One does not make sense without the other; it is yin without yang, Rolls without Royce.

In order to explore the local perceptions and responses to globalization, no method of inquiry is superior to ethnographic field research. Unique among the social science methods, ethnography provides the minute detail and interpretive richness necessary for an adequate appreciation of local life. This requires a deep and reliable understanding of local interpretations of global crisis and their consequences at the level of action. Moreover, there is no such thing as *the* local view. Within any community, views vary since people are differently positioned. Some gain and some lose in a situation of change; some see loss while others see opportunity. But none can anticipate the long-term implications of changes.

AN OVERHEATED WORLD

By now, it is widely recognized, inside and outside of the discipline of anthropology, that whereas ethnography is the richest and most naturalistic of all the social science methods, it is not sufficient when the task at hand amounts to a study of global interconnectedness and, ultimately, the global system. The methods of ethnography must therefore be supplemented. Ethnography is deep and broad in its command of human lifeworlds, but it can equally well be said that it lacks both depth and breadth, that is historical depth and societal breadth. A proper grasp of the global condition requires both a proper command of an ethnographic field and sufficient contextual knowledge – statistical, historical, macrosociological – to allow that ethnography to enter into the broad conversation about humanity at the outset of the twenty-first century. Since human lives are lived in the concrete here and now, not as abstract generalizations, no account of globalization is complete unless it is anchored in a local life world – but understanding local life is also in itself inadequate, since the local reality in itself says little about the system of which it is a part. The tension between the anthropological focus on the non-scalable, local and unique, and a historical and macrosociological perspective on large-scale systems connecting and sometimes clashing with these worlds, should not be seen as an obstacle, but as a resource.

Clashing scales

The road to any imaginable future is paved with unintended consequences. Just as the insecticide called DDT, which was meant to save crops and improve agricultural output, killed insects, starved birds and led to "the silent spring" of Rachel Carson's eponymous book, a foundational text for the modern environmental movement (Carson 1962), so does the car lead to pollution and accidents, the information revolution to the pollution of brains, and fast cultural change itself inspires its dialectical negation in the form of withdrawal and cultural conservatism. Both unintentional side effects and counter-reactions are outcomes of planned changes, and there is no reason to assume that the current crises of globalization were in any way planned or intended. Rather, what we are confronted with, in addition to the aforementioned, are recurrently *clashing scales,* a phenomenon which remains poorly understood. The general formula for scalar clashes is, seen from the vantage point of a resident in Gladstone, Queensland, that

> what is good for the world is not necessarily good for Australia; that which is good for Australia, is not necessarily good for Queensland, what benefits Queensland can be detrimental to the interests of Gladstone, and even what is good for Gladstone (an industrial city) may be bad for me, since increased industrial activity affects my asthma.

Scales clash when large-scale interests overrun local concerns, when universalistic ideologies (e.g. monotheistic religion) threaten small-scale belief systems, or when the ambition to save the climate through global treaties is unconnected to the search for work and economic security in the Sierra Leonean countryside.

In a very general sense, scale simply refers to the scope and compass of a phenomenon – whether it is small or big, short term or long term, local or global. We may nevertheless be more specific. Scale can be taken to refer to a combination of size and complexity (Grønhaug 1978). Social scale can be defined as the total number of statuses, or roles, necessary to reproduce a system, subsystem, field or activity; in other words, if two societies have 10,000 inhabitants, they are of differing scale if their respective divisions of labour vary significantly. Large-scale systems depend on the contributions of many persons and require an infrastructure capable of coordinating their actions, monitoring them and offering a minimum of benefits enabling persons around the system to reproduce it. In this sense, scale is a feature of social organization.

In a different, but complementary sense, scale can refer to cultural and individual representations of society, the world or the cosmos, and there is no necessary congruence between social scale and cultural scale. A society may be embedded in global networks of production and consumption without its residents being aware of their place in a global system. Conversely, residents of societies which are relatively isolated in terms of economic and political processes may be well connected through symbolic communication and possess a high awareness of their place in wider, global systems. The late Fredrik Barth once compared two societies, in which he had done fieldwork, along such lines. The Baktaman of Papua New Guinea lived in small social and cognitive worlds, while the Basseri nomads of Iran were embedded in relatively small-scale economic systems and had a small-scale social organization with a limited division of labour, but at the same time, they had a deep awareness of Persian history, recited classic poets and asked Barth questions about sputniks and the armaments race (Eriksen 2015b).

Finally, temporal scale is important, not least in the context of environmentalism and industry. Environmentalists often assume that industrial capitalism is short-sighted, while only ecological thought takes the long, planetary perspective. However, mining in Australia (and elsewhere) presupposes long-term investments which is sometimes expected to yield profits only decades ahead; and conversely, it is difficult to document large-scale environmentalist movements where actors take decisions solely based on assumed consequences that will only become apparent years after their own demise. The time scale on which people take decisions is relevant in a comparable way to the cultural scale by which they orient themselves, and the social scale in which they are integrated through networks and social organization.

Local life today is almost inevitably multiscalar, and people thus slide between scales many times every day. Sometimes, the scales are connected – if you are in a powerful position, you can change thousands of people's lives far away with a stroke of a pen; but if you spent time with them first, that is likely to influence your decision – but they are often compartmentalized and separate. The tangibly lived life at the small-scale clashes with the large-scale decisions. In a deregulated world increasingly dominated by the large-scale economic interests, frequently in tandem with state apparatuses tailored to promote their interests, large-scale processes tend to shape local lives in ways which are probably unprecedented historically, leading to both acquiescence and forms of resistance, which may take new forms today (Theodossopoulos 2014; Urla and Helepololei 2014).

Apart from following the logic of global capital accumulation, scaling up can also be an efficient way of diverting attention from the actuality of a conflict by turning it into an abstract issue. If your colleagues complain that you never make coffee for your co-workers, you may respond, scaling up a notch, that the neo-liberal labour regime is so stressful and exhausting that the ordinary office worker simply has no time for such luxuries. The world, or an activity, or an idea, changes when you move it up and down the scales. As one of my informants in an industrial Australian city said (perhaps unfairly):

"Those Greenpeace people in Sydney are really good at saving the world, but they don't have a clue as to what to do with real people with factory jobs".

Uneven speed, nostalgia and new boundaries

This special issue is based on the assumption that the fast changes characterizing the present age have significant unintended consequences. Each of the articles shows, through examining events and processes in the post-1991 world, how changes may take unexpected directions, which were neither predicted nor desired at the outset. Reactions and counter-reactions, acceleration and deceleration, hope and nostalgia, fluidity and boundary-making contribute to making the terrain of the early twenty-first century planet bumpy and frequently unpredictable. Although the growth tendencies are indisputable, they vary in significant ways. Some areas are being cooled down, partly as a result of overheating elsewhere. Both Chris Hann and Robert Pijpers show, in their articles about Tázlár (Hungary) and Marampa (Sierra Leone), respectively, how a period of optimism and faith in progress was followed by uncertainty, economic stagnation and decline, withdrawal into identity politics and despair.

Cathrine Thorleifsson, analysing a city which – like Pijpers' Marampa chiefdom – used to rely on mining, shows connections between politics of identity (in this case nationalism) and economic downturns, revealing how the traditional working class has shifted its allegiances from socialism to right-wing nationalism, a pattern replicated in many parts of Europe, including Hann's Hungary.

The deregulation and globalization of markets which took place in the 1990s could lead to a cooling down of local economies which for some reason (failure to compete on a higher scale, lack of technological innovation, remoteness, etc.) were left behind, like Marampa and Tázlár, and this in turn often led to a heating up of identity issues, witnessed at a higher scale in the 2016 Brexit affair and, at an even higher level of scale, in the new European border regimes aiming to stem flows of people across the Mediterranean Ocean. In other locations, neo-liberal deregulation has sped up economic and infrastructural development, mobility and inequality – Majes and Subic Bay exemplify this overheating effect. It should be kept in mind that cooling down, reduced speed, activity and growth (or even degrowth) may be temporary or patchy. The Indian Ocean island-state of Mauritius, which I have followed for three decades, may seem to be an overheated place *par excellence*, with sustained high growth rates in the economy since the mid 1980s. Contemporary Mauritius boasts new shopping malls, highways, hotels, factories and a much improved standard of housing compared to the first years of independence from Britain, which was achieved in 1968. Yet, change is uneven, and a short drive from the hi-tech novelty Cyber City, the trading town of Rose-Hill is virtually unchanged. Like many villages and minor towns in the island, the infrastructure of Rose-Hill is perhaps slightly more dilapidated and worn than in 1990, but it shows few signs of overheating. It is a billabong surrounded by fast streams.

In Elisabeth Schober's analysis of Subic Bay during the same, post-Cold War period, a different picture of the unevenness of overheating emerges: While the Olongapo area cooled down considerably after the departure of the US naval forces in 1992, it has been re-heated more recently by the arrival of the Korean Hanjin corporation and its huge shipyard. A further example is the Estonian mine described by Eeva Keskula, where several layers of temporality – socialist, biographical, neo-liberal and so on – coexist uneasily, and where the predictability of the past has been replaced by a more volatile situation where innovation, not least in the technological realm, is paramount.

In spite of their differences, all these locations give rise to powerful sentiments of nostalgia. The conviction that "things were better in the past" ("the past" often being a time in living memory, between two and four decades ago) is widespread. Notably, according to this narrative, jobs were secure, the economy was predictable, there were incremental improvements to people's lives. They had hopes, however unrealistic, of permanent upward mobility and social development. Often, the scale is recalled as having been manageable, the economy based on local or regional resources rather than the vicissitudes of transnational capital, and change seen as development rather than rupture.

Multitemporality characterizes Astrid Stensrud's analysis of the ways in which locals in the Majes region in Peru make sense of past, present and future. Living in a brand new settlement devoid of a long history, the inhabitants depend on their creativity to create convincing hinges between the past and the future. Similarly, the undocumented migrants described by Synnøve Bendixsen struggle to weave a meaningful narrative out of their disjointed, interrupted and uncertain lives with a past of torment and a future of uncertainty.

Hann shows that in the economically booming times of the prospering 1970s and 1980s, people in Tázlár made good money, but there were side effects in the shape of stress, suicides and alcoholism. It does not seem preposterous to assume that similar ailments may be characteristic of other economically overheated places, such as Majes, or indeed, among people who are stuck in the middle, like Bendixsen's undocumented migrants. Struggling to weave a meaningful narrative out of their disjointed, interrupted and uncertain lives with a past of torment and a future of uncertainty, their lives are also destabilized, but for opposite reasons to those in boomtowns.

The destabilization of borders, which has enabled increased mobility out of Tázlár, has also facilitated migration into Europe, leading to counter-reactions in the shape of right-wing identity politics (Thorleifsson), but also resulting in precarious migrants being trapped in a legal limbo between acceptance and exclusion (Bendixsen). Bendixsen's study of the re-emergence of borders and boundaries in the ostensibly "borderless" post-Cold War world is suggestive of a much broader tendency in this era of "fast-capitalism" (Holmes 2000), deregulated global markets and local marketization. As shown by Leaver and Martin in their comparison between corporate capitalism on Manhattan and corporate groups in Melanesia, entification, or the fixation of flows into bounded entities, is a characteristic of contemporary economic practices, yet while landholder groups in Papua New Guinea become increasingly fixed and bounded, corporations become ever more fluid and fuzzy – owing to global capital flows, new financial instruments and complex ownership structures, their boundaries are less clear than before. Intriguingly, the border work described by Bendixsen in post-Cold War Europe mirrors the analytical model developed comparatively by Leaver and Martin – borders become fixed in some instances, fluid in others, insurmountable for some, easily crossed by others.

The destabilization and restabilization of boundaries, seen in financial upheavals, border regimes and collective identities oscillating between hybridity and fixity, are a key characteristic of overheating, a process of accelerated, but uneven change where different subsystems are chronically out of sync with each other. These disjunctures are related to scale. An analytical perspective attentive to the multiscalar nature of the social world inevitably leads to serious objections towards the standard literature about globalization. By moving up and down the scales, we have endeavoured to combine ethnographic detail with a comparative and global overview, and to relate the scales to each other, hopefully succeeding in making a contribution to a historically informed anthropology of the present world; fast changing, but unevenly, with different scales moving at different speeds, and with ramifications for life-worlds and larger social systems alike.

The disjunctures between scales and temporalities are arguably where the main sites of conflict, and perhaps germs of historical change, are to be located currently. As several of the articles show, slowdowns (or cooling down) in the economic sector can lead to an acceleration (and heating up) in identity politics, and accelerated change in one geographical area may marginalize another, leading to mass unemployment and impoverishment. Conflicting goals, such as growth and sustainability, may similarly lead to economic marginalization. Owing to a political desire to move towards renewable, carbon-neutral energy sources, coal plants have been closed down in several European regions, leading to redundancies and economic downturns similar to the "cooling down" described by Hann, Pijpers and Thorleifsson. If ecological sustainability is given the first priority, jobs may have to be sacrificed, but if full employment is the political goal, sustainability must wait. This tension between "green" and "red" politics mirrors the contradiction between growth and sustainability, and is likely to form the focus of political battles in societies trying to reconcile goals which seem to be contradictory. A cooler world, both in a literal and a metaphorical sense, would by default be slower, less materially affluent and less prolific than the one we currently inhabit. It may also be more multicentric, decentralized and diverse than that of hegemonic neo-liberalism. In any case, the potential for the realization of a less overheated world depends on the outcome of the multiple scalar clashes currently pitting local concerns against translocal interests.

Note

1. This article draws on, and partly overlaps with, sections in Eriksen (2016).

Acknowledgements

The author would like to thank the editor of *History and Anthropology*, an anonymous referee and the Overheating team for excellent criticisms of the first draft.

Disclosure statement

No potential conflict of interest was reported by the author.

Funding

This article is based on research funded by the European Research Council Advanced Grant project "Overheating: The Three Crises of Globalisation" [grant number 295843].

References

Barber, Benjamin. 1995. *Jihad Versus McWorld: How Globalism and Tribalism are Reshaping the World*. New York: Ballantine.
Calhoun, Craig. 2002. "The Class Consciousness of Frequent Travellers: Towards a Critique of Actually Existing Cosmopolitanism." In *Conceiving Cosmopolitanism: Theory, Context and Practice*, edited by S. Vertovec, and R. Cohen, 86–109. Oxford: Oxford University Press.
Carson, Rachel. 1962. *Silent Spring*. Boston, MA: Houghton Miffin.
Castells, Manuel. 1996. *The Rise of the Network Society*. Oxford: Blackwell.
Castells, Manuel. 1998. *End of Millennium*. Oxford: Blackwell.
Chari, Sharad, and Katherine Verdery. 2009. "Thinking Between the Posts: Postcolonialism, Postsocialism and Ethnography after the Cold War." *Comparative Studies in Society and History* 51 (1): 6–34.
Eriksen, Thomas Hylland. 2001. *Tyranny of the Moment: Fast and Slow Time in the Information Age*. London: Pluto.
Eriksen, Thomas Hylland. 2015a. "Globalization and Its Contradictions: Anthropological Research in an Overheated World." In *The Ashgate Research Companion to Anthropology*, edited by Andrew Strathern, and Pamela Stewart, 293–316. Basingstoke: Ashgate.
Eriksen, Thomas Hylland. 2015b. *Fredrik Barth: An Intellectual Biography*. London: Pluto.
Eriksen, Thomas Hylland. 2016. *Overheating: An Anthropology of Accelerated Change*. London: Pluto.
Furedi, Frank. 2002. *Culture of Fear: Risk-taking and the Morality of Low Expectations*. London: Continuum.
Geertz, Clifford. 1986. "The Uses of Diversity." *Michigan Quarterly Review* 25 (1): 105–123.
Goody, Jack. 2012. *Metals, Culture and Capitalism. An Essay on the Origins of the Modern World*. Cambridge: Cambridge University Press.
Grantham, Jeremy. 2011. "Time to Wake Up: Days of Abundant Resources and Falling Prices are Over Forever." *The Oil Drum*. Accessed August 12, 2015. http://www.theoildrum.com/node/7853.
Gray, John. 1998. *False Dawn: The Delusions of Global Capitalism*. London: Granta.
Green, Sarah. 2013. "Borders and the Relocation of Europe." *Annual Review of Anthropology* 42: 345–361.
Grønhaug, Reidar. 1978. "Scale as a Variable in Analysis: Fields in Social Organization in Herat; Northwest Afghanistan." In *Scale and Social Organization*, edited by Fredrik Barth, 78–121. Oslo: Universitetsforlaget.
Hann, Chris, ed. 1994. *When History Accelerates: Essays on Rapid Social Change, Complexity and Creativity*. London: Athlone.
Hann, Chris, and Keith Hart. 2011. *Economic Anthropology*. Cambridge: Polity.
Hobsbawm, Eric. 1994. *The Age of Extremes: The Short Twentieth Century, 1917–91*. London: Michael Joseph.
Holmes, Douglas. 2000. *Integral Europe: Fast-Capitalism, Multiculturalism, Neofascism*. Princeton, NJ: Princeton University Press.
Hornborg, Alf. 2012. *Global Ecology and Unequal Exchange: Fetishism in a Zero-sum World*. London: Routledge.
Kuper, Adam. 2005. *The Reinvention of Primitive Society: Transformations of a Myth*. London: Routledge.
Kwon, Heonik. 2010. *The Other Cold War*. New York: Columbia University Press.
Levinson, Marc. 2006. *The Box: How the Shipping Container made the World Smaller and the World Economy Bigger*. Princeton, NJ: Princeton University Press.
Lévi-Strauss, Claude. 1961[1955]. *Tristes Tropiques*. Translated by John Russell. New York: Criterion.
Lovelock, James. 2006. *The Revenge of Gaia: Why the Earth Is Fighting Back – and How We Can Still Save Humanity*. London: Allen Lane.
Malinowski, Bronislaw. 1984[1922]. *Argonauts of the Western Pacific*. Prospect Heights, IL: Waveland.
Malthus, Thomas. 1982[1798]. *An Essay on the Principle of Population*. Harmondsworth: Penguin.
Morozov, Evgeny. 2012. *The Net Delusion: How Not to Liberate the World*. London: Penguin.

Ostrom, Elinor. 1990. *Governing the Commons: The Evolution of Institutions for Collective Action*. Cambridge: Cambridge University Press.
Ritzer, George. 2004. *The Globalization of Nothing*. London: Sage.
Rowan, Michael. 2014. "We Need to Talk About Growth." *Persuade Me*. http://persuademe.com.au/need-talk-growth-need-sums-well/.
Sahlins, Marshall D. 1994. "Goodbye to Tristes Tropes: Ethnography in the Context of Modern World History." In *Assessing Cultural Anthropology*, edited by Robert Borofsky, 377–394. New York: McGraw-Hill.
Sennett, Richard. 1998. *The Corrosion of Character: Personal Consequences of Work in the New Capitalism*. New York: W.W. Norton.
Soros, George. 2002. *George Soros on Globalization*. Oxford: Public Affairs.
Standing, Guy. 2011. *The Precariat: The New Dangerous Class*. London: Bloomsbury Academic.
Stiglitz, Joseph. 2002. *Globalization and its Discontents*. London: Allen Lane.
Tainter, Joseph. 2014. "Collapse and Sustainability: Rome, the Maya, and the Modern World." *Archeological Papers of the American Anthropological Association* 24: 201–214.
Theodossopoulos, Dimitrios. 2014. "On De-pathologizing Resistance." *History and Anthropology* 25 (4): 415–430.
Trouillot, Michel-Rolph. 2001. "Close Encounters of the Deceptive Kind." *Current Anthropology* 42: 125–138.
Urla, Jacqueline, and Justin Helepololei. 2014. "The Ethnography of Resistance Then and Now: On Thickness and Activist Engagement in the Twenty-first Century." *History and Anthropology* 25 (4): 431–451.
Urry, John. 2003. *Global Complexity*. Cambridge: Polity.
Wolf, Eric. 1982. *Europe and the People without History*. Berkeley: University of California Press.
Zeitlyn, David. 2015. "Looking Forward, Looking Back." *History and Anthropology* 26 (4): 381–407.

Building a city: Korean capitalists and navy nostalgia in "overheated" Subic Bay

Elisabeth Schober

ABSTRACT
Over the course of just half a year, a catastrophic volcanic eruption and an unexpected political victory would come to act upon and dramatically alter the location of Subic Bay in the Philippines. As a consequence, the annus mirabilis of 1991 brought a (temporary) end to more than a century of US tutelage for the Philippines. Subic Bay, an area that had been economically, politically and socially dependent on the patronage of the US Navy, was now undergoing major transformations. The land and infrastructure left behind by the Americans were turned into the Philippines' largest special economic zone, becoming the vanguard platform that allowed for the introduction of an "overheated" form of economic globalization into the Philippines. Amongst the foreign direct investors now active in Subic, a South Korean shipbuilder has become a new hegemon, building a giant shipyard inside the bay that today employs 34,000 Filipino workers. Paying particular attention to how contested gendered relations between foreign sailors and the local population have come "to build this city" during the cold war, the rapidly urbanizing Subic Bay area is analysed through what I call "navy nostalgia": the widespread, yet rather equivocal longing for the return of the US Navy that needs to be read in light of the recent arrival of the South Korean shipbuilder.

Introduction: gendered military legacies in an "overheated" economic present[1]

The city by the bay, the city that rocks, the city that never sleeps ... ("We built this city")

Exceptional news would come to dominate the celebration of the 100th International Women's day in Olongapo City, Philippines. After a city-sponsored parade had marched through the streets in the early morning of 8 March 2014, by 8 a.m. all the NGOs, community organizations and representatives gathered in the City Stadium at the so-called Triangle area, a major commercial node of this urban entity that is home to approximately 200,000 inhabitants. After numerous performances held by the various groups assembled, Mayor Rolen Paulino entered the stage to give a speech. A former employee at the nearby US naval base in Subic Bay which closed down in the early 1990s, Paulino, had only recently been elected into office, and used his time to, amongst other things, coin a new slogan for the city. Instead of "Aim High, Olongapo", the city now marketed itself through "Olongapo, home of the most beautiful women in the world", a catchphrase which could be seen plastered on a number of city-owned buses and on a new wooden gate that had been erected at the outer limits of Barrio Barretto, the thriving red-light district of Olongapo which mainly services Western and East Asian sex tourists and retired US military personnel these days.

At the city stadium, the mayor said[2]:

> I have good news for you. No, it's actually great news! The number of US ships that will make port calls in Subic Bay will double from now on. Olongapo will be open for "Liberty" again, and we will welcome the sailors to our beautiful place. I know that there are some groups here who will not agree, but where will these people be, if the people of Olongapo starve to death?

Then he added, "We will clean up the market area and the beaches. We will make this city safe and clean for the Americans." After this announcement was made, which came in the wake of an official visit made by US ambassador Philip Goldberg to Olongapo just a few days earlier, the organizers of the event once again played the theme song chosen as the soundtrack for the proceedings of the day: "We built this city", by 1980s US band "Starship".

The city that this combo sought to immortalize in their (in)famous song was their home base of San Francisco. Elected "worst song of the 1980s" by the readership of the *Rolling Stone Magazine* in 2011, the cheerful tune by this "sleek corporate band" to many of its US American listeners came to represent the death of a whole era.[3] During the 1960s and 1970s, the urban hub of San Francisco had in many ways become the very apotheosis of a particularly wild strand of US American liberalism: beatniks, hippies, war resisters, actors of the LGBT movement, sex worker activists and many more misfits had come to call this town their home and had thrived in the streets, bars and bookshops of San Francisco. In 1985, when the song was recorded, however, San Francisco had already turned into a much staler affair: it was rapidly transforming into a financial hub, with high rises sprouting up across the city. At the same time, in the aftermath of the Vietnam War, homelessness peaked, and the HIV/AIDS epidemic ravaged entire communities. And with countless rough sleepers never quite rubbing shoulders with the yuppies crowding the streets of this city now, San Francisco slowly came to stand for a particular kind of moral defeat that the cheerful lyrics and tune of "We built this city" perfectly epitomized.

Decades later, when the same song was blasted in the stadium of Olongapo City, amongst some of those who heard it that day, it similarly highlighted a number of contradictions that recent US history has produced in the Philippines. One female resident of Olongapo, who stood next to me during the event, said with a knowing smile, "'We built this city on rock and roll' ... oh yes, the women of Olongapo, they rocked and rolled all night long back then." What she was alluding to was the fact that in the mid-1980s, when this song would have first been played in the many clubs and bars that were lining Magsaysay Drive, an estimated 16,000 Filipina sex workers laboured in the city in order to entertain the US sailors regularly flocking the streets. The women's "labor of love" (Yea 2005) formed the economic base for an urban area that was literally built on the goods and money that the Americans brought to Subic Bay. "The good times", however, eventually rolled on (cf. Sturdevant and Stoltzfus 1992), and in the meantime, a new foreign force has arrived to Subic that makes its own claims over the human and natural resources of the area: South Korean investors, who by many locals are viewed as a poor substitute for the US sailors. As Juan, a waiter at a Korean restaurant, explained to me one day (in a statement that is rather representative for dozens of similar ones that I heard during fieldwork): "In the old days, we were so rich because of the Americans that we could afford to have servants ourselves. Now look at us, we are all servants to the Koreans ...."

Subic Bay today is a coastal urban area[4] that is no longer primarily dominated by the US Navy—even though the US Armed Forces certainly still play an important role not only in economic and political terms, but also in the imagination of the local population. Since their official departure from the area in 1991/1992, Subic Bay has transformed itself into a major hub for the global shipping and shipbuilding industry, with Korean investors, in particular, having made one visible imprint on the landscape of Subic: across the bay from where the old naval base used to be, a giant shipyard, currently employing 34,000 (mostly male) Filipinos, has been erected, which takes up four kilometres of Subic's waterfront. Representing a two-billion dollar investment made by the Korean conglomerate Hanjin Heavy Industries, this shipyard is considered the crown jewels of the Subic Bay Freeport Zone, the highly successful special economic zone that was erected amidst the infrastructure of the old base left behind by the Americans. In the meantime, the shipyard, much like the naval base of the past, has developed a distinct gravitational pull on other populations in the region, with the facility attracting countless new people from far-flung provinces,[5] a process which has also led to a number of unintended social and environmental effects such as a new scarcity of land in Olongapo and Subic Town (cf. Schober in press; Schober 2016b).

Olongapo, it is important to know, is also a city that, for quite a few Manila-based Filipino intellectuals and left-wing activists, is still mainly remembered and talked about as a stain on their national conscience, a "sin city" which was forced to sell its women in exchange for national protection and economic benefits. "The US Navy is largely gone from the area", a scholar from Manila once explained to me, "but the mentality is still there". The particular Subic Bay mentality that he was referring to, I believe, has to do with the dream of easy money to be made in a moment's time which is nowadays often juxtaposed with the backbreaking, dangerous and lowly paid work available at the Korean shipyard these days; and it is a powerful dream indeed in an area that has seen so much wealth come and go. In light of stories of the occasional 50-dollar-tip left at bar tables by US sailors, and of local women departing for the United States with their sailor husbands in tow, amongst the residents of the Subic Bay area the South Koreans are often not considered a viable alternative for the region's many problems. They are too stingy, I was told on many occasions, they want too much without giving back, they push their workers too hard to make quick profits, and to make matters worse, they seclude themselves from the people of the area, seeking to avoid getting drawn into local patron–client relationships in the way the Americans often did.

In this article, I will delve into the curious phenomenon hinted at above: the widespread, yet rather equivocal nostalgia in Subic Bay for the US Navy that needs to be read in light of the recent arrival of the South Korean shipbuilder and the kind of rapid changes it has brought in its wake. Nostalgia, as Olivia Angé and David Berliner have recently pointed out, is often a reaction to a "sense of temporal acceleration prompted by unprecedented social and economic transformations", with nostalgia, in the particular setting I explore, perhaps best understood as "an act anchored in present context that says a lot more about contemporary social configurations than about the past itself" (Angé and Berliner 2015, 2, 3; see Thorleifsson, 2016, for another articulation of this phenomenon).[6] While Subic Bay is nowadays certainly marked by economic "overheating" in the sense that ever new foreign direct investors make their way to the region to benefit from cheap labour and the informal no-union policy at work in the Freeport Zone (Chan and Kelly 2004, 150), in Olongapo the putative hyper-exploitation of male Filipino workers is often countered with tales of how much better things used to be in the past, when the Americans were still around and used local female bodies instead.

Such remarkable local perceptions and interpretations of Subic's past and present, I believe, need to be read within the context of what Heonik Kwon has called the "decomposition of the cold war", that is, "the diverse and locally specific ways in which the cold war is coming to an end" in different regions of the world (2010, 10).[7] Along the same vein as Kwon, who urges us to re-investigate our common understanding of the cold war as a single, conherent phenomenon that came to a clear end in 1991, I shall argue that the (uneven) decomposition of one political order in the Philippines (i.e. the phase of outright US militarism that ended in 1991) has in fact *not* led to a neat rupture with the past. Instead, recent rapid politico-economic changes have caused a situation in which new post-US military realities have merely been stacked on top of half-digested painful pasts, inadvertently triggering a number of social fermentation processes in this key site for Philippine economic growth. In the particular ways in which the (gendered) legacy of the US Navy is being rhetorically chartered by some of my informants in an effort to contest the claims for primacy that are being made by Korean investors, we can arguably discern how the current "overheated" era of economic boom in Subic Bay represents both a breach with the past, and a (somewhat contorted) continuity with how things were formerly done.

Declarations of (in-)dependence: Subic Bay and the US Navy

> Few places in the world have had as long and as intimate a relationship with the United States as Olongapo. (Seth, *New York Times*, April 23, 1988)

In the midst of US colonial rule over the Philippines (1898–1946), a term was coined by William Howard Taft, before he became the 27th president of the United States, that has in the meantime become a bit of an embarrassment to US citizens: Taft, in his capacity as the first American Governor-General of the Philippines, referred to the local population by using the term "our little brown brothers". Specifically, Taft argued that "'our little brown brothers' (…) would need 'fifty or one hundred years' of close supervision 'to develop anything resembling Anglo-Saxon political principles and skills'" (Loewen 2014, 836). Such statements, pointing to a significant history of paternalist racist justifications for the subjugation of the Philippines to US interests, were then spun around amidst the drink-soaked banter of US sailors making "liberty" calls in Subic Bay, who adapted this phrase in a way that added a sexist layer to the contentious words of "little" and "brown": "little brown fucking machines powered by rice" became a popular slur used by the sailors to talk of the Filipina sex workers they encountered—an insult which was even printed onto T-shirts and sold to the Americans in Olongapo City (Santos 1992, 40).

Reflecting on the women thus portrayed by their customers can give us an indication of how racist paternalism, uneven sexual relations on the ground and high politics were at times mutually constitutive in the historical US–Philippine encounter before and amidst the cold war.[8] This social aggregation, drawing together diverse scales, resonates in a number of other locations in Asia where the US military has touched ground, which typically led to a series of "base encounters" (Schober 2016a) involving US soldiers, local women and men. Moon, in her book *Sex Among Allies* (1997), based on research conducted in the South Korea of the early 1990s, has shown how the sex industry catering to the US military in the Korean context served both local economic interests and fed into the larger security system that the United States has built up in the Asia-Pacific region.[9] When I engaged in fieldwork nearly two decades later on the US military presence in and near Seoul, I was struck by the overwhelmingly negative depictions of US soldiers in South Korea. I tried to make sense of this phenomenon as an expression of "violent imaginaries"—a concept I use to refer to the social practice of making sense of US militarism through the reconfiguration of individual acts of gendered violence committed by soldiers into an issue that pertains to the nation. This practice came to play a crucial role in the globally connected Korean social movement against US bases in the country, which, incidentally, has also forged numerous ties to anti-base activists in the Philippines (cf. Schober 2016a). And indeed, during later fieldwork in Olongapo (in 2013/2014), I saw many similarities between the Philippine experience and the South Korean one I had studied earlier; however, some crucial differences came to puzzle me as well, which primarily had to do with the fact that my informants in Olongapo seemed to at times hold incredibly positive views of the US Navy, which contrasted starkly with the situation I had experienced in Seoul.

While a first naval port had already been erected in the Subic area in the late nineteenth century by Spanish imperial forces, this terrain was later taken over by the US Navy after the Spanish–American War in 1898, and eventually occupied by Japanese troops during the Second World War. When the Philippines attained its independence from the United States in 1946, Subic Bay and the adjacent town of Olongapo remained under US jurisdiction for quite a few more years (Olongapo was officially only turned over to the Philippines in 1959). The US naval facility in Subic Bay kept expanding over the next few decades and came to stigmatize the entire region as a hotbed of prostitution and violence, with tens of thousands of Filipina sex workers attending to the needs of the American soldiers in the clubs, bars and motels of Olongapo and its twin city of Angeles, which was located next to Clark Air Base, some 80 km away. As Reynato An Cabatit, the author of *The Making of Olongapo* (1985), notes:

> The rapid proliferation of the R&R Industry, labeled "institutionalized prostitution" by a sociologist from UP, brought dollars to the coffers of Olongapo, along with the dreaded social disease, and a host of other problems, including what was termed as the "dehumanization of the weaker sex" (…). In such a setting, girls could be sexually abused, cheated, exploited, ostracized, and even killed, and "no one would give a damn". (Cabatit 1985, 93; cf. Sturdevant and Stolzfus 1992)

"Entertainment" was provided to sailors for many decades in the area, which inevitably bore other fruits as well: thousands of so-called Amerasian children were fathered by US

Americans, who more often than not abandoned their offspring together with their Filipino mothers. Some estimates say that 10,000 of them live in Olongapo alone (cf. Moon 1997, 35). And indeed, meeting Amerasians in the Olongapo of today is not exactly a difficult feat: the ethnically mixed composition of this city is one of the most blatant ways in which the legacy of the US naval presence in the area can be felt into the present (which, incidentally, is also very different from the South Korean situation, where Amerasian children have for the most part been given up for transnational adoption and have thus vanished from Korean soil). Consequently, the very fact that the presence of Americans can, in spite of the current status of Subic as a "post-base" area, be traced all the way into the most intimate family ties of so many people in Subic Bay has created an incredibly uneven and at times nearly schizophrenic relationship of unreciprocated love–hate between Olongapo's residents and its former military neighbours.[10] Quintessentially, despite the fact that Olongapo is located on Philippine territory, decades after the US Navy has departed, many of its Filipino residents still seem to view themselves as residing in a city that is in some ways extraterritorial to their country—a feeling that was arguably only solidified with the arrival of foreign direct investors to the area.

In sum, ever since the beginning of the inclusion of the Philippines into the US American sphere of the capitalist world economy, the local population of Subic Bay did not only find itself in highly asymmetrical financial relationships with the wealthy Americans at the base nearby. The particular role that this area came to play amidst US cold war geopolitics also meant that locals got ever more personally and intimately tied into and invested in the hegemonic power in ways that went way beyond mere economic calculations. In the imagination of many people residing in the area, the US Navy came to figure as the all-powerful patron, with Subic's inhabitants trying to make a life for themselves by attaching themselves as clients, friends, lovers or potential wives to the sailors flooding their town.

Of ruptures and continuities: from naval base to Korean shipbuilding hub

While 1986—the year that long-time military dictator Marcos was deposed in the midst of the so-called People Power Revolution—has often been attributed as *the* watershed moment and turning point in recent Filipino history, others disagree with that timeline:

> For the Philippines, the new era had begun not with the fall of Marcos who looted the country's treasury of at least $10 billion, most of it never recovered, but with the departure of the Americans from the bases (…). The fall of Marcos, the one-time darling of American presidents and CIA chiefs for his uncanny ability to talk democracy while bullying and robbing his own people, was only the dramatic opening, a prelude, to the real struggle for change. (Kirk 1998, 6)

The year of 1991, a time of many upheavals worldwide, indeed brought a rather dramatic discontinuity to the Philippines in general, and to Subic Bay in particular. After Mt. Pinatubo, a massive volcano in the area, erupted on 15 June 1991, 20,000 military dependents were evacuated from the nearby Clark US air base to Subic in a matter of a few days. With the "natural" disaster[11] destroying Clark beyond redemption and striking at a particularly critical moment—talks between the United States and the Philippines over the renewal of leases for US military installations in the country had been stalling amidst growing public dissent—the seemingly unthinkable happened: on 13 September

1991, the Philippine Senate voted against a contract renewal. After forty-seven years of continuous heavy military presence in the country, the US Armed Forces had to abandon their bases now, which marked the end of a century of direct US American dominance over the Southeast Asian nation (cf. Simbulan 2010). "What the (U.S.) anti-base activists were not able to do in two decades, Mt. Pinatubo did in one day", a popular local joke of those days sums up the dramatic events (Santos 1992, 32) that would bring so many changes to Subic Bay.

For Olongapo and the other areas adjacent to the bay, the closure of the base first seemed to spell economic doom. In all, 42,000 jobs were lost overnight that were directly linked to the base. And Olongapo—with its many restaurants, shops and entertainment facilities solely catering to US sailors and their dependents—threatened to become a ghost town. Richard Gordon, Mayor of Olongapo City at that time, remembers that first day in a documentary on the base transformation:

> I went out for a walk that morning, the next day already (after the last U.S. Navy ship had left) at 7 o'clock. And I must admit (…) I was really scared. Because at Magsaysay Drive, which used to (be) a hustle and bustle of activity, (with) thousands of people coming in every morning, going to work—(now) there was nothing. There was nothing![12]

Due to a massive campaign spearheaded by Gordon and supported by thousands of volunteers that protected the base facilities from looting,[13] however, within a year's time the abandoned base was turned into the Subic Bay Freeport Zone, with the era of US militarism giving way to what Gonzalez has called "the postcolonial fictions of neoliberalization in Subic Bay" (2010, 64). The infrastructure left behind by the Americans—such as the airport, the road system, the many warehouses and the port facilities—proved to be invaluable assets for such a political–economic endeavour. And so did the proven willingness of Subic's residents to accommodate (and incorporate) wealthy outsiders in their midst. The first few years of the Freeport were somewhat uneven, however, with companies such as Federal Express and Acer amongst the investors to make use of the prime land and the tax incentives offered at Subic Bay, who then ended up pulling out of the area again after a relatively short-time frame had passed (cf. Kirk 1998, 89ff; Reyes 2015). The largest coup was only landed in 2006, when South Korean company Hanjin signed a 50-year-lease and built its shipyard facility in the Bay area, making it the single largest foreign investor in the Special Economic Zone, and by extension, in the Philippines (cf. Sison 2009).

The conversion of a military base into a flourishing Special Economic Zone has been interpreted by some commentators as a heroic act that reinstated the country's sovereignty, as a small miracle achieved through the hard labour of the locals after so many decades of US military domination in the region (cf. Mydans 1996). Other more critical commentators have pointed out hidden continuities amidst apparent changes. Already in 1995, for instance, a Visiting Forces Agreement was signed between the Philippines and the United States, which granted US Forces visiting rights to Subic Bay again; an understanding that was further deepened by the signing of the Enhanced Defense Cooperation Agreement (EDCA) on 28 April 2014. The 2014 agreement, critics say, gives the US Armed Forces nearly unrestricted access to Philippine military installations, and is "a key aspect in the comprehensive American military build-up throughout the Indo-Pacific region, as part of the US pivot to Asia aimed at subjugating China to its diktats"

(Pastrana 2016). In Subic Bay, the recent signing of EDCA has been used to announce that strategic sections of the Freeport Zone will be designated for military usage again, a significant backtrack from previously enthusiastic statements that the old base in Subic Bay would only be serving civilian purposes from now on. The demilitarization of Subic Bay for the sake of economic development, however, has been an uneven affair even before EDCA was signed, as a closer look at the major Korean actor Hanjin may reveal.

Exporting a Korean capitalism of the barracks

In April 2012, the South Korean corporation Hanjin closed a deal with Huntington Ingalls Industries (a key US defence private contractor), opening

> the door to large-scale servicing of United Sates military ships [in Subic Bay] for the first time in almost 20 years. In a news release announcing the deal, Huntington Ingalls said the companies "will work together in providing maintenance, repair and logistics services to the U.S. Navy and other customers in the Western Pacific region". (Whaley 2012)

With the company's revenue partly being made up by military contracts such as these, it is perhaps not surprising that the physical terrain of the shipyard is equally as much a high security space as the naval base used to be, as the access to the shipyard is heavily regulated by the presence of private security personnel and the Philippine armed forces.

Leaving these concrete material manifestations of the shipyard as militarized space behind, the history of the corporation that owns the shipyard can also give insights into the interweaving of big business and war in East and Southeast Asia and into a specifically Korean 'capitalism of the barracks' (Schober 2016a) that played a fundamental role in the country's economic ascend during the cold war era. Ever since military dictator Park Chung-hee took charge of the country in 1961, South Korea began its spectacular climb from being an economic basket case in the mid-twentieth century to effectively functioning as a sub-imperial economic and political force in Southeast Asia these days. South Korea's close alignment with the United States and its military engagements in the Asia-Pacific region certainly played a pivotal role in this; Hanjin, for instance, would climb up into the ranks of top Korean players during the Korean War as a shipping business catering primarily to the US military. Much of Hanjin's fortunes were then made during the Vietnam War, when the company, together with other *chaebol* (such as Hyundai), was responsible for transporting goods for the US Armed Forces between Korea and Vietnam (cf. Lie 1998, 64). "South Korea's submilitarism in Vietnam", writes Lee Jin-kyung, "was a significant factor in securing South Korea's position as a sub-imperial force within the U.S.-dominated global capitalism in the years following the end of the Vietnam War" (2009, 657).

With South Korea's unprecedented climb from the periphery of the world economy to its very core in a matter of decades, its role as a sub-empire in the wider Asia-Pacific region eventually reached all the way to the Philippines. While male labour migrants from countries such as the Philippines have been recruited to work in South Korean factories since the late 1980s (cf. Seol and Han 2004), thousands of young Filipinas have come to labour as entertainers in the clubs nearby US military bases in Korea since the 1990s, when the red-light districts catering to galvanized iron (GIs) in their own country dwindled in size (cf. Cheng 2010, Yea 2005). And with Filipino labour increasingly on the move between the two countries, it seems that it was just a matter of time until Korean capital would follow suit. Under these conditions, Hanjin could ultimately benefit from the two countries' common history of being part of the U.S.' "empire of bases" (Johnson 2004).

With 34,000 Filipinos currently working at the Korean-owned shipyard in the Philippines, the shipbuilder Hanjin is the undisputed foreign economic actor in Subic Bay these days. Hanjin's financial might, however, does not translate directly into popularity amongst the local population, which can partly be attributed to the particular labour management practices that Hanjin has exported to the Philippines alongside much of its shipbuilding. Involving "flexible" labour regimes that translate into much precarity for the local workforce (cf. Standing 2011; Hann and Parry 2017; see also Kesküla, 2016), extraordinarily long working hours, frequent shouting, cussing and the occasional physical abuse directed at workers, labour relations at the shipyard have also been strained by the high number of accidents at the shipyard, with more than 5000 occurring between 2006 and 2010 alone (Robinson 2011). Thirty-eight workers are known to have died between 2006 and 2014 through work-related accidents (Datu 2014). Also, recruitment patterns have been a source of contention: while Hanjin originally sourced its labour locally during the first wave of hirings, the company then gradually began to recruit its workers from faraway provinces like Mindanao or Northern Luzon instead, with one reason presumably being that the workforce available in the Subic area is used to higher wage levels than Hanjin was prepared to pay.

Elsewhere, I have explored how social distinctions made along ethnic lines at the shipyard, and the discrimination resulting from such strategies play themselves out, which have arguably also led to dangerous contradictions arising amidst the cultural gaps between Korean and Filipino understandings of how to work (Schober 2017). In such a way, Hanjin's shipyard is a place that may alert us to the often destructive consequences of the "overheating" (Eriksen 2016) of economic domains that comes with the introduction of neoliberalism-taken-into-higher-gear in a place like Subic. South Korean investors, due to the historical trajectory outlined above, which has turned their home country into a major economic force in Southeast Asia through the successful capitalization of a history of patron–client relationships with the United States—are certainly in a privileged position vis-à-vis their Filipino workers, which allows them to enforce an imported work process that is aimed at making the production of ships cheaper, faster and more efficient.[14]

"They never left": Navy nostalgia and uncertain livelihood quests

"If there was no port, Subic Bay would be nothing", Rosalie tells me. She is a 26-year-old resident of Olongapo, who until recently used to work at an English language school catering to South Korean students. Given her experience working for Koreans, for a little while Rosalie also contemplated getting an administrative job at the shipyard, but then changed her mind due to stories she had heard about accidents at that facility, and how the Korean corporation allegedly was trying to cover those up. "It was the talk of town a few years ago", she said, "that they pay 10,000 Pesos to the families to keep them quiet about the dead". These rumours concerning undisclosed deaths at the shipyard eventually made her change her mind: "I wouldn't want to get involved in covering up accidents myself", she says. During a visit at the shipyard, when she was being interviewed for a job opening, she was also taken aback by the prospect of having to work alongside so many young men: "They were very rude", she said, "hundreds of them staring at me". Nowadays, she works a number of part-time jobs instead, and hopes to find a way to go abroad and find a job overseas.

She would also not be opposed to the idea of meeting a US sailor here in Subic, she says. Whenever a ship comes in, she and her female friends make sure to be out and about in the touristic parts of the Freeport Zone, or on Olongapo City's Magsaysay Drive, where they hope to encounter the sailors. Business and bar owners in the area will on such days hang up posters and banners in the windows of their shops: "Subic Bay Welcomes (name of ship)", and people will flock the streets to catch a glimpse of the American men. "When you see these young, muscular Navy guys walking down the street in their uniforms ...", Rosalie says, then pauses and giggles. People in Olongapo welcome the return of the Navy, she says, because many still remember the good old days. There were well-paid jobs to be had, and the sailors spent like crazy whenever they were out partying. An aunt of hers used to work in the clubs, then got married to a sailor and lives in the United States now, so "it can work, you can get lucky", she reassures me, after I express some doubts about these men functioning as an entry ticket to a new life in the United States.

People from Olongapo have a reputation for being very optimistic but also a bit lazy, she says, that is why conglomerates like Hanjin in the end decided to hire workers from faraway provinces instead, she believes; such outsiders bring a different work ethic to the table, given that they have not been "spoiled" by the US Navy as the residents of Olongapo have. Olongapo, Rosalie reflects to me, is perhaps really just a fishing village that grew too quickly, the implication of this being that the idea of "easy money" to be made in a matter of moments, the notion of catching that last big fish, is deeply ingrained into the thinking of the local population when it comes to the foreign forces in their midst.

Ramon is in his mid-20s, too, and just like Rosalie, his life has been marked by his city's intimate ties with the United States. In the 1980s, Ramon's mother, who was working for a small company in a distant province, received an offer by a friend of hers to work at a bar she owned in Olongapo. "If only one could turn back time ...", Ramon says, but the fact remains that his mother chose to quit her job and move to Olongapo: "When she was still young, she really wanted to marry an American. One of her dreams ...." Instead of fulfilling that desire, she became pregnant by one of the customers at the bar, a US sailor who would leave Subic Bay and never financially support Ramon or his mother. Ramon says he holds no grudges against his father, though, which he largely attributes to a meeting with him when he was still in elementary school: "Even though we are not together, I guess I'm still lucky. Because I have a loving mom and even though I just met my dad once, he really appreciated me. He showed me the love of a father."

What he is referring to here is his one real-life encounter with his father (they have in the meantime re-established contact via the internet), which he described to me in the following way:

> They (were) just having a good time, on Magsaysay Drive, you know, like the military do (*laughs*). (...) My mom, she just saw him (on the street). "Oh, it's him". And she quickly went home and then got me, (saying) "I'm gonna let you see someone", and when we got to the bar, then my mom whispered into my ear, "Hey, go to that man, he's your Dad" (*laughs*). And I was a kid, just followed the order. And then I went there, "Hey, hey, Sir",

> something like that. "Are you XX? I'm Ramon, I'm your son." He knows he has a baby (in the Philippines). And then, quickly, he lifted me up (*to show his son to his sailor friends he was drinking with*). No question at all. Because when I was young, we had the same features—the same face, like my brothers in the U.S. So it was easy to see, "oh yes, that's my son!" (*laughs*) That's why, you know, I never had a bad feeling for him, even though he didn't support me.

Ramon, like Rosalia, is trying to make ends meet financially these days by patching together a number of jobs. "I'm the provider at home", he explains, "I really need to have a job; a *good* job, you know, so that I can also help my family." That "good" job that he is referring to, it seems, is not be found at the Korean shipyard for him, either: "At first, when I heard there was gonna be a big company here ... a lot of people were excited because it will give jobs. But over time, they discovered the situation there is not good. And it's hard (work), no?" A lot of young men from his neighbourhood got jobs at the shipyard in the late 2000s, and for a while he was contemplating it, too, but was then dissuaded by how most of his friends were gradually quitting their jobs:

> Suddenly, they stopped working there. Because they said the treatment there is very bad. I don't know if it's a cultural thing. They said that it's Korean culture, they tap you on the head (= *hit you*). That's okay in Korea, but in the Philippines, it's a big No No.

He finds himself frustrated by how economic development in the area has not translated into better jobs for people in Olongapo and suggests that perhaps foreign direct investors like Hanjin should have to first hire the people of Olongapo, rather than give jobs to more compliant newcomers from distant rural areas. "It's still developing, the Philippines ... well, I hope I will still be alive when ... (*laughs*). Progress here, you know, it takes too long!" And until "progress" through foreign direct investment can be felt in people's lives, Ramon believes, people in Subic will always dream about the US Navy as their other option to improve their lives. Female friends of his, in particular, he says, easily succumb to the idea that the Navy ships will bring a better future for them along: (*In a high-pitched voice:*)

> "Ah there's an American ship! Let's go to Pier 1, let's meet some guys there". You know, it's really sad, makes me feel sad for the situation, but who am I to stop it. They need to eat, they have families to provide, there are needs.

Finally, I ask Ramon whether he believes that the US Navy will make a formal return to the area, as many people in the wake of the signing of the EDCA agreement seem to hope and believe, and he answers in a straightforward manner:

> They never left! (*laughs*) It's just a treaty. Paper. They never left. The Philippines will always need the U.S. Especially now that the Chinese are hitting us. (...) Some are excited for the U.S. to be back here. And some disagree. But no matter what's their reaction, the U.S. is still here, living with us. They never left.

Conclusion: "We rose from the ashes of Mt. Pinatubo"

A place like Olongapo City is bound to bring up complicated gendered legacies, with Subic Bay's residents often viewing the historical (and uneven) transformation from military base to civilian Freeport rather differently than social actors who would like to see the Philippines finally disentangled from its uneven relationship with the United States. While visiting Olongapo's City Museum, for instance, I was particularly struck by one display room that features the contours of an entertainment district drawn on its walls, and a life-size mannequin dressed up as an exotic dancer positioned next to a dancing pole, while a mannequin representing a Filipino man leers at her from the distance. This representation is a surprisingly direct and honest appraisal of the city's particular role in the "bases of empire" (Lutz 2009) that the United States has spun across the globe during the twentieth century. And indeed, the museum employee I encountered during my visit went even further in his endorsement of the US Navy: After the eruption of the volcano, he told me, the city was in despair, but "we rose from the ashes of Mount Pinatubo", only to add moments later, after we had begun to talk about the Freeport Zone, its Korean shipyard, and the kind of jobs it was providing to the area, "but they are not as good, these jobs, as they were with the Americans".

The abandoned US naval base, which covered the equivalent of the landmass that forms Singapore (ca. 68,000 ha), represents a huge and important facility for the Philippines, and indeed, many of the social, economic and environmental problems that the original facility brought along have not entirely gone away, but have just diversified and transformed themselves over time. Much of the same thing can be said of the US military's presence in Subic Bay: while I expected a clear-cut transition from base to foreign investor hub when I set out on my field research, I was continuously struck by the many continuities I experienced in Subic in the end. Instead of serving as *the* prime example of a successful transformation from military to civilian usage (as it has often been hailed by visitors of the area), Subic Bay, upon closer examination can rather be held up as a case that shows the ongoing and multifarious entanglement of strategic economic sites in the workings of a larger assemblage for which the term "U.S. military-industrial complex" (cf. Turse 2008) may prove to be a rather feeble label. Subic Bay, in all its social, economic and political complexities, may also serve as a prime example of how the cold war order did not simply vanish into thin air in the early 1990s, but is rather, in Heonik Kwon's terms, still decomposing at different rates and speeds today. In this particular corner of the world, as we have seen, this gradual rotting away of the past has given space to the strangest fermentation processes, with the future of Subic Bay now partially laying in the hands of new foreign actors that hail from Northeast Asia. To be sure, since the landmark year of 1991 and the political and economic upheavals it brought, Subic Bay's history has been accelerating without a clear direction to be made out just yet, with this "loss of a clear script for the future" (Eriksen, introduction) giving rise to what I have labelled "navy nostalgia".

While Korean investors have been particularly apt at strategically utilizing their old and wide-ranging connections with the US military and its installations in the Philippines, their interventions in Subic have certainly not been greeted with anonymous approval. This may be the most unexpected bubble yet to emerge from the decomposition of the former US domination of the Philippines: paradoxically, it is local memories of the "good old days" when the US Navy was still around in Subic Bay that have served as a form of resistance to the kind of unhampered super-exploitation of the Filipino workforce that these East Asian investors have brought to the area. The economic overheating, work-related accelerations and political discontinuities that have come to act upon Subic with the introduction of a particularly rampant form of globalization, in such a way, are countered with a longing for old stabilities that sits rather uncomfortably with some of the realities of that particular past.

Notes

1. As part of the ERC-Advanced-Grant project "Overheating. The three Crises of Globalisation", I have conducted seven months of field research in Subic Bay, where between September 2013 and April 2014 I explored the impact of the South Korean shipyard on the communities nearby. Names of individuals—unless they are public figures—have been anonymized according to anthropological standards. I wish to thank Thomas Hylland Eriksen, David Henig and the anonymous reviewer for their incredibly useful comments on earlier versions of this article.
2. The speech was given in Tagalog, so I relied on the on-site translation of my research assistant here to capture his words.
3. http://www.rollingstone.com/music/pictures/readers-poll-the-10-worst-songs-of-the-1980s-20111006/1-starship-we-built-this-city-0260875.
4. Subic Bay is a colloquial term, and does not correspond to an exact administrative unit. The actual bay encompasses two urban areas—Olongapo City and Subic town—which, while being adjacent to each other and nominally both part of the province of Zambales, fall under different jurisdictions, as Olongapo is governed independently.
5. A 42.4% population increase has been noted in Subic Town alone between 2000 and 2010, with the neighbouring areas of Castillejos and Olongapo having equally seen a rise in residents that can partially be attributed to the lure of the shipyard. Data found at National Statistics Office of the Republic of the Philippines (http://web0.psa.gov.ph/).
6. For other influential anthropological renditions of the term nostalgia, see, for instance, Stewart (1988), Rosaldo (1989) and Herzfeld (1997, 139ff).
7. In a brilliant passage of his book *The Other Cold War*, Kwon writes that

   > in some regions, cold war politics was viewed primarily as the business of the state and their alliances, largely unconnected to the routines of the civic order, whereas in other places people had to live the cold war as part of their everyday lives in their most immediate, intimate domains. The history of the global cold war consists of a multitude of these locally specific historic realities and variant human experiences, and this view conflicts with the dominant image of the cold war as a single, encompassing geopolitical order. (2010, 7)

   Bayly's work (2007) on the complex interplay of (post-)socialism, (post-)colonialism and capitalism in today's Asia is equally of relevance here, as is Chari and Verdery's theoretical intervention (2009) on the connections between post-socialism and post-colonialism, in which they argue for the emergence of "a single analytical field—'the (post) Cold War'" as a new lens, which in their view will allow us to ask "how Cold War representations have shaped and continue to shape theory and politics" (18).
8. The gendered histories of the US–Philippine meeting, and how the small-scale and intimate feeds into large-scale geopolitics can be exemplified by General Douglas McArthur's love affair with a young Filipina. McArthur, who is today still revered in both the Philippines and South Korea for the role he played in the liberation of both countries from Japanese occupation during the Second World War, would in 1930 meet a young Filipina actress called Elizabeth Cooper. Cooper, who was only sixteen years old at that time, became McArthur's mistress, and followed her 50-year-old lover to Washington D.C. The relationship lasted for three years, at the end of which McArthur allegedly handed Cooper 15 000 dollars and a ticket back home to the Philippines, which Cooper refused to make use of, choosing to stay in the United States instead.
9. Moon's book is a key contribution to a growing body of literature on the issue of prostitution proliferating nearby US military bases, much of which has been inspired by the pioneering work of feminist Cynthia Enloe (e.g. 1989). US imperialism, in this literature, is often seen as a project that is held in place by a form of virulent masculinity that is enacted by soldiers in the contact zones near US bases with the aim of dominating the local population via the bodies of women—an understanding of prostitution which runs rather contrary to notions

put forward by "pro-sex work" scholars such as Agustin (2007), Kempadoo and Doezma (1998) or Weitzer (2000). In my own attempt to navigate these long-raging victimhood vs. agency debates around the subject of prostitution/sex work, I have sought to map out "the terrain where personal aspirations, collective imaginaries, and various temporal orientations come up against a local architecture (of prostitution) that has attached itself to the globe-spanning infrastructures of the US Armed Forces" (Schober 2016a, 90).
10. This is perhaps best epitomized in a joke about the Philippine anti-base movement that I heard in Olongapo: instead of simply saying "yankee go home", like their Korean counterparts would, the Philippine activists are said to scream, "yankee go home, but take me with you".
11. As with most so-called natural disasters, there seems to have been a human-made element to the Mt. Pinatubo eruption, too, as geothermal drilling taking place on the volcano shortly before the eruption has on occasion been blamed, a narrative I have explored further elsewhere (Schober 2016b). For an introduction into the rather large field of the anthropology of disaster, with which I cannot fully engage for the purposes of this article, see e.g. Oliver-Smith (1996) or Hoffman and Oliver-Smith (2002).
12. See "The Subic Bay Story. Rising Above the Storm" http://www.youtube.com/watch?v=sYWtvUc604w&feature=relmfu.
13. Nearby Clark Air Base fell victim to massive looting after the eruption of Mt. Pinatubo—for an account of the looting, see Kirk (1998).
14. Comparable arrangements have also been observed by Jaesok Kim in his book *Chinese Labour in a Korean factory* (2013), some sections of which highly resonate with Korean labour management tactics I learned about in Subic Bay; tactics which, Kim similarly argues, "had been formulated through the Korean historical experiences of the Cold War, oppressive military government, and authoritarian work culture as a result of the military regime" (11).

Disclosure statement

No potential conflict of interest was reported by the author.

Funding

This work was supported by European Research Council [grant number 295843].

References

Agustin, Laura. 2007. *Sex at the Margins: Migration, Labor Markets, and the Rescue Industry*. London: Zed Books.
Angé, Olivia, and David Berliner. 2015. "Introduction. Anthropology of Nostalgia – Anthropology as Nostalgia." In *Anthropology and Nostalgia*, edited by Olivia Ange and David Berliner, 1–15. London: Berghahn.
Bayly, Susan. 2007. *Asian Voices in a Postcolonial Age. Vietnam, India and Beyond*. Cambridge: Cambridge University Press.
Cabatit, Reynato An. 1985. *The Making of Olongapo*. Manila: Soller Press.
Chan, Fong Yin, and Philip F. Kelly. 2004. "Local Politics and Labor Relations in the Philippines. The Case of Subic Bay." In *Labour in Southeast Asia. Local Processes in a Globalized World*, edited by R. Elmhirst and R. Saptari, 129–157. London: Routledge.
Chari, Sharad, and Katherine Verdery. 2009. "Thinking Between the Posts. Postcolonialism, Postsocialism, and Ethnography After the Cold War." *Comparative Studies in Society and History* 51 (1): 6–34.
Cheng, Sea-ling. 2010. *On the Move for Love. Migrant Entertainers and the U.S. Military in South Korea*. Philadelphia: University of Pennsylvania Press.
Datu, Randy V. 2014. "Security Tightens at Hanjin Shipyard over Workers' Drug Use." *Rappler*, October 6. http://www.rappler.com/nation/71234-security-tightens-hanjin-shipyard-workers-drug-use.

Enloe, Cynthia. 1989. *Bananas, Beaches and Bases: Making Feminist Sense of International Politics*. London: Pandora.

Eriksen, Thomas Hylland. 2016. *Overheating. Understanding Accelerated Change*. London: Pluto Press.

Gonzalez, Vernadette. 2010. "Touring Military Masculinities. U.S.-Philippines Circuits of Sacrifice and Gratitude in Corregidor and Bataan." In *Militarized Currents. Toward a Decolonized Future in Asia and the Pacific*, edited by Setsu Shigematsu and Keith Camacho. Minneapolis: University of Minnesota Press.

Hann, Chris, and Jonathan Parry, eds. 2017. *Regular and Precarious Labour in Modern Industrial Settings* (Max Planck Studies in Anthropology and Economy series). London: Berghahn Press.

Herzfeld, Michael. 1997. *Cultural Intimacy*. New York: Routledge.

Hoffman, Susanna M., and Anthony Oliver-Smith. 2002. *Catastrophe and Culture. The Anthropology of Disaster*. Santa Fe: SAR Press.

Johnson, Chalmers. 2004. *The Sorrows of Empire. Militarism, Secrecy, and the End of the Republic*. New York: Metropolitan Books.

Kempadoo, Kamala, and Jo Doezma. 1998. *Global Sex Workers: Rights, Resistance, and Redefinition*. New York: Routledge.

Kesküla, Eeva. 2016. "Temporalities, Time and the Everyday: New Technology as a Marker of Change in an Estonian Mine." *History and Anthropology* 27 (5).

Kim, Jaesok. 2013. *Chinese Labor in a Korean Factory. Class, Ethnicity, and Productivity on the Shop Floor in Globalizing China*. Stanford: Stanford University.

Kirk, Douglas. 1998. *Looted. The Philippines After the Bases*. New York: St. Martin's Press.

Kwon, Heonik. 2010. *The Other Cold War*. New York: Columbia University Press.

Lee, Jin-kyung. 2009. "Surrogate Military, Subimperialism, and Masculinity: South Korea in the Vietnam War." *Positions* 17 (3) 1965–1973.

Lie, John. 1998. *Han Unbound. The Political Economy of South Korea*. Stanford: Stanford University Press.

Loewen, James W. 2014. "The Nadir of the Negro." In *Race and Racism in the United States. An Enceclopedia of the American Moasic. Vol. 1 (A–E)*, edited by Charles A. Gallagher and Cameron D. Lippard, Santa Barbara, 835–838. Greenwood: ABC-CLIO.

Moon, Katharine H. S. 1997. *Sex Among Allies: Military Prostitution in U.S.–Korea Relations*. New York: Columbia University Press.

Mydans, Seth. 1988. "Olongapo Journal; At an Old Port of Call, a New Scourge." *New York Times*, April 23. http://www.nytimes.com/1988/04/23/world/olongapo-journal-at-an-old-port-of-call-a-new-scourge.html.

Mydans, Seth. 1996. "Subic Bay, minus U.S., becomes a Surprise Success." *New York Times*, November 23. http://www.nytimes.com/1996/11/23/world/subic-bay-minus-us-becomes-surprise-success.html.

Oliver-Smith, Anthony. 1996. "Anthropological Research on Hazards and Disasters." *Annual Review of Anthropology* 25: 303–328.

Pastrana, Dante. 2016. "US and the Philippines move rapidly to implement military deal." *World Socialist Website*, February 26. https://www.wsws.org/en/articles/2016/02/26/phil-f26.html.

Reyes, V. 2015. "Legacies of Place and Power. From Military Base to Freeport Zone." In City and Community (early online version). http://onlinelibrary.wiley.com/doi/10.1111/cico.12097/full.

Robinson, Tammy Ko. 2011. "South Korea's 300 Day Aerial Sit-in Strike Highlights Plight of Precarious Workers in Korea and the Philippines." *Asia-Pacific Journal*. http://www.japanfocus.org/-tammy_ko-Robinson/3644.

Rosaldo, Renato. 1989. "Imperialist Nostalgia." *Representations* 26: 107–122.

Santos, Aida F. 1992. "Gathering the Dust. The Base Issue in the Philippines." In *Let the Good Times Roll. Prostitution and the U.S. Military in Asia*, edited by Saundra Pollock Sturdevant and Brenda Stolzfus, 32–44. New York: The New York Press.

Schober, Elisabeth. 2016a. *Base Encounters. The US Armed Forces in South Korea*. London: Pluto Press.

Schober, Elisabeth. 2016b. "Indigenous Endurance Amidst Accelerated Change? The U.S. Navy, South Korean Shipbuilders and the Aeta of Subic Bay (Philippines)." In *Identity Destabilised: Living in an Overheated World*, edited by Thomas Hylland Eriksen and Elisabeth Schober. London: Pluto Press.

Schober, Elisabeth. 2017. "The (Un-)Making of Labour. Capitalist Accelerations and Shattered Bodies at a South Korean Shipyard in the Philippines." In *Regular and Precarious Labour in Modern Industrial Settings*, edited by Chris Hann and Jonathan Parry (Max Planck Studies in Anthropology and Economy series). London: Berghahn Press.

Schober, Elisabeth. In Press. "Between a Rock and a Stormy Place. Land and Labour in the Philippines." In "Economies of Growth or Ecologies of Survival", Special Issue of *Ethnos*. Online: http://www.tandfonline.com/doi/abs/10.1080/00141844.2016.1169204#.V2-ugbQkJo0

Seol, Dong-Hoon, and Geon-Soo Han. 2004. "Foreign Migrants and Social Discrimination in Korea." *Harvard Asia Quarterly* VIII (1): 45–50.

Simbulan, Roland G. 2010. "People's Movement Responses to Evolving U.S. Military Activities in the Philippines." In *The Bases of Empire. The Global Struggle Against U.S. Military Posts*, edited by Catherine Lutz, 145–180. New York: New York University Press.

Sison, Bebot Jr. 2009. "Hanjin to invest additional $86 million in Subic facility." *The Philippine Star*, June 8. http://www.philstar.com/Article.aspx?articleId=475488&publicationSubCategoryId=66.

Standing, Guy. 2011. *The Precariat: The New Dangerous Class*. London: Bloomsbury Academic.

Stewart, Kathleen. 1988. "Nostalgia – A Polemic." *Cultural Anthropology* 3: 227–241.

Sturdevant, Saundra Pollock, and Brenda Stoltzfus. 1992. *Let the Good Times Roll. Prostitution and the U.S. Military in Asia*. New York: The New York Press.

Thorleifsson, Cathrine. 2016. "From Coal to Ukip: The Struggle Over Identity in Postindustrial Doncaster." *History and Anthropology* 27 (5).

Turse, Nick. 2008. *The Complex. How the Military Invades our Everyday Lives*. New York: Holt.

Weitzer, Ronald, ed. 2000. *Sex for Sale: Prostitution, Pornography, and the Sex Industry*. New York: Routledge.

Whaley, Floyd. 2012. "Philippines Role May Expand as U.S. Adjusts Asia Strategy." *New York Times*, April 29. http://www.nytimes.com/2012/04/30/world/asia/philippines-role-maygrow-as-us-adjusts-asia-strategy.html?pagewanted=all.

Yea, Sallie. 2005. "Labour of Love – Filipina Entertainer's Narratives of Romance and Relationships with GIs in U.S. Military Camp Towns in Korea." *Women's Studies International Forum* 28: 456–472.

Mining, expectations and turbulent times: locating accelerated change in rural Sierra Leone

Robert J. Pijpers

ABSTRACT

In 2006 the iron mines in Marampa Chiefdom, in the Northern Province of Sierra Leone, re-opened. This event sparked a widespread feeling of excitement and hope among the local population, and gave rise to a landscape of expectations in which memories of both relative prosperous and "dark" pasts were invoked and imaginations of a better future flourished. However, soon after the re-opening and initial development of the mines, it appeared that the expected opportunities would not materialize everywhere and for everybody. Frustration, disappointment and loss of hope became part and parcel of the dynamics in this place, which is seen as a hot-spot, a notion that is applied to highlight the numerous frictions and negotiations within this investment landscape. This paper examines this momentum of rising expectations in the hot-spot by scrutinizing its connection to the area's recent past of boom and bust, the increased global demand for raw materials, especially from China, national development agendas and life-cycles of mining operations. Subsequently, some spatial and social dynamics of accelerated change in Marampa will be discussed. Exploring these dynamics allows to see accelerated change in these investment landscapes from a diverse angle. Through highlighting these temporal, spatial and social dynamics of change in the hot-spot, the paper argues that overheating, a phenomenon often associated with accelerated change, may play out not only as a result of accelerated change, but also as a result of deceleration and the experience of being excluded from the potential opportunities of change.

Introduction – "we were expecting good things to happen"

We were expecting good things to happen, but look at the youth passing by now, none of them belong to any job. It is a lot that we expected to see, but we are very disappointed.

Santigie Kamara lives in Rogbaneh, a village on the Southern side of the London Mining iron ore mining concession in Marampa Chiefdom, Sierra Leone. This statement was part of a comparison he made between the situation today with life before and after the war (1991–2002). It followed an explanation of how life before the war was good, how it got disrupted throughout the war, but slowly stabilized again afterwards. When London

Mining re-opened the iron ore mines in 2006, after three decades of closure, good things were expected to happen: jobs, infrastructural development, improved living standards and better schools would all be the result of the rising opportunities. And indeed, notwithstanding statements such as the above, many things changed.

"Lunsar is developing now, it is a good thing. It's only the people without a job that are complaining", a local inhabitant of the chiefdom said to highlight the recent developments in Lunsar, the main town of Marampa Chiefdom. He referred to the changes that could be seen in the chiefdom, such as improved infrastructure, job opportunities and construction work. "You can feel it", someone else present at the same conversation added, thereby referring to the good vibes and the hopes and expectations for the future that can be sensed in the town.

These diverging, yet co-existing, perceptions of accelerated change, in the context of large-scale mining in Marampa, are central to the analysis in this paper.[1]

The purpose of this paper is two-fold. The re-opening of the iron ore mines by London Mining in 2006 propelled a period of accelerated change and gave rise to a "landscape of expectations". This paper examines this moment by scrutinizing its entanglement with the area's (recent) past of boom and bust, and contextualizing it in wider national and global developments. In doing so, the field is approached as a temporal site where memories of previous periods of growth and decline, characterized by the development, presence and termination of resource extraction, become interwoven with experiences in the present and imaginations of the future. This situation can be well captured by the idea of historicity which Hirsch and Stewart (2005, 262) describe as "a human situation in flow, where versions of the past and future (of persons, collectives or things) assume present form in relation to events, political needs, available cultural forms and emotional dispositions". "Historicity in this sense is the manner in which persons operating under the constraints of social ideologies make sense of the past, while anticipating the future" (Hirsch and Stewart 2005, 262).

Secondly, the paper also shows how at one moment in time, boom and bust, accelerated change and cooling down, can feature simultaneously. Besides rising expectations and hope, after several years of mining operations, local inhabitants in Marampa increasingly expressed disappointment and frustration with the lack of those opportunities which they had expected. The horizons of progress and development that were so clearly visible to many appeared increasingly distant to some. These double-bounded dynamics in Marampa offer an opportunity for global comparison, as they relate well to contemporary processes of acceleration and deceleration, of hope for progress on the one, and disenchantment on the other hand, that unfold in multifaceted ways around the world (Eriksen 2016b). In order to analyse the different experiences of accelerated change and cooling down within Marampa's current mining boom, of both the flow and closure of the opportunities brought by this particular form of globalization (cf. Meyer and Geschiere 1999; Geschiere and Nyamnjoh 2000), different temporal, spatial and social aspects of the dynamics of change in this Sierra Leonean chiefdom are analysed. As I will show in the next section, using the notion of the hot-spot allows for doing so.

Zooming in on accelerated change and cooling down in Marampa will not only contribute to an emerging body of literature within an anthropology of resource extraction, it also sheds further light on the emergence and dynamics of overheating, a phenomenon described as "unevenly paced change where exogenous and endogenous factors combine to lead to instability, uncertainty and unintended consequences in a broad range of institutions and practices, and contribute to a widely shared feeling of powerlessness and alienation" (Eriksen 2016a, 16). The analysis here shows that overheating in Sierra Leone is first and foremost a (paradoxical) result of cooling down, of deceleration and the experience of being excluded from the expected change. In other words, locating (the experience of) accelerated change in Marampa highlights that in the case of rural Sierra Leone, the sudden emergence of change, or the speed of change, in itself does not result in a feeling of powerless, alienation and disappointment, but rather the perceived exclusion from the opportunities associated with this moment of change.

Marampa Chiefdom: from growth pole to hot-spot

Marampa Chiefdom, located in the Northern Province of Sierra Leone,[2] is a relatively rural chiefdom, with the majority of the people depending on small-scale, often subsistence level, activities, such as farming and trade, although formal wage employment, mainly in the iron ore mines, is a much desired option. As will be discussed in more detail in the next section, extensive iron ore mining took place in the past. From the 1930s to 1975, the Sierra Leone Development Company (DELCO) operated the mines, a period that is under the current conditions of mining vividly remembered and drawn upon in various discussions. With the re-opening of the iron ore mines in 2006 by the London-listed company London Mining, there was a growing hope that subsistence-level activities were something of the past and a positive future was ahead. Expectations of employment, access to consumer goods, better education for the next generation, a general improvement in standards of living and improved access to material goods flourished. In other words, expectations about (material) improvements in life were omnipresent. And, as I mentioned in the introduction, a multitude of physically visible changes did occur. Not only did the chiefdom's main town Lunsar rapidly urbanize due to the high influx of job seekers, the availability of public water, the opening of restaurants and shops, increase in motorized transport, the establishment of an electricity network and infrastructural improvements are just a few examples of the immediately visible changes. Many of these changes were perceived positively, and indeed, it is not difficult to imagine the difference it makes when dust roads are asphalted and bread sold along these roads is not covered in dust anymore, or when previously bumpy rides on motorbikes suddenly become smooth and fast.

The developments in Marampa seem to fit well into the notion of the growth pole, which is a central element of the World Bank's Growth Poles programme in Sierra Leone (Kayonde, Alexandre, and Speakman 2013). This programme assumes that economic development concentrates around a particular geographical feature, economic hub or a key industry from which the generated prosperity spreads to the surrounding areas (Kayonde, Alexandre, and Speakman 2013, 6). And indeed, even though the World Bank indicates growth poles of a much larger geographical span, areas surrounding large-scale investments, such as the iron ore mines in Marampa, developed into economic focal points. However, the relation between mining and development is more complex and ambiguous, and the term growth pole, with its focus on increased economic and demographic growth and its reliance on the spread of prosperity, obscures processes other than growth that also take place in these investment landscapes. Investments, after all, affect social, political, economic and physical landscapes in a variety of ways and people respond to, influence and act upon these changes with different interests, concerns and strategies. Besides, the term growth pole does not problematize the social and spatial division of the assumed generated of wealth, even though this is highly problematic as part of the population is excluded from the growth and experiences stagnation or even decline (cooling down). Above, I referred to two different perceptions of Marampa's current situation of accelerated change – one of them highlighting disappointment and a feeling of exclusion, the other one emphasizing that "Lunsar is developing now", thereby stressing the improvements that can be witnessed. Growth pole approaches do not allow acknowledging to the full extent the co-existence and entanglement of these two different perceptions and developments. Moreover, taking into account how large-scale investments generate spaces open to negotiation between different forms of power and authority (cf. Sikor and Lund 2009) and may thus create fields of friction (Tsing 2005), using notions such as "growth pole" leads our attention away from the micro-politics, the numerous contestations and negotiations that take place within these investment arenas. A more appropriate concept to characterize investment landscapes is that of the hot-spot; a concept that sees these environments as contested space, characterized by processes of accelerated change and an increased density of activity and claims, where various forms of power are used, re-enforced and contested and processes of inclusion and exclusion unfold.[3]

Thus, in order to understand the double-bounded and complex realities of change in Marampa Chiefdom, it is important to look at the multitude of dynamics that emerge in the creation and frustration of expectations, in the experience of change and cooling down. In order to do so, the following sections explore some temporal, spatial and social dynamics of accelerated change in this hot-spot. First, I start with the temporal dimension by scrutinizing how the contemporary rise of expectations of change in Marampa should be contextualized in a history characterized by periods of boom and bust.

Memories and imaginaries: the creation of a landscape of expectations

The re-opening of the iron ore mines in Marampa Chiefdom in 2006 fitted well in Sierra Leone's national development agendas that were developed in the post-war period. In 2008, the Sierra Leone government launched the Agenda for Change (GoSL 2008), a policy document and national development agenda that would lead Sierra Leone out of poverty and back on the track of economic development. In 2013, this agenda was followed by the "Agenda for Prosperity: the road to a middle-income country" (GoSL 2013). Both agendas are Poverty Reduction Strategy Papers (PRSPs)[4], and build upon previous post-war policies, such as the National Recovery Strategy (GoSL 2002), especially in the realm of economic recovery. In doing so, these national agendas continued to emphasize the role of the private sector in economic recovery and development. Large-scale investments in agriculture and natural resource extraction are seen as crucial in the country's projected progress. As touched upon in the previous section, such policy approaches are facilitated by perspectives promoted by institutions such as the World Bank that see large-scale investments, drivers of development and economic change (Robertson and Pinstrup-Andersen 2010; Deininger et al. 2011; Kayonde, Alexandre, and Speakman 2013). Consequently, the government has in the post-war period attracted several large-scale investors, of which London Mining was one.

AN OVERHEATED WORLD

Even though iron ore prices were relatively low when London Mining started its operation in 2006, the history of iron ore mining in Marampa enabled the company to start an operation at relatively low costs. As I discuss in more detail elsewhere (Pijpers, forthcoming), due to the availability of tailings (residual material after processing of the ore) that could be re-processed, and a considerable amount of weathered, and therefore easily processable, material, London Mining was able to acquire funding even under difficult global market conditions. In addition, during the first years of the operation, developments on the world market for iron ore turned more favourable and enabled a growing industry in Marampa Chiefdom. Iron ore prices rapidly rose, reaching a peak of over 180 USD per ton in 2011–2012, compared to about 100 USD per ton in 2005. Not coincidentally, these rising prices corresponded with an extraordinary increase in domestic infrastructural investment in China and its rapidly growing steel industry, and thus an increased demand for raw materials. London Mining depended largely on China's consumption, with all of their production of 2012 and 2013 being sold to China testifying to that (London Mining Plc 2014).

The national post-war discourse of economic development, change and prosperity and the influx of investments, such as London Minings' iron ore mining operation, that bring along a modern and large infrastructure, triggered high expectations in rural Sierra Leone. These developments would finally enable people to move away from the country's recent history of crisis, characterized by Marampa Chiefdom's Paramount Chief Bai KobloQueen II as a time of "darkness":

> Since the closure (of the mines) from 1975, Marampa chiefdom has turned a ghost town. Marampa chiefdom has turned one of the darkest cities in the world, darkest city in Sierra Leone. We have been in the wilderness.

Whereas many parts of the world entered a period of stability with the end of the cold war in 1991, this year had a radically different meaning for Sierra Leone as it witnessed the beginning of a decade-long civil war (1991–2002). The war broke out after a long period of social and economic decay, in Marampa symbolized and expedited by the closure of the iron ore mines in 1975. Also the brief re-opening of the mines in the 1980s by Austro-Minerals (1982–1985), an Austrian mining company, did not turn the tide of the increasingly difficult situation in the area. This period of economic decline and political turbulence was contextualized in both regional/global developments, such as the oil shocks in 1973–1974 and 1979–1980, as well as internal political struggles for regime survival based on a patronage system at the detriment of a sustainable economic strategy (FasholeLuke and Riley 1989; Reno 1997). Years of discontent and frustration eventually led to the outbreak of the civil war in 1991. The impact of the war cannot be overemphasized, as it left a deep scar on Sierra Leone society and symbolizes a long and devastating crisis. Yet, interestingly, and contrary to what one may expect, in the contemporary situation in Marampa it is mostly the closure of the iron ore mines that is taken as an initial reference point to this time of crisis. The war is obviously acknowledged and not forgotten, yet, the re-emergence of iron ore mining in the present and people's concerns, desires, imaginations and expectations of this development is framed in memories and experiences of past mining activities. Thus, whereas the closure of the iron ore mines in the 1970s is related to the emergence of a period of darkness, the re-opening of these mines in 2006 is associated with the ending of it.

Considering the area's recent history of devastating crisis, it is not surprising that the reopening of the mines and the material manifestations of change led to a rise in expectations and hope, and fed into a local discourse on how life was changing for the better. Moreover, besides the area's recent history of darkness, contemporary imaginations of a future positive were also nursed by memories of a more prosperous history. After all, the Northern Province of Sierra Leone, including Marampa Chiefdom, had experienced periods of economic growth and industrial development before the crisis started (van der Laan 1965; Fage 1969; Lanning and Mueller 1979; Kamara 1981). In Marampa, this period of relative prosperity, of economic growth and industrial development, was directly related to the initial establishment of the iron ore mining industry in the 1930s.

When iron ore was discovered in Marampa in 1926 during the geological surveys commissioned by the British Empire, large-scale iron ore extraction by the Sierra Leone Development Company (DELCO) soon commenced. The mines attracted numerous of people from all around the country and, as Jarrett argued in 1956, the town closest to the mines (Lunsar) developed from a "tiny village of about half a dozen huts in the 1920's [...to] until today its population is estimated at about 15.000" (1956, 153). Local people in contemporary Marampa vividly and positively remember this previous period of iron ore mining, whether by direct experience or through oral history. Frequently, these memories are expressed in phrases such as "During DELCO there was no problem" and "Just imagine, we had a good living with the DELCO". More than being reflections on the past, these comments have to be seen as strategic statements in the context of contemporary discussions regarding the presence and performance of the chiefdom's current iron ore miner, London Mining (Pijpers, forthcoming). Subsequently, they both refer to a past in which there was hope for a better future, a period with high "expectations of modernity" (see Ferguson 1999), as well as they allow people to make claims towards the company, express dissatisfaction and voice imaginations of a future positive. Logically, not everybody does this in similar ways. Through processes of celebrating and silencing certain past periods (see also Trouillot 1995), different groups of actors, such as companies, local communities and politicians, stage different elements of Marampa's history in order to legitimize their actions, strengthen their position, negotiate possibilities in the present and make claims towards the future (Pijpers, forthcoming).

This brief history of Marampa sketched out above shows how the contemporary field is embedded in a multitude of developments at different scales, such as the Chinese infrastructural development project, the global commodity crisis that emerged around 2010, a civil war, national and local politics embarking of social economic recovery and a complex global development apparatus projecting different development ideologies. Moreover, it also illustrates how the chiefdom's history of boom and bust, characterized by resource extraction, actively feeds into the contemporary social situation in Marampa. As such, it illustrates how the presence (or absence) of mining, whether in the past, present or future (in this case in all three), casts its influence over the creation of not only physical, but also social, political and economic landscapes.

The role of time and temporality is increasingly prominent in studies on natural resource extraction. Like this paper on accelerated change and cooling down in Marampa, these studies highlight this dimension of time and temporality in multiple instances, such as the relations between different actors involved in resource extraction, the integration of local lifeworlds into global economies, the changing (uncertain) circumstances triggered by this integration, and the prominent role of expectations of what present and future resource extraction may bring.

Besides the ground-breaking work of Ferguson, who in *Expectations of Modernity* (1999) focuses on the lives of Zambian miners on the Copperbelt in a period of economic decline after Zambia's economic boom in the 1960s and 1970s, Weszkalnys, also concerned with the temporality of resources and resource extraction, discusses the role of hope and expectations of an "oil economy without oil" (2008, 474) in Sao Tomé e Príncipe. She demonstrates how the assumed presence of oil generated a number of activities by numerous stakeholders in anticipation of a (potential) oil future, one of these activities being the management of expectations (Weszkalnys 2008). Halvaksz (2008) also discusses temporal questions in mining communities, in his case those brought about by mine closures. He argues that "mines are not merely extracting minerals, but are also marking time and space with their appearances" (Halvaksz 2008, 21), and that the expectations of current and future mining projects are "as much about creative engagement of humans with a physically transformed as they are about historical and cultural experiences" (Halvaksz 2008, 21). Moreover, focusing on industrial mining companies, Hilson (2011), Teschner (2013) and Luning and Pijpers (forthcoming) illustrate how mining companies' operations are influenced by, among other things, social histories of mining of various scales and legacies of industrial predecessors. Furthermore, Kesküla (in this special issue, 2016) analyses how miners' discourse of new mining technologies and tempo and rhythm of work opens an opportunity to engage with different temporalities of socialism and neoliberalization. Additionally, Knapp and Pigott (1997) highlight the role of material culture in tracing the evidence of the social life of miners and mining areas. And indeed, in Marampa, the numerous remains of the Delco mining period (still intact houses, bygone industrial infrastructure, the still standing and frequently used Lunsar town hall) are by many people considered as traces of a better past with the more "thick" social engagement (Ferguson 2006) of a concerned and caring company. What is thus of additional interest in this case is that, besides signifying an industrial past, these remains are appropriated and deployed in present negotiations of a future positive.

Taking into account the entanglement of past, present and future that is highlighted in this paper, as well as in the studies discussed above, the contemporary field of resource extraction can be fruitfully approached as a temporal site, as "a processual configuration through which time and space continuously interweave to chart out new analytical terrains" (Dalsgaard and Nielsen 2013, 3). In this temporal site, versions of both past and future are configured into a particular social situation and become meaningful in relation to present events and imaginations. Hirsch and Stewart (2005, 262) capture such a situation elegantly with the term historicity: "the manner in which persons operating under the constraints of social ideologies make sense of the past, while anticipating the future". Slightly rephrasing this definition, one can argue that given people's (or institutions') contemporary and future challenges, ideologies and imaginations, the past is appropriated in multiple ways that serve these ideologies, challenges and imaginations in strategic ways. This approach of historicity has recently been applied to studies of austerity and crisis in Europe, showing how "across Southern Europe, people are looking to the past to inform coping strategies or conjure strength, to express fear or to provide glimpses of hope for the future" (Knight and Stewart 2016, 4). As we have seen, similar processes are at hand in Marampa, a space of change, contestation and competition, where the recent mining boom offers many opportunities, but where people are also afraid to be excluded from these opportunities.

Zooming in on the hot-spot: spatial and social divisions of change

The previous section stressed how periods of boom and bust have succeeded each other in Marampa and how imaginations of resource extraction in the past, present and future play a role in informing people's contemporary experiences of accelerated change and give shape to ideas of how life should look like. This section continues the focus on the intertwinement of accelerated change and cooling down and on the varying experiences of change within Marampa's current moment of rising expectations and new opportunities by looking at several spatial and social features of Marampa's accelerated change. In other words, this section asks where and for whom do processes of accelerated change and cooling down occur? This allows us to see not only periods of boom and bust succeeding and informing each other over time, but also to scrutinize how dynamics of boom and bust can feature simultaneously within one particular period of accelerated change in a particular place.

In or outside – where is the change?

Although Marampa as a whole may experience accelerated change, commonly manifested in material improvements, the spaces where these signs of progress occur vary. Taking the mining concession as a starting point, since mining is the driving force of change here, there are three main zones to be distinguished: (1) rural areas outside the concession, (2) rural areas inside the concession and (3) an urban area outside the concession. As the discussion of these zones below will show, in all three of them the impacts (positive and/or negative) are perceived differently.

Manonkoh is a village located just outside the London Mining concession area. Even though it had been included in the concession during the initial phase of the operation, after two years, during which the annual surface rent was paid to the landowners, London Mining relinquished this part of the concession as they did not intend to use it for mining activities. As a consequence, expectations and hope for access to opportunities in the community vanished and disappointment and frustration rose. During a group discussion in the village, the following statement exemplified this process:

> When London Mining came to Lunsar they went to the surrounding villages to ask the young people to come and brush. We were promised employment, but nobody is employed. We are also outside the concession area. They [London Mining] paid surface rent for two years, but then we were moved outside the concession area. We are just suffering for nothing, we have no benefits. The other villages that are inside the concession have more benefits. But those people do not expose what they are gaining from the mining people and we are not allowed to attend any meetings in the other villages.

The statement makes explicit that a large-scale investment may open up many opportunities and benefits, but the degree to which these affect an individual or group, in this case a village, varies greatly. Discussions in Manonkoh highlighted how community members perceived to be only experiencing the negative consequences of the mining operation, which is mainly attributed to their exclusion from being inside the concession. In

Golubs' words, when reviewing Jacka's ethnography of the people living just outside of the main area affected by the Porgera gold mine in Papua New Guinea (2015), people in Manonkoh are "outside the benefit zone, [yet] inside the impact zone" (Golub 2015). Many of the problems the community members listed were related to the flooding of a lake nearby which destroyed many crops, to their missing out on the surface rent payments and to the lack of employment in the mining. This opposed to villages that are inside the concession area and that serve as their reference points. Here, it is believed and argued, people enjoy a variety of benefits, such as surface rent payment, job opportunities and more philanthropic kinds of support, although the exact gains seem to be concealed with secrecy.[5]

However, moving on towards the kind of villages the people from Manonkoh referred to (the second zone that covers the rural areas inside the concession), there were also complaints about the loss of land and livelihoods, despite being compensated for this.[6] Even though being inside the concession area implied certain rights for compensation and surface rent payments,[7] this appeared to be not to the satisfaction of all. Maforki is such a village. The settlement itself is located on the fringes of the concession, but the village land falls within the concession. Many of the benefits that are expected occurred here: surface rent payments, compensation for the loss of crops, the refurbishment of the school and a job here and there. Yet, upon visiting Maforki, complaints were multiple and appeared to be of a similar nature as those in Manonkoh. The issues and frustrations here even resulted in a "strike" (an attack on several facilities of the mining company) and a serious conflict between the village on the one hand and local authorities, such as the local police unit and the Paramount Chief, on the other. It was claimed by company staff and local authorities that the case of Maforki was instrumental to some "big men" in the community, trying to gain support of mostly disappointed young men through highlighting, or as some argue, instigating, conflict between the communities and London Mining. In any case, the example of Maforki illustrates the complex dynamics of change as, despite several positive developments in this village, the benefits that community members envisaged clearly did not materialize in a satisfactory way.[8]

When visiting the areas both inside and outside the concession, it becomes clear that many of the visible changes actually occur in the urbanizing centre Lunsar, located outside the concession. Here economic activities developed, businesses started-up and grew, the market supplied more and more people with food and other items, roads were constructed and communal structures re-habilitated and refurbished. "Lunsar has style now", a local salesman working in a small convenient store appealingly characterized the situation to me once. In a similar way, one of the town councillors, the late Papa Kamara, described the situation as follows:

> People are moving well in the community, there is rapid development in the community: solar lights, streets, water in the township. It's better than before, life is improving and everyday Lunsar is becoming more populated, everyday people are coming for jobs.

We expected better things to happen – for whom is the change?

Statements such as the one above by the town councillor highlight the pride in the recent developments and the ongoing improvements of life in the town. But these statements often heard in the urban centre of Lunsar also contrast sharply with those in the villages around, with the other zones of accelerated change that I distinguished (rural areas outside the concession and rural areas inside the concession). The reasons for this spatial division of the positive effects of accelerated change, and thus for the creation of developing and cooled down areas, lie in the social division of it and its dependency on local financial flows, flows that concentrate in Lunsar for a variety of reasons.

First of all, many of the improvements that can be instantly recognized are due to public investments, either by London Mining, the chiefdom authorities or by a state body. By being a residential, political and economic hub in the chiefdom, Lunsar is the focal point of these material improvements, as opposed to the rural areas where relatively few people live. In the past years Lunsar has had its market place renovated and the town hall refurbished by London Mining and the (local) government has initiated projects ensuring that the central roads would be paved with asphalt and electricity supply established. Although infrastructural projects are carried out in the rural areas (London Mining has for example constructed water wells in several villages and refurbished schools), these investments have been limited in comparison to Lunsar. Yet, more importantly than these investments, it is the increased circulation of money in Lunsar. "It's only the people without a job that are complaining" the local resident quoted in the introduction assured me. Whether that is factually correct or not, it highlights the importance of wage employment in this area, which has in rural Sierra Leone since long been offered by mining companies (Swindell 1975). Not surprisingly, the (temporal) dynamics of the labour requirements of mining operations and, subsequently, the social background of their staff have an interesting role to play.

Employed or made redundant?

Different stages of mining operations require different activities and workforces. Moreover, the particular approach to extraction that a mining company uses should be situated in the wider context at a particular moment, as large-scale resource extraction is entangled in local, national, regional and global developments.[9] Fluctuations in the global commodity markets, the development of new extraction techniques, national, regional and global political agendas, the local social context (think for example about the outbreak of a viral disease) or the sudden boom in competitive markets are just a few examples that may influence the way in and the extent to which a resource is extracted. These dynamics have a direct influence on the work force and could result in increasing or decreasing the amount of labourers who are recruited. Moreover, the common (and thus calculable) cycle of a mining operation also impacts upon the amount and the kind of labour that an operation requires.

One could distinguish several phases of a mining operation: prospecting, exploration, development, production and reclamation. Naturally some of these stages could be sub-divided, development could be split up, for example, in mine-site design on the one hand and construction on the other. For our purpose and in the context of iron ore mining in Marampa, there are three stages important to the local dynamics of expectations and change: exploration, development/construction and production.

During the exploration phase, in which a company is trying to map out its deposit, the amount of labour that is required is limited. Local demands may therefore be limited as well; the operation has not started yet and expectations are still to be fulfilled. In Marampa this was well illustrated by the way discussions in 2013/2014 all focused on London Minings' operation, thereby almost ignoring the presence of another mining company, Marampa Iron Ore, which was still in its exploration phase. When the development phase of London Minings' operation commenced in 2006, a considerable amount of unskilled and low-skilled labour was recruited, as the earlier quotations from the discussion in Manonkoh illustrate. Construction work took place, bushes were cleared, drivers for vehicles were sought, compounds brushed and offices painted. During this period a relatively large amount of "locals" could thus hope for and also found employment in the mines. Naturally, these developments also began to attract people from all over the country, trying to find opportunities in this booming area.[10] However, after this initial infrastructural work conducted under the development phase had been finished, more skilled labour was demanded for the production phase. As a result, part of the workforce was laid off, made redundant and part of it replaced by skilled labour, which is often sourced from outside the local communities where the required skills are not available. Consequently, the opportunities imagined by local inhabitants living in the proximity of the mines seem to be disappearing. Disappointment, frustration, hopelessness and, at times, physical expression of anger, as it was the case with the "strike" in Maforki, are the result.

Many of the "new" employees of the company thus came from outside the chiefdom, from other rural areas in the country, but most often from the capital where they received their education. These "strangers" usually settle in the urban centre. Here they can not only find housing more easily, but also entertainment, facilities like electricity and football cinema's and social contacts. It is here where a fair share of their money is spent and therefore also where money can be made. It is thus a place where not only public, but also private investments take place and may become profitable. But salaries through wage employment do not constitute the only financial flow that is directly linked to the mining operations.

Financial compensation

Another source of mining-related income is the payment of crop compensation to farmers and the yearly surface rent payment to the landowners. Considering that crop compensation is a one-time payment, the importance of this source of money is relatively small. The potentiality of the payment of the yearly surface rent, however, is considerably larger. At first sight, this payment may be more connected to the rural areas, since this is where the land leased by London Mining is located. However, this financial flow also has important urban ties.

As part of the land-lease agreement, London Mining (as any other mining company) pays a yearly surface rent. In Sierra Leone, 50% of the surface rent is paid to the landowners directly.[11] The 2013 surface rent, paid to a total number of eight landowning families, was approximately 150,000 USD. This is a considerable amount of money, especially in rural Sierra Leone. However, only eight landowning families received surface rent payment and all eight represented a different village (some of them owning land in more than one village). Considering that villages comprise of several families, many families did not see anything of the surface rent money. Moreover, with the surface rent being received by the head of the family, the money is most often limitedly distributed even within the family itself and thus does not spread extensively within the village network. Furthermore, several landowners do not permanently reside in the villages where they own land, but often have houses in urban areas, such as Lunsar or Freetown. During meetings in one of the villages within the concession, a resident of this village illustrated this, arguing that "most of them don't even stay in the village, but in Lunsar of Freetown. He [referring to a landowner] is only here when he hears of something beneficial". This marginal redistribution of financial compensation within villages and families to a particular stakeholder or party, implies that a larger amount of people residing in rural villages do not receive any direct benefits from the mining operations, something which they surely had hoped for and expected. In addition, due to the lack of basic education many of these people are not suitable for the companies' workforce once more skilled labour is required.

Considering the spatial and social division of the direct benefits from the mining operations and of the related material changes, it has become clear that not everywhere and not by everyone in this hot-spot is the current period of accelerated change experienced in the way it was imagined and expected. Moreover, the strike in Maforki, the complaints in Manonkoh, the considerable new wealth of landowners and the temporality of employment are all examples of the complex reality of growth and change in this hot-spot. In other words, through combining several temporal, spatial and social dynamics, we see that in a time of accelerated change, when indeed much is changing, a pocket of people develop that rather experience a relative cooling down or an exclusion from the changing world around them. It is exactly this paradox in locating accelerated change that provides some interesting perspectives on overheating, which I will turn to in the next and final section.

Overheating in a hot-spot: a matter of getting cold?

In this paper, I have set out to scrutinize the current situation of accelerated change, spurred by a large-scale iron ore mining investment, in Marampa Chiefdom in Sierra Leone. First of all, I have analysed Marampa as a landscape of expectations and as a hot-spot, a contested space characterized by accelerated change and an increased density of activity and claims, where power is deployed in various forms and processes of inclusion and exclusion unfold. Subsequently, inspired by debates regarding the role of temporality in the field (see for example Trouillot 1995; Hirsch and Stewart 2005; Dalsgaard and Nielsen 2013; Knight and Stewart 2016), in particular in mining environments (see, among others, Knapp and Pigott 1997; Ferguson 1999; Halvaksz 2008; Weszkalnys 2008), I discussed how local inhabitants' current desires for the future are entangled in a (recent) history of boom and bust. This discussion resonates well with Kesküla's analysis (this issue) in which she shows how in an Estonian oil-shale mine multiple temporalities exist simultaneously and how the mine's working environment renders certain moments and periods more prominent and influential than others. As I discussed in this paper, in the case of Marampa, periods of progress and development, of stability and growth, on the one hand, and of crisis on the other, have succeeded each other. In the contemporary situation, people actively draw upon this history in order to make sense of the present and make claims towards a better future, thereby appropriating history in particular ways. These processes are not similar to all groups in society as different groups have different interests and celebrate and silence different pasts in order to negotiate different futures (Pijpers, forthcoming).

Furthermore, besides the occurrence and experience of growth and accelerated change, a number of people simultaneously experience a form of cooling down, of stagnation and deceleration. As change was expected, this situation leads to frustration, disappointment and at times tension between different individuals, communities, political authorities and the company. It may lead to what Eriksen (2016a, 16) has termed overheating, the "unevenly paced change where exogenous and endogenous factors combine to lead to instability, uncertainty and unintended consequences in a broad range of institutions and practices, and contribute to a widely shared feeling of powerlessness and alienation".

The features of change in Marampa discussed here have mainly focused on material improvements in public and private life. They are immediate changes in livelihood conditions, such as better access to education, access to finance and improved infrastructure. Although it is outside the scope of this paper, it is still important to point to the fact that several of the phenomena discussed here may have more profound social effects in society. An example briefly stipulated upon previously is the rise of a fierce identity politics, due to the influx of strangers and an increased competition of resources (mainly jobs). Additionally, the relations between landowners and land-users, or between autochthones and strangers (some of them being new, but some of them may have also lived in the area for generations) experience profound shifts due to the dynamics of the rise of a large-scale economy in a small-scale society. This, however, is a topic to be explored elsewhere, as this paper focused on locating accelerated change, or the lack thereof, in time and place.

The phenomena I discussed regarding the spatial and social dynamics of accelerated change are not exclusively applicable to Sierra Leone. It is widely recognized, most recently in analyses that situate labour in debates on large-scale investments and development, that the development of new economies causes shifts in, for example, labour practices and may benefit certain groups, yet may cause new challenges to others (see for an excellent example Li 2011). In this analysis, I show how these processes play out in a marginalized part of the world, where any kind of change is desired as the starting point is so rudimentary. The opening up of new opportunities gives rise to hot-spots where fierce competition over these opportunities emerges. My analysis demonstrates how this hot-spot is constituted, among other things, through particular temporal, spatial and social dynamics. The intertwinements of past memories and futures desires, the creation of centres and peripheries and the different groups and individuals that are either benefiting or losing out all contribute to contested space which features both an inclusion and exclusion of the accelerated change that takes place.

Besides contributing to debates regarding the local perceptions and responses to globalization (Eriksen 2016b), and to a growing body of literature within an anthropology of mining, the particularities of processes of accelerated change and cooling down in Marampa also provide an interesting perspective on the way we may look at overheating (Eriksen 2016a). Interestingly, whereas overheating is often considered to emerge as a feature of accelerated or an uneven pace of change, my ethnography illustrates how overheating can also emerge due to a lack of change or due to an exclusion from the change that is expected or witnessed. People's frustration, uncertainty and powerlessness, mainly occurs in the zones and among the groups that are excluded from both the observed developments elsewhere (places that are in close proximity) and the improved future that was hoped for and expected. Thus, in this case, the concern is not with accelerated change as such (not the emergence of a large-scale mining industry), but the incapability to, or the exclusion from, participating in and benefitting from the opportunities associated with accelerated change. Subsequently, overheating may be seen not only as the result of too fast or unevenly changing lifeworlds in general, but in particular as the result of a feeling of exclusion from the changes unfolding, an exclusion from the promises of a better future.

Acknowledgements

Many thanks go to Thomas H. Eriksen, the editor and an anonymous reviewer for their helpful comments on drafts of this paper. Naturally, my appreciation also goes to all of those who I engaged with during fieldwork. Field research for this paper was conducted in 2013–2014 as part of the research project "Overheating: the three crises of globalisation", at the Department of Social Anthropology, University of Oslo.

Notes

1. This paper draws upon fieldwork conducted in May 2013 and between October 2013 and July 2014, prior to the outbreak of the Ebola virus in West Africa in 2014 and the dramatic fall of the iron price starting in December 2013. Per 16 October 2014, London Mining PLC went under administration and, although Timis Corporation has taken over the Marampa mines, the future of the operation is uncertain. Even though these recent developments are not taken into the analysis here specifically, as will become clear, they fit well into the boom and bust dynamics studied.
2. Sierra Leone's political administration is divided into provinces (4) and districts (14), governed by (decentralized bodies of) the national government on the one hand and chiefdoms (149), governed by Paramount Chiefs, on the other. The boundaries between these distinct spaces of governance often cross and overlap, resulting in situations in which multiple political authorities engage in decision-making processes, such as regarding the establishment of large-scale investments.
3. This is a reworked version of an earlier conceptualization proposed in Pijpers (2014).
4. PRSPs are policy documents that describe macroeconomic, structural and social policies and programs to promote growth and reduce poverty. As an initiative of the IMF and World Bank, they are prepared by governments and are crucial to the IMF's economic and financial programs in low-income countries. See for more information http://www.imf.org/external/np/exr/facts/prsp.htm.
5. For more detailed studies on secrecy in Sierra Leone, see e.g. Ferme (1999, 2001) and Shaw (2000, 2002).
6. A methodological reflection is crucial here. Although the statements made in these villages are sincere, they have to be seen as part of a larger strategy to ensure a better future. As a researcher, being able to move between local communities, political authorities and company staff and management, I could serve as a translator of, in this case, community interests. It is, therefore, crucial to acknowledge the context in which negative or positive reflections on the situation are made. This makes people's opinions not less relevant, on the contrary, I would argue, as they illustrate expectations, desires and frustrations that are crucial for understanding hot-spots.
7. In Sierra Leone, like in most other countries in the world (the US being a well-known exception), sub-surface rights are vested in the state, whereas surface rights can be with either the

state, local authorities or local land-owners. This means that while a local land-owner can own the surface rights, the interest of the state in natural resource extraction may overrule these rights. In such cases, surface rent needs to be paid to the owners of the land. Naturally, all property destroyed by a mining operations is required to be compensated as well.
8. The emphasis on "satisfactory" is important here. The experience of development and progress is entangled in imaginations and expectations. Life did improve a great deal in many of these villages compared to 2003, when I first visited the area after the war. However, according to local communities, improvements have not been sufficient and satisfying.
9. See e.g. Park and MacDiarmid (1975), Dumett (1998), Ferguson (2005), Hilson (2011), Appel (2012), Sosa (2012), Kirsch (2014), Golub (2014), Welker (2014) and Luning and Pijpers (forthcoming).
10. It is not surprising that large-scale investments attract considerable amount of people who seek employment. Unemployment is a serious issue in Sierra Leone and large-scale investments offer a good proportion of the few employment opportunities available. This has serious consequences, as the pressure on both investors as well as on local environments increases. The influx of strangers from elsewhere in Sierra Leone creates, e.g., tension as local populations fear that others will be picking the fruits of the investments. This may result in a fierce local identity politics based on ideas of autochthony and belonging (Pijpers, 2016).
11. The remaining 50% is divided over four other recipients: the Paramount Chief 15%, the District Council 15%, the ?Chiefdom Administration 10% and the Constituency Development Fund (under the responsibility of the local Member of Parliament) 10%.

Disclosure statement

No potential conflict of interest was reported by the author.

Funding

This work was funded by the European Research Council (ERC), project number 295843.

References

Appel, H. 2012. "Walls and White Elephants: Oil Extraction, Responsibility, and Infrastructural Violence in Equatorial Guinea." *Ethnography* 13 (4): 439–465.
Dalsgaard, S., and M. Nielsen. 2013. "Introduction: Time and the Field." Special Issue of *Social Analysis* 57 (1): 1–19.
Deininger, K., D. Byerlee, J. Lindsay, A. Norton, H. Selod, and M. Stickler. 2011. *Rising Global Interest in Farmland: Can It Yield Sustainable and Equitable Benefits?* Washington, DC: The World Bank.
Dumett, R. E. 1998. *El Dorado in West Africa*. Athens/Oxford: Ohio University Press/James Currey.
Eriksen, T. H. 2016a. *Overheating: Coming to Terms with Accelerated Change*. London: Pluto Press.
Eriksen, T. H. 2016b. "Overheating: The World Since 1991." *History and Anthropology*. doi:10.1080/02757206.2016.1218865.
Fage, J. D. 1969. *A History of West Africa*. Cambridge: Cambridge University Press.
FasholeLuke, D., and S. P. Riley. 1989. "The Politics of Economic Decline in Sierra Leone." *The Journal of Modern African Studies* 27 (1): 133–141.

Ferguson, J. 1999. *Expectations of Modernity: Myths and Meanings of Urban Life on the Zambian Copperbelt*. Berkeley: University of California Press.

Ferguson, J. 2005. "Seeing Like an Oil Company: Space, Security, and Global Capital in Neoliberal Africa." *American Anthropologist* 107: 377–382.

Ferguson, J. 2006. *Global Shadows: Africa in the Neoliberal World Order*. Durham, NC: Duke University Press.

Ferme, M. 1999. *The Underneath of Things: Violence, History, and the Everyday in Sierra Leone*. Berkeley: University of California Press.

Ferme, M. 2001. "Staging Politisi: The Dialogics of Publicity and Secrecy in Sierra Leone." In *Civil Society and the Political Imagination in Africa: Critical Perspectives*, edited by J. L. Comaroff, 160–191. Chicago: The University of Chicago Press.

Geschiere, P., and F. Nyamnjoh. 2000. "Capitalism and Autochthony: The Seesaw of Mobility and Belonging." *Public Culture* 12 (2): 423–452.

Golub, A. 2014. *Leviathans at the Gold Mine: Creating Indigenous and Corporate Actors in Papua New Guinea*. Durham, NC: Duke University Press.

Golub, A. 2015. "Outside the Benefit Zone, Inside the Impact Zone: Jerry Jacka on Mining and Social Change in Porgera, Papua New Guinea." *American Anthropological Association: Anthropology Book Forum – Open Access Book Reviews*. http://www.anthropology-news.org/?book-review=outside-the-benefit-zone-inside-the-impact-zone-jerry-jacka-on-mining-and-social-change-in-porgera-papua-new-guinea.

GoSL (The Government of Sierra Leone). 2002. *National Recovery Strategy Sierra Leone 2002–2003*. Freetown: Government of Sierra Leone.

GoSL (The Government of Sierra Leone). 2013. *The Agenda for Prosperity: Road to Middle Income Status. Sierra Leone's Third Generation Poverty Reduction Strategy Paper (2013–2018)*. Freetown: Government of Sierra Leone.

GoSL (The Republic of Sierra Leone). 2008. *An Agenda for Change. Second Poverty Reduction Strategy (PRSP II) 2008–2012*. Freetown: Government of Sierra Leone.

Halvaksz, J. A. 2008. "Whose Closure? Appearances, Temporality and Mineral Extraction in Papua New Guinea." *Journal of the Royal Anthropological Institute* 14 (1): 21–37.

Hilson, G. 2011. "Inherited Commitments: Do Changes in Ownership Affect Corporate Social Responsibility (CSR) at African Gold Mines?" *African Journal of Business Management* 5 (27): 10921–10939.

Hirsch, E., and C. Stewart. 2005. "Introduction: Ethnographies of Historicity." *History and Anthropology* 16 (3): 261–274.

Jacka, J. K. 2015. *Alchemy in the Rain Forest: Politics, Ecology, and Resilience in a New Guinea Mining Area*. Durham: Duke University Press.

Jarrett, H. R. 1956. "Lunsar: A Study of an Iron Ore Mining Center in Sierra Leone." *Economic Geography* 32 (2): 153–161.

Kamara, J. N. 1981. "Informal Credit Among Coffee/Cocoa Farmers in the Upper Moa Basin, Eastern Province of Sierra Leone: A Case Study." In *Some Socio-Economic Structures and Related Grass Roots Problems in Rural Sierra Leone*, edited by J. Kamara, and H. Turay, 116–136. Freetown: Njala University.

Kayonde, S., L. H. Alexandre, and J. F. Speakman. 2013. *Sierra Leone – Growth Pole Diagnostic: First Phase of the Growth Poles Program*. Washington, DC: World Bank Group. http://documents.worldbank.org/curated/en/2013/11/19678109/sierra-leone-growth-pole-diagnostic-growth-poles-program-phase.

Keskula, E. Forthcoming. "Temporalities, Time and the Everyday: New Technology as a Marker of Change in an Estonian Mine." *History and Anthropology*.

Kirsch, S. 2014. *Mining Capitalism: The Relationship Between Corporations and Their Critics*. Berkeley: University of California Press.

Knapp, A. B., and V. Pigott. 1997. "The Archeology and Anthropology of Mining: Social Approaches to an Industrial Past." *Current Anthropology* 38 (2): 300–304.

Knight, D. M., and C. Stewart. 2016. "Ethnographies of Austerity: Temporality, Crisis and Affect in Southern Europe." *History and Anthropology* 27 (1): 1–18.

van der Laan, H. L. 1965. *The Sierra Leone Diamonds: An Economic Study Covering the Years 1952–1961*. Oxford: Oxford University Press on behalf of Fourah Bay College, the University College of Sierra Leone.

Lanning, G., and M. Mueller. 1979. *Africa Undermined*. New York: Penguin Books.

Li, T. M. 2011. "Centering Labor in the Land Grab Debate." *The Journal of Peasant Studies* 38 (2): 281–298.

London Mining Plc. 2014. *Annual Report 2013. Producing High Quality Iron Ore for the Global Steel Industry*. London: London Mining Plc.

Luning, S., and R. J. Pijpers. Forthcoming. Governing Access to Gold in Ghana: In-depth Geopolitics on Mining Concessions. *Africa*.

Meyer, B., and P. Geschiere. 1999. *Globalization and Identity: Dialectics of Flow and Closure*. Oxford: Blackwell Publishers.

Park, C. F., and R. A. MacDiarmid. 1975. *Ore Deposits*. San Francisco: Freeman.

Pijpers, R. J. 2014. "Crops and Carats: Exploring the Interconnectedness of Mining and Agriculture in Sub-Saharan Africa." *Futures* 62 (part A): 32–39.

Pijpers, R. J. 2016. "Politics of Localness: Claiming Gains in Rural Sierra Leone." In *Identity Destabilised: Living in an Overheated World*, edited by T. H. Eriksen, and E. Schober. London: Pluto Press.

Pijpers, R. J. Forthcoming. "Lost Glory or Poor Legacy? Mining Pasts, Future Projects in Rural Sierra Leone." In *Mining History: Corporate Strategies, Heritage and Development*, edited by J. B. Gewald, J. Jansen, and S. Luning. London: Routledge Studies in Culture and Development.

Reno, W. 1997. "War, Markets, and the Reconfiguration of West Africa's Weak States." *Comparative Politics* 29 (4): 493–510.

Robertson, B., and P. Pinstrup-Andersen. 2010. "Global Land Acquisition: Neo-Colonialism or Development Opportunity?" *Food Security* 2: 271–283.

Shaw, R. 2000. "Tok af, lef af': A Political Economy of Temne Techniques of Secrecy and Self." In *African Philosophy as Cultural Inquiry*, edited by L Karp, and D. A. Masolo, 25–49. Bloomington: Indiana University Press.

Shaw, R. 2002. *Memories of the Slave Trade: Ritual and the Historical Imagination in Sierra Leone*. Chicago: University of Chicago Press.

Sikor, T., and L. Lund. 2009. "Access and Property: A Question of Power and Authority." *Development and Change* 40 (1): 1–22.

Sosa, I. 2012. "Responsible Investment Case Studies: Newmont and Goldcorp." In *Governance Ecosystems: CSR in the Latin American Mining Sector*, edited by J. Sagebien, and N. M. Lindsay, 201–213. London: Palgrave.

Swindell, K. 1975. "Mining Workers in Sierra Leone: Their Stability and Marital Status." *African Affairs* 74 (295): 180–190.

Teschner, B. 2013. "How You Start Matters: A Comparison of Gold Fields' Tarkwa and Damang Mines and their Divergent Relationships with Local Small-Scale Miners in Ghana." *Resources Policy* 38: 332–340.

Trouillot, M. R. 1995. *Silencing the Past: Power and the Production of History*. Boston, MA: Beacon Press.

Tsing, A. L. 2005. *Friction: An Ethnography of Global Connection*. Princeton, NJ: Princeton University Press.

Welker, M. 2014. *Enacting the Corporation: An American Mining Firm in Post-Authoritarian Indonesia*. Berkeley: University of California Press.

Weszkalnys, G. 2008. "Hope & Oil: Expectations in São Tomé E Príncipe." *Review of African Political Economy* 35 (117): 473–482.

Temporalities, time and the everyday: new technology as a marker of change in an Estonian mine

Eeva Kesküla

ABSTRACT
This paper explores the relationship between men and mining technology in an Estonian oil shale mine. It traces the linear time of socialism and postsocialism, arguing that for Estonian miners, the end of socialism might not have been as radical of a change as changing the mining technology in early 2000s. The introduction of the new technology changed the nature and perception of miners' work, as well as the opportunities of controlling the everyday tempo of work. The way miners talk about new technology (*novaia tekhnika*) opens a window for exploring the different temporalities of socialism and capitalism. It allows seeing the way the time, through the state and the market, shapes small time of the everyday, the tempo of and rhythm of work. The wider changes from socialism to neoliberal capitalism which alter workplace relations, and create new class structures, are most acutely experienced at the nexus where new technology changes the rhythm and pace of work, the bodily activity of production which Bourdieu calls tempo. Furthermore, the introduction of new technology has implications to the job security and health of miners.

Introduction

"We now have new technology, we have contemporary machines, the work is much more efficient now, cleaner, faster and warmer", the Estonian oil shale miners often told me during my fieldwork in 2010–2011. The old, rusty Soviet technology has been replaced by contemporary, diesel-fuelled efficient bright yellow machinery from Germany, Poland and Finland. An old miner, born in 1922, who had a chance to visit the mine many years after his retirement, explained,

> The work that I did and what my son does now are totally different. He could wear a shirt and tie to the mine if he wanted to. But the way I was sweating, taking off even my undershirt, with a spade in my hand, it was like Gulag, only without guards.

For the Estonian miners, new technology was a key indicator of change among a plethora of other recent changes. In Estonia, as elsewhere the former socialist block, the 1990s were marked by fast penetration of international capital, privatization, reorganization of economy, including deindustrialization, raising questions about new temporal orders. While political scientists were often talking about 1991 as a rupture, expecting a linear transition from socialism to capitalism, anthropologists have emphasized that there was no clear breaking point between socialism and postsocialism, and it is more fruitful to talk about gradual transformations (Burawoy and Verdery 1998; Verdery 2002). Furthermore, before the collapse of the Soviet Union, no one was expecting change, everything was forever, until it was no more (Yurchak 2006).

These processes do not characterize only the postsocialist area but also postcolonial spaces (Chari and Verdery 2009). Today's overheated world can be described as one of acceleration and intensified contact between different locations, due to new technological solutions as well as a Post-Cold-War geopolitical order, hypermobility of capital and flexible production. Population growth and increased energy consumption in the last decade are signified by the increased volume of mining, bringing about tensions regarding land, labour and the environment (Eriksen 2016a). In the time of economic crisis, labour and its relation to technology become a key site of contestation. Speeding up economic activities and natural resource extraction go hand in hand with the unpredictable economic cycles and crises in capital accumulation that create uncertainty about the future and opportunities of social reproduction. The times of crisis and acceleration also emphasize simultaneous multiple coexisting contradictory and disjunctive temporalities. With that in mind, changes in mining technology in Estonia raise questions of wider significance. What are the implications of the penetrations of new temporalities, new narratives of nationalist times and regimes of labour discipline? How do the global, local and the everyday interplay and how is it experienced locally? What are the implications in a society where the meaning of labour has changed so radically?

In this article, I argue that there are multiple temporalities present in the life of Estonian miners and the space of the mine. Besides the monumental, historical and linear time marked by the changing systems of political economy and narratives of modernity and labour, there is the time of the mine. In the mine time, there is the linear time that is periodized as the time before and after the introduction of the new technology, *novaia tekhnika*, as the miners call it. There is also the cyclical time of production. While fully considering the radical changes in the political economy of the former socialist bloc and the impact it had on peoples' everyday life, I suggest that in the everyday of the miners, the introduction of the new technology was just as significant breaking point in history as was 1991. New technology, while being a manifestation of the bigger changes in the global geopolitics and economy, had a radical impact on the local level, challenging the existing narratives based on labour. The socialist and the capitalist exist side by side in work organization, one more visible in some aspects than in others, coexisting and intertwining, and intertwining with the cyclical time of the production process, breaking down the idea of a linear time from socialism to postsocialism.

Anthropology and time: capitalism, national time, labour, mining

The accelerated time–space compression and globalization have made anthropologists pay attention to time and temporalities, in particular to how capital circulation affects the working of time as national time is penetrated by the time of globalization. As Sassen (2000) points out, the national state constitutes the master temporality of historic time, which is losing out to the global temporal order in the making.

As we observe the global economy transcend the authority of the national state even as it roots itself into national territories and institutions, we see more clearly that "national economy" is only a particular territorialization of capital – a particular spatiotemporal order. (16)

Furthermore, the speeding up of time and its unevenness have become a focus of study along with techniques of creating and managing particular time regimes. Moments of economic crisis rupture the everyday routines and make people engage with multiple temporalities that coexist simultaneously – to draw on the past to while the future is perceived as uncertain and the present intimidating and suspended (Knight and Stewart 2016) manifested by both messianic and practical everyday time coexisting in politics (Palumbo 2016). While the global time is to a different extent penetrating local temporalities, this does not result in homogenized global, ultra-speedy time but rather the coexistence of different timescapes in one location. Ssorin-Chaikov (2006) describes heterochrony as different temporalities where "a linear historicist time is part of the picture but it borders and even partially overlaps with other temporalities", as a crossing point of several temporal disjunctures that extend beyond the scope and the terms of a particular site/span.

Describing modern time, Bear (2014) argues that it can be defined as multiple divergent representations and techniques of time and rhythm, which are increasingly in conflict with each other. The deep collective representations of social time form time-maps that bring together questions about navigating in time to the long-term fate of ethical and political relations. In modern time, the most dominant of these temporalities is the abstract time-reckoning of capitalism that forms the basis for "the universal measure of value in labour, debt, and exchange relationships" (5) and is in conflict with people's experiences and everyday social rhythms of time. Time becomes the key measure of the value of labour and objects, expressed in contradictory rhythms of capital accumulation, financial markets, production and consumption. Acts of labour by capitalists, traders, financiers and workers mediate these contradictions in social rhythms. Through labour, workers create surplus value for the market but are simultaneously affected by the cycles where production halts. Workers' bodily movements throughout the day, the weariness or speed of their bodies influences the movement of capital. "Labouring in/of time" indicates the body's encounter with the material world, a creative act to reconcile and mediate conflictual social rhythms, representations and non-human time, creating new time spaces.

As the natural resource sector has been expanding at an unprecedented speed, and the overheated and contested field is bringing about significant social, economic and environmental changes, mining has been increasingly analysed in relation with time. In the Perm region in Russia, the regional company extracting oil from the depths of the earth supports local cultural heritage projects that emphasize the similarity of the geological depth of oil with the historical depth of the local culture (Rogers 2012). Wind and solar power productions in Greece are seen as extractive economies harnessing resources for the benefit of foreign companies in the times of crisis, making local farmers feel as if they were returning to past colonial relationships and suffering (Argenti and Knight 2015). Exploring the potential of future oil in Sao Tome and Principe, Weszkalnys (2015) traces the unevenness of development and long periods of dormancy and the particular temporal regimes that characterize the industry. Rather than a linear story of progress, there are pauses or excess of time before the next temporal acceleration of capital accumulation caused by the contradictions in the disjunctive temporalities of state, science, geology and markets. In Congo, mining coltan ore, "a mineral that has enabled the most current and perhaps the most revolutionary forms of spatial–temporal acceleration in human history" (28), is connected with temporal dispossession where the local Congolese people are unable to produce future and predictable time themselves (Smith 2011). Economic crisis, fluctuation of global natural resource prices and the unpredictability of opportunities for livelihoods, social reproduction, environmental security and stable futures make mining a particularly fruitful field of studying heterochronic temporalities.

The national and regional time

Before looking at the life and time of miners, let me introduce the larger temporalities that have influenced Estonia and the mines. The Estonian national narrative, rather than being linear, was about revisions, reversals and repetitions throughout the twentieth century. First Estonian Republic (1918–1939) built its nationalism rejecting former rulers of the country, the Russians and the Germans, on Estonian peasant identity and connection with land. The Soviet occupation rejected the previous bourgeois nationalism, promoting socialist internationalism and fast industrialization. After becoming newly independent in 1991, Estonian elites tried to restore the values of the First Republic, re-creating the myth of the nation based on Estonian language and peasant past. As a consequence, Russian speakers, especially the Russian-speaking industrial working class, became an enemy within, a symbol of past injustice of the Soviet occupation (Keskūla 2015).

Like many other Eastern European countries, the economic policy of "shock therapy" was introduced after 1991. As Stenning (2011) points out, neoliberalization in Central and Eastern Europe was one of the most radical projects of implementing ideas of free market, and these ideas were embedded in the wider notion of the "Washington Consensus" derived from the policies of international financial institutions, such as the World Bank, the International Monetary Fund (IMF) and the European Bank for Reconstruction and Development (EBRD). In Estonia, the liberal market economy and re-joining Europe were seen as the only right and imaginable aims and in the national master narrative, successful market reforms signified the end of history (Fukuyama 1992) where justice had been restored and the country returned to its only rightful track.

The time of oil shale, a brown sedimentary rock that miners were digging to burn in thermal power plants, had a story that did not share the same temporality with the national time. Oil shale has been a paradoxical case of "the survival of the unfit" since the mining of it has continued despite its low energy efficiency and highly polluting nature, mostly supported by geopolitical circumstances (Holmberg 2008). Although mining was started during the 1920s, it significantly expanded when the mines were nationalized after the Second World War and Estonia's incorporation into the Soviet Union (Järvesoo in Mettam and Williams 1998). The fast pace of development in the oil shale industry demanded import of labour from the Russian-speaking areas of the Soviet Union (Vseviov 2002). In the 1960s, about 80% of the energy that was produced was exported to other parts of the Soviet Union (Pihlamägi 2010). As living conditions and salaries improved, mining became an attractive profession, glorified all over the Soviet Union and respected locally (Vetik 2002). Forty per cent of the population of the mining town Kohtla-Järve worked in oil shale extraction and processing by 1989

(Valge 2005). Perestroika encouraged the Estonian national movement, which was often framed as an environmental movement (Auer 1998) portraying mining as an alien polluter. The Russian-speaking mine workers suddenly experienced a double shock of losing their privileged status as workers and as Russian speakers. High unemployment, accompanied with social problems including the spread of HIV and drug use in the region touched every family and neighbourhood in some way, making life unpredictable. The newly founded state did not grant citizenship to those who were not descendants of the First Estonian Republic, placing most of the Russian-speaking industrial labour force in permanent uncertainty.

The mines, however, kept working the way they had before. Production that reached 30 million tonnes in 1980 dropped to a yearly 11–15 tonnes in 2000s (Varb and Tambet 2008), but in the 1990s, no mines were closed and staff reductions were insignificant. Although privatization was discussed and almost executed, it did not happen due to lack of financially sound investors and strong public opposition. The director of the conglomerate of mines who had been working in mining all his life did little to change the management of the company. The same trade union leader kept leading the trade union, with the disappearance of the Communist party, the same local politicians quickly formed new parties and were still running the town. Miners, engineers and managers kept doing their work as they had before, driving to the mine on the company bus, descending to the underground on an underground train, playing cards. They did their hard physical work on hand drills, shovelling oil shale to conveyor belts where it had fallen off the clumsy scraping conveyor, cutting holes to the seam with a massive cutting device invented in Ukraine in the 1960s. The same piece rate pay system that had been in place in the Soviet era was maintained. Things started changing only in 1999, when the old director, seventy-two years old by then, was replaced with a new energetic leader. As part of the national plan of optimizing the energy and mining sector, multiple mines were closed and staff gradually reduced from 10,000 in 1999 to about 3000 by 2010. For the remaining miners, the biggest change, however, was the introduction of new mining machinery.

Of machines and men

New technology meant renewing most of the machinery in the mine and replacing rail transport and conveyers with more contemporary wheeled machines produced in Poland and Finland. Instead of the underground train, miners now rode Mercedes minibuses, still good for playing cards. The hand drills and face-cutting machines were replaced with giant yellow trucks with drills on them, that the miner operates from levers, buttons and a mini-computer attached to the machine. If a hand drill could drill two meters deep into the face area, the drilling-car could do up to seven. Clumsy scraping conveyors that were transporting oil shale from the face area to bigger belt conveyors, were replaced with more flexible wheeled loading cars with buckets that could take up to four cubic meters of oil shale to the bigger conveyor belt in one go.

This was a radical change for miners who have a very particular relationship with their machines. Mollona (2005) has shown how machines are not seen as external tools of production in a steel factory in Sheffield. Rather, they are "symbolic extensions of the workers' bodies, metaphorical appendages of their sexuality, powerful technologies of enchantment and markers of social status" (35). In the Estonian mines, each miner had one main machine that they were using, and miners sometimes jokingly said that the machine was dearer to them than their wives. The intimate relationship between the man and the machine is demonstrated, for instance, in the memoirs of the hero of socialist labour, a miner Aksel Pärtel, who started implementing mechanized mining machinery in the 1970s. He describes a capricious machine sent from a Soviet factory that made equipment for coalmines. It took him and his brigade weeks of work to rebuild the machine so that it was suitable for oil shale mining. Nevertheless, the machine had the habit of breaking down just as important officials were visiting. Over time, Pärtel and his colleagues mastered the stubborn machine and even when new and better machines were introduced, the old one still remained the most comfortable and dearest to them (Pärtel 1972). Many of the older men who had to invent new ways to make the machinery function better, loved the creativity the machines allowed in their work.

But the relationship was not, however, only that of romantic love. The machine was the feeder of the miner and helped him to earn his living, working piece rate. Therefore, miners pushed the machines as hard as they could, occasionally breaking electricity cables or other parts in the rush to earn more money. The miners thought that underground servicemen were never repairing the machines fast enough and that it was terribly unfair when part of their salary was cut when they had repeatedly broken the machine. They were bitter about the wearing out of the machines and sometimes expressed it quite visually. For example, a miner had written *"Bez tormazov"*, without breaks, on his loading machine that had a problem with breaks wearing and not being as sensitive as they used to be in the beginning. Thus, miners were always balancing on the border of working in the fastest and most efficient way or pushing the machine over the edge. Besides being the mechanized extensions of bodies that the workers applied embodied skills to, they seemed to have a mind of their own, which the worker needed to tame to make the machine cooperate. The machine can be their best teammate or the unreliable comrade, breaking down in the middle of the greatest rush. The relationship with the machines is related to the speed and the tempo of the work which will be discussed in more detail below. The mining machinery, on the one hand, part of the wider capitalist project of increasing profit and making the mine more efficient, is, on the other hand, the miner's closest companion. Following mining machinery as the manifestation of various temporalities allows a deeper insight into small and large historical changes as objects have their own temporalities and rhythms (Bryant 2014). But considering the intimate relationship with machinery, what were the different temporalities and meanings of the new technology?

Meanings of *novaia tekhnika* (new technology)

When following the temporal representations and meanings of new technology in the mine, three distinct simultaneous temporalities could be identified: two related to the narrative of progress and labour in high modernity and one to the precarization and dispossession of the working class.

First of all, the story of introducing *novaia tekhnika* was the story of progress, the continued story of high modernity and linear movement towards a better and more efficient life. All production managers and engineers were talking about the increased efficiency of work. Also miners themselves were using this narrative frame, for example, blasters were boasting how they can now blast four rather than two meters of face area in one go. The old miner was exaggerating when telling that one can now work in a shirt and tie. But nevertheless, there was an enormous difference whether to hold a heavy, vibrating and moody hand drill or to sit in a comfortable seat, pushing buttons, directing the mechanical drill to the right place in the face area. Many aspects of physical labour in miners' work have now largely been removed. The current machinery signified progress. The head mechanic of one of the production departments was convinced in fact the Soviet Union collapsed because the ageing leaders in power were reluctant to introduce new technology and did not let the keen youth do it. When the Soviet Union produced their Ladas and Moskwiches without any changes, in the West, cars changed every few years. In his opinion, this kind of development and progress was also important to run the mine successfully. This is an example of the crossing over of the political history and history of the technology, where the development of technology seems to have crucial importance for the development of political history. In the big picture, however, mine workers continue the narrative of high modernity characteristic of the Soviet Union where the progress in industry and technology eventually leads to a better life. Nevertheless, the counterhistory where the Soviet Union has collapsed and capitalism with its more efficient forms of management has taken over is equally narrated through the idea of technological process.

The second narrative about technology resonates with another grand Soviet symbol, that of miner, the hero, doing hard physical work. While the narrative of the new technology is challenging the idea of physical labour, it nevertheless simultaneously and in a contradictory manner, reinforces it. If earlier the miner was paid for hard physical work, then after the introduction of new technology, he was paid to carefully operate the expensive machinery. New technology changed the image of the miner doing hard work. Miners feel that the basis of their entitlements is hard work, expert skill, sacrificing their health and living a short life. In return, miners want respect and money (Kesküla 2012). The Soviet order idealized the noble proletariat, and miners who were doing hard work and risking their lives became the ideal representation of a worker. They represented pure socialist masculinity, the socialist idea of a man bound up in the image of a miner, embodied most famously by Stakhanov (Ghodsee 2011). Therefore, at home, in their mining towns and in the wider society, miners still claimed respect based on hard work and were bragging less about the new technology in the mine. New technology was juxtaposed with working conditions that were still hard. Drawing on Soviet discourses and other temporalities allowed miners to maintain respect in the community, although in the neoliberal order hard work did not equal hard physical work and in the larger society, manual labour was no longer valued.

Thirdly, in contrast to the linear temporalities of progress and labour were the new trends affecting labour, such as outsourcing.

> The mines have invested hundreds of millions of Estonian kroons to buying new mining technology. Today we have fewer, but more powerful and reliable machines, productivity is higher than it was by several times. This means that there are fewer repair works. As the machines are more complicated and require higher qualifications from servicemen, we have decided to use the help of the specialists from the machine production factory. Buying the service and repair provision from the purveyor is a widespread practice today.

This was the message in the local newspaper in October 2009, together with the announcement that further 150 service workers would be made redundant. Previously, an extraction department would consist of miners proper who were engaged in drilling, blasting and loading the oil shale and service and maintenance staff working in the underground garage doing regular and emergency maintenance and repair work of the machinery, taking great pride in their technical skill and considering themselves irreplaceable in guaranteeing the smooth work of the miners. The announcement about lay-offs signified a larger trend where servicemen were losing their role as the creative developers and carers for the equipment, the doctors of machines. As outsourcing machine maintenance was seen as a cheaper option, bigger repair works were increasingly done externally. Hence, the meaning of work after the new technology was not changing only for miners who actually operated the new machines but also for support staff. When miners proper claimed their respect as hard workers, maintenance staff emphasized their skill. When many of them were laid off and others outsourced and deskilled, the inequalities between underground workers engaged in different labour increased significantly.

Labour in Estonia was following the global trend, becoming more precarious and more stratified (Silver 2003; Standing 2011). New forms of work have appeared, such as part-time, limited in time, interim and subcontracting, in order for firms to meet the demands of free trade and the logic of competitiveness, cutting down on labour costs (Procoli 2004). Directly linked to the introduction of new technology, the machines help to explain the bigger changes that are taking place. Thus, within the space of the mine, the introduction of new technology helps to see three different and simultaneous temporalities at work. In discourse, new technology continues the representations of the linear modern Soviet narrative of progress and centrality of labour although now simultaneously represented by two contradictory discourses of advanced technology and physicality of male work. When looking at the actual changes in the labour organization, new technology is linked with the global trends of increased labour outsourcing and precarious work. But besides these large narratives clashing in the space of the mine, there is also the micro-time of the everyday.

Negotiating the everyday of work

Besides the different layers of linear time of socialism–postsocialism, old technology–new technology, socialism and the market, there is the cyclical time of production. Production moves from mine development to the preparation of face area, to drilling, to blasting, to loading, to separating the oil shale from the rock and transporting the oil shale to power plants. Every twenty-four hours, the same cycle is repeated never stopping, unless a breakdown somewhere along the line causes the halt of the whole cycle and industrial downtime. Within the cyclical time, the same movements are repeated – drill-move on, drill-move on, or the pendulum swings of the loading machinery going back and forth.

In his classic work on industrial time, Thompson (1967) claims that modern machine production and capitalism introduced new ways of perceiving time and organizing work discipline. In the pre-industrial world, time was task-oriented, dictated by the rhythms of nature. Intense labour alternated with long periods of idleness, and no strict line was drawn between work and life. In factory production, a greater synchronization of tasks was needed which resulted in stricter work discipline through time. Other ethnographies have shown how flexibility and task orientation still prevail in factories (Parry 1999) or look at ways of challenging the strict factory time by small everyday subversive actions (Ong 1987). Ethnographies of socialist factories have emphasized that instead of a steady rhythm, production process is characterized by a rush at the end of the month (Burawoy 1988). In the Estonian mine, which was operating on clock-time since its establishment, new technology nevertheless brought about changes to the tempo of the everyday work. While miners still maintained their agency through negotiating the tempo and risk of labour in relation to their wages, both the tempo and risk had increased.

If one were to enter the mine on a random afternoon, and look at how men work, the tempo of the work would really seem daunting to an onlooker. The loading machines, TORO-s, drive along the tunnel connecting the face area and the conveyer belt in an incredible speed. Seeing the big machine driving closer, its bucket full of oil shale, pieces falling off under its wheels and then bouncing off in every direction, the machine kicking up dust, one would want to be careful and step away from their path, especially so when miners are driving back from the conveyer belt in reverse gear, not seeing what is behind them. *Bez tormazov*, without breaks, as someone had written on one of the machines. New machinery was not only more efficient but was also capable of moving faster and further, hence speeding up of work. Miners on loading machines drive back and forth for the whole shift, stopping only if the conveyer belt stops or the miner needs a little pause for coffee or sandwiches. Old miners who have visited the mine and looked at the new technology notice that although the work is physically easier, the tempo is morally draining, needing constant attentiveness and fast reactions.

This is not to say that miners were not working fast in socialism or before the new technology. Piece work, as well as socialist competitions, the urge to beat another brigade or set a new record motivated men to work quickly. In theory, miners were tightly imprisoned in the production cycle and the reward of piece work. But in reality, even in an environment strictly regulated by the production process and pay system, there was still room for playing with the tempo. Looking at the rhythms of gift-giving, Bourdieu (1977) focuses on the time between a gift and a counter-gift. Reciprocating too early or too late can lead to the breakdown of the social relationship. "Even if an action is heavily ritualised, as in the dialectic of offence and vengeance, there is still room for strategies which consist of playing with time, or rather tempo, of the action" (7). In other words, even in the most stringent social situations, the agent can play with tempo for his own benefit. Similarly, playing with time is used as a strategy in the production of objects. Even in the middle of work rush, artisans and chefs aim to control their rhythms of bodily movement cultivating a display of unhurried competence (Herzfeld 2004). This is similar to controlling tempo in the process of production, workers' strategies of controlling the process to a certain extent and de-totalizing the system of production. Similarly, in the face of the recent economic crisis, ways of challenging and shaping time have acquired a new significance. Ringel (2016) describes time-tricking as a set of strategies to bend time according to one's own needs, for juggling conflicting temporal orders and creating alternative ideas about time. Besides attempts to shape and reinterpret the past, tricking time shapes the future, attempting to "accelerate, decelerate, interrupt or delay some particular future content of time" (5) and specific temporal rhythms and structures that order social life in the future. While Bourdieu and Ringel describe the attempt to seize control over long-term future by playing with tempo or time, for Estonian miners on piece wage, their main agency was expressed in playing with the micro-tempo within the shift, the longest term of consequences being expressed in the salary at the end of the month.

Miners have to calculate the number of pieces they do very carefully. If they do too much, the management reduces piece rates or warns them by decreasing the monthly bonus. Nevertheless, miners cannot work fast until they have done a certain number of pieces and then slack off because if being seen idle, the underground foreman would find them another task. Therefore, it is important to know how quickly to work. It needs experience and careful calculating to balance the good salary and keeping the piece rates as they are. Even if a miner would want to take it easy and do less, it has to be done in a measured constant slow pace, not to be caught by the underground foreman. A common strategy is to work hard during the first half of the month to ensure a decent salary and then relax but to keep a particular tempo to avoid tedious tasks such as shovelling rock outside one's own workplace. The act of balancing, controlling the micro-tempo is what piece workers can exercise regardless of the new technology. In the case of time workers, consider the following example.

In his book "Men, Stone and Machines" (1972), a Hero of Socialist Labour, Aksel Pärtel, describes his problems with workers who were not paid a fixed salary based on time. When experimenting with the new mechanized way of mining, a brigade of five time workers was sent to him to set up a conveyer belt.

> They knew how to work in exactly one tempo and balance on the edge that differentiates idling from the kind of work which has a small but perceivable benefit for society. The first thing they did at the start of the shift was a have thorough rest. It is not easy to sleep with eight degrees and underground dampness. One has to be with very strong health or be completely drunk. The second reason was not likely. It was not possible that all the members of the brigade were pissed every morning. One tipsy guy could somehow sneak into the mine under the cover of others, but not a whole bunch. (56)

Due to fewer workers and stricter control, this kind of rhythm of work was no longer possible in 2010. The service and maintenance men working in the underground garage received a time wage. Their work days were usually busy and fast, but they could afford breaks, meals, occasional joking and chatting. They knew exactly how much a routine job would take them. If no unplanned emergency repairs were needed, they had enough time for both work and leisure. If something happened to a machine, the steady rhythm of servicemen's work was broken. They needed to rush to repair the machine and stay for an extra shift if a repair is urgently needed. However, in 2009, some servicemen were transferred to another department formally, to cut their salary. They still kept working in the same department side by side with their colleagues but for a smaller salary. To express their anger and dissatisfaction, these men were doing the bare minimum they could, as slowly as possible, slightly reminding Pärtel's time workers from the 1970s. When earlier they would go and help a colleague after their own tasks were done, they would now sit down at the computer of the underground garage, playing Solitare. If Pärtel's sleeping brigade was not particularly motivated to work in the situation of full employment, the contemporary servicemen were not motivated due to the restructuring that they have undergone. Increased outsourcing and constant rumours about additional restructuring and lay-offs meant that they had no control of the global time characterized by precaritization of labour. Their only remaining strategy was to reclaim the small time of the everyday. As Bear notes (2014), such everyday acts of labour are the site where the contradictory temporalities of global capitalism, cycles of consumption and production and the small rhythms of everyday meet and are mediated. But as her own ethnography of austerity regimes on an Indian river shows, labour is not only about navigating time but also about navigating the risk of accidents.

Gambling with tempo is, however, not only about optimizing the salary and labour, but also gambling with health and the official health and safety rules. Miners' work is always balancing on how much one can take out of the *novaia tekhnika* versus how much to follow *tekhnika besopasnosti*, occupational Health and Safety rules. There were silent agreements in the mine that some rules do not need to be followed. For example, to drive the wheeled loader TORO back to the face area, according to *tekhnika besopasnosti*, one would have to turn around the machine to drive it back. This would, however, slow down the loading process considerably and no one did that. The young miner who did was forced to leave his job rather quickly, as the salary of loaders is divided between everyone in the shift and the experienced miners did not want to see a drop in their salary because of some slow guy who stuck to the rules. The blasters were supposed to mark the area of blasting with plastic cones to forbid anyone to enter the area. "When there is no management around, to be honest, I simply do not use the cones, because it takes time to lay them out and pick them up later again, but I am paid by amount of blasting that I do in my shift ... " Memoirs of the record-breaking brigade leaders from the Soviet time indicate that health and safety rules were not always followed then either; there was even an agreement in the management that the health and safety inspector would not be visiting the brigade of the fastest tunnelling miners during the month when they were supposed to break the record (Keskula 2013).

Although miners were always trying to work as fast as possible, and the rules of *tekhnika besopasnosti* were always ignored to a certain extent, *novaia tekhnika* and new ways of organizing work have opened up new possibilities for taking risks. For example, blasters were transferred to piece rate system together with introducing the new technology and the blaster who admitted ignoring health and safety above, actually believed that it was dangerous and wrong for blasters to work piece rate. Therefore, the general speeding up of the production process also affects the miners' attitude to health and safety and encourages them to take more risks with more potentials for the rhythm of the everyday to be broken by an accident.[1]

There were also other health implications after the introduction of new technology. When the old technology had used electric power, electricity cables were feeding the machines that were operating, the new ones were powered by diesel. This meant that miners breathed in poisonous diesel fumes that the old ventilation system of the mine could not cope with, making them sleepy and less prone to accidents. New technology made production faster but allowed miners on piece rate to slightly negotiate the tempo. For miners on time rate, time was similarly faster due to reduction of staff, but within the group, workers reclaimed their time differently, depending on whether their job had been restructured. But the labour process was not only about optimizing time and money but also of one's health through risks that one now needed to take, mediating the different temporalities though the labouring body.

Conclusion

As ideas of globalization and time–space compression have become common knowledge, anthropologists' task is to show how socially embedded practices play out the effects of globalization in different ways in particular localities (Eriksen 2016b) and how modern time can be described (Bear 2014). While earlier studies expected the homogenization of time in the accelerated space, recent research in anthropology has rather emphasized the heterochronic nature of modern time, particularly in relation to the capitalist boom and bust cycles and the contradictory rhythms that are built into them. As Eriksen states in the introduction to this special issue, overheating refers to heat as well as speed. The speed would finally make the engine overheat and grind to a halt unless changes are made.

Mining brings about the intensification and overheating in some locations while cooling down in others. While the decreased volume and significance in Estonian mining means that time is cooled down in some ways, introduction of the new machinery meant that the tempo of the everyday speeded up and thus became overheated. Overheating is not only affecting global processes unevenly but within the coexisting multiple temporalities of a particular space, it affects some temporalities more than others, resulting in the simultaneous speeding up and cooling down of tempo and time. Not only economic crisis but also other significant changes in the way of life, such as the introduction of new infrastructure or technology, put people in situations where the future time is increasingly unpredictable, making them try their best to creatively trick time.

Labour, and particular spaces where it takes place in cooperation with human and non-human actors, allows a space where to observe the characteristics of overheated modern capitalist time where the global, national and the everyday times come together and create spaces for people to play with time to the extent that they can, even if crisis challenges perspectives of future and hope.

This article has attempted to bring together the literature on capitalist time, national time as well as the minute tempo of the everyday. If the 1990s indeed brought about such a speeding up and overheating of the world, the postsocialist space with fast changes and mining as the archetypical socialist labour might be the key places where to look for locally manifested multiple temporalities. In the mine, multiple temporalities exist together. The case of Estonian miners shows that the rupture might not lay in the breaking point of socialism versus capitalism, but might appear in later manifestations of capitalist management, such as investing in new and more efficient machinery. I have argued that for the underground miners, introducing the new technology was just as significant of a change as the 1991 change in political economy. The change in technology creates an intersection of the linear historical time, the time of the new machines, the cyclical time of production with its speeding up and slowing down and the workers and his machine's individual tempo, playing with time. New technology changes the nature of their job and encourages nostalgia for the way miners used to be seen. It makes work easier physically, but also speeds it up and encourages more potential accidents and permanent damage to workers' health. All these changes point to multiple temporalities, that of modernity, where work is easier and technology is developing, to that of capitalism, where work is more efficient and fewer men are needed. These all form different layers and break the routine of the everyday, the tempo of work and bodily movement.

Note

1. In absolute terms, accident rate in the Estonian mines has decreased in comparison with the previous decades. The statistics, however, does not consider the significant reduction of staff in the mines. Furthermore, injuries that are not very serious are usually not recorded as a common agreement between mine management and workers and tend to happen 'in the garage' or 'at home'.

Acknowledgements

This research was conducted during my doctoral studies funded by the Estonian Centre for Academic Mobility. I would like to thank my supervisors Frances Pine and Mao Mollona for advice on the earlier draft of this paper. I also received helpful feedback from Jonathan Parry, Rebecca Prentice, Jessie Sklair, Theo Rakopolous, Tim Martindale, Sergei Oushakine, John Schoeberlein and Laura Adams.

Disclosure statement

No potential conflict of interest was reported by the author.

Funding

This work was supported by Eesti Teadusagentuur [PUT1263]; Sihtasutus Archimedes [PhD studies grant].

References

Argenti, Nicolas, and Daniel M. Knight. 2015. "Sun, Wind, and the Rebirth of Extractive Economies: Renewable Energy Investment and Metanarratives of Crisis in Greece." *Journal of the Royal Anthropological Institute* 21 (4): 781–802.
Auer, Matthew R. 1998. "Environmentalism and Estonia's Independence Movement." *Nationalities Papers: The Journal of Nationalism and Ethnicity* 26 (4): 659–676.
Bear, Laura. 2014. "Doubt, Conflict, Mediation: The Anthropology of Modern Time." *Journal of the Royal Anthropological Institute* 20 (S1): 3–30.
Bourdieu, Pierre. 1977. *Outline of a Theory of Practice*. Cambridge: Cambridge University Press.
Bryant, Rebecca. 2014. "History's Remainders: On Time and Objects After Conflict in Cyprus." *American Ethnologist* 41 (4): 681–697.
Burawoy, Michael. 1988. "Piecework Hungarian Style." In *On Work*, edited by Ray Pahl, 190–209. Oxford: Blackwell.
Burawoy, Michael, and Katherine Verdery. 1998. *Uncertain Transition: Ethnographies of Change in the Postsocialist World*. Lanham, MD: Rowman & Littlefield.
Chari, Sharad, and Katherine Verdery. 2009. "Thinking Between the Posts: Postcolonialism, Postsocialism, and Ethnography After the Cold War." *Comparative Studies in Society and History* 51 (1): 6–34.
Eriksen, Thomas Hylland. 2016a. *Overheating. An Anthropology of Accelerated Change*. London: Pluto Press.

Eriksen, Thomas Hylland. 2016b. "Overheating: The world since 1991." *History and Anthropology*. doi:10.1080/02757206.2016.1218865.

Fukuyama, Francis. 1992. *The End of History and the Last Man*. London: Hamish Hamilton.

Ghodsee, Kristen Rogheh. 2011. *Muslim Lives in Eastern Europe: Gender, Ethnicity, and the Transformation of Islam in Postsocialist Bulgaria*. Princeton, NJ: Princeton University Press.

Herzfeld, Michael. 2004. *The Body Impolitic: Artisans and Artifice in the Global Hierarchy of Value*. Chicago, IL: University of Chicago Press.

Holmberg, Rurik. 2008. *Survival of the Unfit Path Dependence and the Estonian Oil Shale Industry*. Linköping: Linköping University.

Keskküla, Eeva. 2012. "Mining Postsocialism: Work, Class and Ethnicity in an Estonian Mine." PhD diss., Goldsmiths, University of London.

Keskküla, Eeva. 2013. "Fiddling, Drinking and Stealing: Moral Code in the Soviet Estonian Mining Industry." *European Review of History: Revue europeenne d'histoire* 20 (2): 237–253.

Keskküla, Eeva. 2015. "Reverse, Restore, Repeat! Dynamics of Class and Ethnicity and the Russian-Speaking Miners of Estonia." *Focaal* 72: 95–108.

Knight, Daniel M., and Charles Stewart. 2016. "Ethnographies of Austerity: Temporality, Crisis and Affect in Southern Europe." *History and Anthropology* 27 (1): 1–18.

Mettam, Colin W., and Stephen Wyn Williams. 1998. "Internal Colonialism and Cultural Divisions of Labour in the Soviet Republic of Estonia." *Nations and Nationalism* 4 (3):363–388.

Mollona, Massimiliano. 2005. "Gifts of Labour. Steel Production and Technological Imagination in an Area of Urban Deprivation, Sheffield, UK." *Critique of Anthropology* 25 (2): 177–198.

Ong, Aihwa. 1987. *Spirits of Resistance and Capitalist Discipline: Factory Women in Malaysia*. Albany: State University of New York Press.

Palumbo, Berardino. 2016. "Debt, Hegemony and Heterochrony in a Sicilian City." *History and Anthropology* 27 (1): 93–106.

Parry, Jonathan. 1999. "Lords of Labour: Working and Shirking in Bhilai." *Contributions to Indian Sociology* 33 (1–2): 107–140.

Pärtel, Aksel. 1972. *Mehed, Kivi ja Masinad* [Men, the Stone and Machines]. Tallinn: Eesti Raamat.

Pihlamägi, Maie. 2010. "Policy of Transition: Industry in the Estonian SSR During the First Post-War Five-Year Plan (1946–1950)." *Acta Historica Tallinnensia* 15: 146–166.

Procoli, Angela. 2004. *Workers and Narratives of Survival in Europe: The Management of Precariousness at the End of the Twentieth Century*. Albany: State University of New York Press.

Ringel, Felix. 2016. "Can Time Be Tricked? A Theoretical Introduction." *The Cambridge Journal of Anthropology* 34 (1): 22–31.

Rogers, Douglas. 2012. "The Materiality of the Corporation: Oil, Gas, and Corporate Social Technologies in the Remaking of a Russian Region." *American Ethnologist* 39 (2): 284–296.

Sassen, Saskia. 2000. "Spatialities and Temporalities of the Global: Elements for a Theorization." *Public Culture* 12 (1): 215–232.

Silver, Beverly J. 2003. *Forces of Labor: Workers' Movements and Globalization Since 1870*. Cambridge: Cambridge University Press.

Smith, James H. 2011. "Tantalus in the Digital Age: Coltan ore, Temporal Dispossession, and "Movement in the Eastern Democratic Republic of the Congo." *American Ethnologist* 38 (1): 17–35.

Ssorin-Chaikov, Nikolai. 2006. "On Heterochrony: Birthday Gifts to Stalin, 1949." *Journal of the Royal Anthropological Institute* 12: 355–375.

Standing, Guy. 2011. *The Precariat: The New Dangerous Class*. London: Bloomsbury Academic.

Stenning, Alison. 2011. *Domesticating Neo-Liberalism: Spaces of Economic Practice and Social Reproduction in Post-Socialist Cities*. Chichester: Wiley-Blackwell.

Thompson, E. P. 1967. "Time, Work Discipline and Industrial Capitalism." *Past and Present* 38: 56–97.

Valge, Janek. 2005. "Kohtla-Järve hilissotsialistlik segregatsioon" [The Segregation of Kohtla-Järve in Late Socialism]. MA thesis, in Department of Geography. Tartu University, Tartu.

Varb, Nikolai, and Ülo Tambet, eds. 2008. *90 aastat Põlevkivi Kaevandamist Eestis: Tehnoloogia ja Inimesed* [90 Years of Oil Shale Mining in Estonia: Technology and People]. Tallinn: GeoTrail KS.

Verdery, Katherine. 2002. "Whither Postsocialism?" In *Postsocialism: Ideals, Ideologies, and Practices in Eurasia*, edited by C. M. Hann, 15–28. New York: Routledge.

Vetik, Raivo. 2002. "The Cultural and Social Make-up of Estonia." In *National Integration and Violent Conflict in Post-Soviet Societies*, edited by Pal Kolsto, 71–105. Oxford: Rowman & Littlefield.

Vseviov, David 2002. "Kirde-Eesti urbaanse anomaalia kujunemine ning struktuur pärast Teist maailamsõda" [The Formation and Structure of the Urban Anomaly in Northeast Estonia after WWII]. PhD diss., Tallinn Pedagogical University.

Weszkalnys, Gisa. 2015. "Geology, Potentiality, Speculation: On the Indeterminacy of First Oil." *Cultural Anthropology* 30 (4): 611–639.

Yurchak, Alexei. 2006. *Everything was Forever, Until It Was No More: The Last Soviet Generation*. Princeton, NJ: Princeton University Press.

The refugee crisis: destabilizing and restabilizing European borders

Synnøve K. N. Bendixsen

ABSTRACT
Drawing on fieldwork among irregular migrants in Norway, this article examines how borders are constructed, reproduced and contested by a variety of actors, using techniques, institutions, laws, policies and social interactions at different scales. It indicates the shifts in border regimes following the alleged weakening of national borders after the Cold War. The implementation of European integration, for instance through the Schengen Agreement, has made it increasingly difficult for undocumented travellers to cross the external Schengen borders, and within the nation-states, internal boundary processes facilitate, obstruct and set yardsticks for migrants' entrance to society. Drawing on scholars who have explored the spatial dimensions of border controls (delocalization), the temporal dimension, and the role of non-state actors in shaping border policies (denationalization), I investigate borders through three critical moments for migrants: the movement to Europe, the waiting in Europe and the (potential) return.

Our ability to maintain an area free of internal border controls depends on our ability to effectively manage our external borders. Today we are proposing a set of recommendations to ensure that, at all external borders of Greece, controls are carried out and brought in line with Schengen rules. At the same time, we take note of the efforts of the Greek Authorities to improve the situation and are reminding that all parts of the Commission's comprehensive plan need to be applied to face the unprecedented pressure at Europe's external borders. The objective of the European Commission and of the Member States is to safeguard and strengthen Schengen. We will only save Schengen by applying Schengen. (Dimitris Avramopoulos, EU commissioner for Migration, Home Affairs and Citizenship, February 2016)[1]

When one country decides to close a border, its neighbour is left with the problem. That is not my Europe. (Angela Merkel, February 2016)[2]

Please open the border. (Slogan from migrant protest in Athens, February 2016)[3]

Introduction

What would be Europe's current equivalent of Ellis Island, Nova Scotia's Pier 21 or Checkpoint Charlie? That these zones of arrival today are iconic and have popular museums suggests that they represent a lost time (Walters 2006). These spaces operated not only as territorial gateways, but as arrival, reception and integration points (Walters 2006, 198). At Ellis Island and Nova Scotia's Pier 21, authorities checked the health conditions of migrants, and migrants became connected to both public and private networks that could arrange work and housing. These spaces were both nation-state borders and entrance points to the *society* (Walters 2006). Checkpoint Charlie marks the border between the two Berlins during the Cold War, and today's museum exhibits photos and stories of Germans deceiving the East German border guards in order to flee without the legal documents that would authorize their movement. Tellingly, for the migrants fleeing to Europe today, the equivalent museum could perhaps be said to be the first underwater sculpture museum in Europe, Museo Atlantico, off Lanzarote (inaugurated February 2016). The Raft of Lampedusa, a statue placed on the seafloor, carries thirteen passengers modelled on migrants who arrived in Europe, and also features figures walking towards the European shore.

At the beginning of the 1990s, influential voices spoke of a "borderless world" and celebrated what seemed to be a de-bordering of the state due to globalization processes. A decade later, social scientists argued that the relevance of territoriality had shifted rather than being weakened (Andreas 2000) and that borders were as important as ever, continuously changing their forms, structures and techniques. Balibar (2002, 84–85) calls this the "ubiquity of borders" and describes an order where borders are not disappearing, but are proliferating, becoming "a grid ranging over the new social space" instead of taking the shape of a line separating the bordered from outside. At the same time, borders have been destabilized since the 1990s. Increased mobility (however selective), the formation of the passport-free Schengen area and the expansion of the European Union, cheap calls and cheap flights, undocumented migration and tourists who overstay their visa, have perforated borders that might formerly have seemed stable. Yet this destabilization is being countered by a restabilization, or reconfiguration, of borders, which is what this article is about.

This article examines how borders are constructed, reproduced and contested by a variety of actors, using techniques, institutions, laws, policies and social interactions at different scales. The implementation of European integration, for instance through the Schengen Agreement, has made it increasingly difficult for undocumented travellers to cross the external Schengen borders, and within the nation-states, internal boundary processes facilitate, obstruct and set yardsticks for migrants' entrance to society. Drawing on scholars who have explored the spatial dimensions of border controls (delocalization), the temporal dimension and the role of non-state actors in shaping border policies (denationalization), I investigate borders through three critical moments for migrants: the movement to Europe, the waiting in Europe and the (potential) return. I will indicate how, at different scales of border production, a variety of actors act upon different intentions and competences as well as different technologies and techniques.

The data for this article derives from fieldwork with irregular migrants living in Bergen and Oslo, Norway (2011–2013). During this period, I spoke with irregular migrants who were mostly male, of various ages and from different ethnic and national backgrounds. Some arrived in Norway by themselves, while others arrived with their family. As the asylum process can take a relatively long time, several migrants had been living in Norway for more than two years before they were even categorized as irregular migrants.

Since a premise for this special issue is accelerated change, it may be relevant to point out here that circumstances, practices and policies concerning migration into Europe change. The Syrian refugee crisis, notably, emerged only after my fieldwork. Yet, the following analysis of bordering, boundedness and precarity is no less relevant today than at the time of fieldwork. Indeed, the situation is more acutely overheated than before, with the number of displaced persons worldwide reaching the highest level since the Second World War.

Studying the ever-moving border

In 2012, Greece built a razor-wire fence along a short section of its border with Turkey where migrants frequently crossed. In October 2015, Hungary sealed its border with Croatia in an effort to reroute migrants passing through the country to get to Western Europe. The border to Serbia had already been closed. In February 2016, Turkey closed its border to an estimated 70,000 refugees fleeing Aleppo, although Turkey had previously allowed hundreds of thousands of Syrian refugees to enter and remained open "for emergency situations", according to Turkish officials.[4] These are a few examples of the physical barriers built during what is arguably the most serious refugee crisis since the aftermath of the Second World War; they are an effort to, if not control, then at least divert or deter migrants. In the postcolonial new world order, border controls have not only intensified through various technologies and materialities, but have also become a core question in discourses of European and national identities, frequently linked to the (un)sustainability of the welfare state and the economy in general. The political landscape of Europe is currently characterized by a proliferation of nation-states' efforts to immobilize people, xenophobic backlashes and the rapid rise of extreme-right political movements, as well as cross-border activism, humanitarian volunteer efforts and new political solidarities. The "refugee crisis", which should not only be understood as the heightened number of people trying to reach Europe across the Mediterranean but also the intra- and inter-governmental responses to these efforts, has caused anxiety on both the political right and left, albeit marked by very different logics ("we are being overloaded" versus "we are losing our humanity").

In this atmosphere of anxious border fortification, there has also been a proliferation of empirical studies of borders.[5] Alternative ways of studying borders under conditions of globalization include examining the performativity of walled states (Brown 2010), and the bordering Europe referred to as the "illegality industry" (Andersson 2014). The multiplicity of borders (e-borders, offshore borders, juxtaposed borders, smart borders; Rumford 2010, 952) has been linked to the securitization of immigration (Bigo 2002), and to how the border has become a "spectacle" due to the politicization and securitization of migration (De Genova 2002).

The border is both a temporal and a spatial experience. Borders are experienced differently depending on one's legal status, country of origin, ethnicity, race, gender, age, etc. (Anderson 1996; Balibar 2002; Rumford 2006; Nyer 2010; Fassin 2011). Time and temporality play important parts in border management (Nyer 2010): for some, the border can mean impediments, delays, and increased waiting times while for others it signifies swift movement and speedy processing as a "trusted" traveller (Nyer 2010). As Balibar puts it, borders are "polysemic" (2002, 82), in that "borders never exist in the same way for individuals belonging to different social groups" (2002, 78–79).

Balibar's argument that borders no longer exist (if they ever did) only "*at the edge of the territory*, marking the point where it ends" but "have been transported *into the middle of political space*" (2009, 109) seems obvious today. Borders are everywhere, they are "not to be conceived only as edges of territory, zones of connectivity, or even spaces of governance" (Rumford 2006, 166). Inspired by Mezzadra (2015) views the border as a social relation mediated by things, rather than a thing in itself. As a consequence, he views borders as "complex social institutions, which are marked by tensions between practices of border reinforcement and border crossings" (Mezzadra 2015, 128). For this article, Mezzadra's argument (2004) that while social and economic processes inevitably shape migration patterns, borders are also shaped and produced by migrants' agency is particularly relevant.[6] In the current border crisis, anthropologists need to examine how and when borders are made socially relevant, examining both how people's action may construct, maintain and erase borders (Rumford 2008; Reeves 2014) and the multiscalar context in which these actions must be understood.

It can be useful to distinguish between borders and boundaries (Barth 1969; Kearney 1991; Fassin 2011), where borders are external frontiers and boundaries are the internal social categorizations (Fassin 2011). I make this distinction in order to critically study the process of destabilizing and restabilizing borders, the production and reproduction of borders at various scales and the interrelatedness of these processes. While some researchers highlight that borders in Europe are rescaled from the nation-state level to the level of the city (Rumford 2006), I argue here that there is an interdependent scaling process between the various levels of control and movement. Border controls, immigration control and security checks are part of the sovereign techniques both responding to and preceding migrant movements (Nyers 2015). Further, migrants are not only reacting to controls but are also initiators of new (literal and metaphorical) ways of pursuing movement. This insight means that it is important to examine the various dimensions of border production at various scales and their interrelatedness.

Bordering Europe after the Cold War

The EU has been described as the largest reconfigured political space since the period of the British Empire, and the currently largest experimentation in postnational and supranational polity building (Wilson 2012). Yet there is a paradox in European integration: the decreased importance of borders is based on those borders simultaneously being recognized (Diez 2006, 237; Green 2013). EU's regionalization process, which promotes European regions in order to counteract individual states' bordering techniques, has not reduced borders, but has rather led to the proliferation of new ones (Wilson 2012, 174; Green 2013). For example, the tendency of nation-states in Europe to build walls is a performance both of states' sovereign power and of the inability to control which people reach the territory (Brown 2010).

Since about 1990, European politics of border control have changed dramatically. The efforts of five EU Member States (Germany, France, the Netherlands, Belgium and Luxembourg) to expand the single market by abolishing the internal borders in the mid-1980s resulted in the Schengen Agreement, signed in 1985, which established common rules regarding visas, the right to asylum and checks at external borders.[7] The special EU Council summit in Tampere (1999) initiated negotiations about the creation of a Common European Asylum System (CEAS). The Schengen area, defined by the European Commission Home Affairs office as an "area without internal borders", has gradually come to include other EU and European Economic Area member states.

Yet, the eradication of nation-state borders simultaneously introduced "compensatory measures": external border controls were strengthened, and cooperation in the field of asylum and immigration increased. This is part of the new forms of connectedness we are seeing today (Eriksen 2016): the EU and its member states have expanded both their cooperation and individual actions related to external relations policies, partnerships with third countries, "internal security", the exchange of information and monitoring, setting standards, cooperation with EU neighbours and what the EU calls the fight against "cross-border crime".

The increased European cooperation on migration in the 1990s has been attributed to the growing movement of refugees from the Balkans and the former communist countries in Eastern Europe to a number of member states, in particular Germany. This trend of responding to the movement of migrants and refugees has continued: as a direct response to the growing number of refugees in July 2012, the EU accepted a reform of the Schengen Treaty that allowed Schengen countries to once again carry out passport checks for arrivals at national borders "for a limited period". Similarly, in 2015, some EU member states re-established "exceptional" border controls: for instance, passport controls were reintroduced between Denmark and Sweden. This indicates that the regulation of internal and external EU border controls is not only a process constructed by European political elites, but also initiated and shaped by actors at the nation-state level. The culture of border control produced by Schengen is not essentially about constructing a post-national community, but rather recognizes the central role of national governments (Zaiotti 2007). Moreover, the reintroduction of border controls also suggests the role of migrant movements in shaping EU and European nation-states' policies and border management. The connectedness of local realities, here migrants' mobility, with large scale processes must, as Eriksen (2016) argues, be studied through multiscalar analysis.

Although Norway is not a member of EU, it takes active part in "Europeanization" by closely following EU's migration regime development since the 1990s (Brekke 2012): Norway generally adapts its migration policies and legislation to that of the EU. Since 2000, Norway has been part of the Schengen area, and that year it also implemented the EURODAC registration system.[8] Norwegian immigration authorities apply the Dublin agreement, and up to one in five asylum seekers is turned back to their first country of application within Europe (Brekke 2012).

The current right-wing Norwegian government presumes that migrants respond to policies and legislation. In December 2015, the government proposed a series of restrictive measures, including a 48-hour asylum application procedure, restrictions on family reunification, a list of allegedly safe countries and an increased use of temporary protection. These restrictions are supposed to make it "less attractive" to seek asylum in Norway and to restrict the number of asylum-seekers arriving in the country.[9] Yet whether and how migrants respond to such measures remains a theoretical discussion (Brekke 2012; Hagen-Zanker and Mallett 2016). What is clear is that the number and the background of the migrants directly influence Norwegian migration policy and legislation (Brekke 2012).

Scholars argue that in this process, European states have shifted their migration accountability *up* to forms of international or supranational cooperation (Guiraudon and Lahav 2000). However, accountability and control mechanisms for migration have simultaneously moved *inwards* towards the societal level: nation-states have shifted their focus from territorial border marking to a politics of boundary production and assertion *within* the nation-state. The dismantling and deinstitutionalizing of the physical borders within Schengen have entailed a dismantling of controls and distinctions marking those who have the right to be there versus those illegally present. Several of the former functions of external national border controls have increasingly been delegated or redistributed to practices that reaffirm, sustain and produce social boundaries. It remains to be seen whether such restabilizations of nation-state boundaries will lead to increases in racialized policies and policing.[10] For instance, boundaries and control over access to resources are frequently communicated through social and cultural distinctions between "us" and "them".

In order to investigate how borders and boundaries are being reshaped, reconstructed and reconfigured in the tense, overheated world of the early twenty-first century, I now examine how irregular migrants' lives get entangled with these national and supranational rules and practices. Irregular migrants are particularly interesting in the discussion about borders because the construction of some migrants as "irregular" contributes to leaving them in a legal limbo, living perennially on the border. Furthermore, although migrants' agency and performances of migration are often ignored, they are also part of the border management at the national and supranational scale. Indeed, to grasp the connectedness and consequences of such connectedness at the level of migrant's action we need to combine an ethnographic method with sufficient contextual knowledge (Eriksen 2016).

Crossing the nation-state borders: the journey

During my fieldwork with irregular migrants in Oslo, I meet Lubaid, a Palestinian twenty-five-year-old who had been in Norway for two years. He had grown up in a Lebanese refugee camp. Lubaid told me that his journey to Norway started with him being stuck for seven months at the Dubai International Airport. He added, as if reading my thoughts: "yes, it was kind of like the movie 'the Terminal'."[11] He said that Dubai did not let him in, and because neither Lebanon nor Palestine would accept him, his only option was Europe. Lubaid had acquired some European acquaintances in the refugee camp, and phoned them. They called the Dubai the United Nations High Commissioner for Refugees field office, which sent its officers to the airport to interview him. Still, Europe would not let him in because that would create a precedent, Lubaid said. In the end, through a process which was not entirely clear to me, he entered Dubai, but "since they don't want Palestinians there", he added "I needed to get out as soon as possible. I worked some months, without getting much pay. I was given food and housing because he [the employer] paid also for my residency stay."[12] Then Lubaid bought a forged passport with his own name. He eagerly added:

> a good passport with a real stamp – so it was really expensive. I wasn't nervous because I had spent all that time at the airport before, so I knew it well. I first flew to Turkey – then I decided

on Norway (...) I went to Sweden first – I bought a plane ticket on the internet, for a good price. At the airport in Turkey they asked questions – who I was going to visit?

He answered: "my girlfriend, do you want to see a picture of her?" In Sweden he was the only person standing in a different queue – they looked at him, but still: "I managed to not look nervous." In Stockholm, he found a place to sleep on the internet. Then he hitched a ride to Norway. He had thought that Norway was a country where human rights were respected, which is what he had heard from NGOs in the refugee camp, and he also referred to the efforts of Norwegian medical doctors in Gaza. These were his reasons for choosing Norway. At the airport in Dubai, he had met a lawyer from Belgium who had tried to persuade him to seek asylum in Belgium, but he had decided against it, going to Norway instead – a choice which he now regretted.

In Lubaid's story, the crossing of state borders is defined materially and technologically: it is done in the passport line at the airports, on train platforms or ferries. But it is also socially constructed: the implementation of passport controls at the local scale (for instance the airport) includes non-material techniques, such as the controller's assessment of whether or not someone is nervous. Crossing a state border at an airport is a practice that combines having the right materials (a good passport), attitude (not being nervous) and know-how (where to go, how to cross and which responses are more likely to be believed by the passport inspector).

Lubaid's statement that he was not nervous because he had acquired the necessary knowledge of how to perform in front of the border guards alludes to how these sites rely on a constructed image of a citizen or lawful border-crosser. Performance at the airport borders represents an existential moment of crisis (Johnson et al. 2011), where identity claims are adjudicated and performance is evaluated. The relation to the border that Lubaid performs is not that of an illegal trespasser. His border-crossing performance introduces the migrant as an additional actor in the interaction between border agents and state bureaucrats in the complex decision-making process determining "where, how, and on whose body a border will be defined" (Wonders 2006, 66). The practices of those determined to cross the border, with or without legal documents, also shape the production of the border at the local scale. Indeed, migrants' actions are so powerful that they shape border policies at both EU and nation-state levels.

Since the 1990s, the "border game" (Andreas 2000) between officials and migrants has been professionalized (van Liempt and Sersli 2013) as a result of an amplified technologization of border management, including biometric passports (the introduction of which in Norway began in 2005), electronic ID cards, e-passports, carrier sanctions, cooperation and re-admission agreements, joint border patrolling, safe third country agreements and forced detention and removal (Bigo and Guild 2005; De Genova 2010). Document controls are increasingly carried out by private parties such as airlines, which face sanctions when transporting people without legal documents, a process which has been called the shifting out of European nation-states' responsibility in the field of migration (Guiraudon 2001). The use of EU bodies, such as Europol and Frontex, to target smugglers is increasing (European Commission 2015), and is to become part of the Common Security and Defence Policy operations. EU's management of borders also includes a criminalization of smugglers through penal sanctions of both smugglers and migrants (van Liempt and Sersli 2013) and through the media spectacle of migrants arriving on boats, which links perceptions of organized crime, migrant smuggling, bogus asylum seekers and migrants as victims.[13] The European Union's alleged plans to criminalize charities, humanitarian volunteers and those helping migrants can also be added to recent development of border management.[14]

Unlike Lubaid, most migrants are not stuck for months in an airport, but several have spent unwanted time in a country where they had no intention of building their future, and where they therefore devoted their time to efforts to continue their journey to their desired destination. In an otherwise accelerated world, the lives of people migrating and applying for asylum is characterized by waiting, positioned in a limbo of uncertainty as to when their waiting will end and future life will start, inhabiting what Eriksen calls the "disjunctures between speed and slowness" (Eriksen 2016). Waiting comprises a certain form of temporality (Bendixsen and Eriksen 2017). In the accelerated capitalist world, to wait is to waste time and thus should be evaded (Bendixsen and Eriksen 2017). Waiting has become one local effect of policies and management of migration at the nation-state and supranational EU scale.

Like Lubaid, several migrants I spoke with expressed regret that they applied for asylum in Norway. This regret followed the rejection of their asylum application: they regretted the fact that they had not applied for asylum for example in Germany where they – at that moment in time – were certain that they would have been accepted. While many thought they had made a wrong move at some point of their journey, others did not believe that ending up in Norway was a choice of their own. The latter thought that their arrival in Norway was a consequence of various moments of decisions, events or misfortunes during the journey, and that these had been out of their own control, as they had been in the hands of the helper or smuggler. Elias, an Ethiopian man whose asylum application had been rejected, said:

> you know, your destination sometimes ends in the wrong country. Of course, it was not chosen by me, but unfortunately, you know, when the people take you, they just take you where they need to go or maybe sometimes where you need. As for myself there was someone who took me here, so that's why I came here, unfortunately.

European politicians and leaders frequently argue that the nation-state's policies towards asylum seekers and how they are accommodated (materially speaking) have consequences for the decisions refugees make before and during the journey about their target destination. In Norway, as in other countries, there is a general presumption that refugee movements can be steered by limiting welfare rights for asylum seekers and by introducing stricter acceptance procedures and actively enforcing return policies.

At the EU level, the goal of the CEAS has been to harmonize asylum law in the EU, so as to avoid so-called "asylum shopping". The term "asylum shopping" has been used to describe both migrants' efforts to reach a particular country in Europe where they are thought to have a higher chance of having their asylum application accepted and the practice of making multiple application claims in different Schengen states. These migratory practices were part of the impetus behind the EU decision to harmonize the asylum process to avoid different assessments of asylum claims. The Dublin Convention, signed in 1990, establishes the principle that one member state should be responsible for examining an individual's asylum application (Guild 2006).[15] Later, the Dublin II and Dublin III regulations clarified the Member State's responsibilities. These introduced more detailed regulations of family reunification and prohibited member states from transferring anyone to a country where they would be at risk of inhuman and degrading treatment.

With the Dublin regulations, the EU sought to avoid having a migrant move from one country to another to apply for asylum.[16] Such efforts to reduce secondary movements inside the Schengen area have later come to include inducements to ensure that applicants are registered properly, and that Member States have reception conditions in line with EU law and fundamental rights. However, the ongoing migration movement signals the failure of the system to produce equal standards for asylum procedures, accommodation, approval of asylum claims, and for the general treatment of migrants by police and the authorities (Hagen-Zanker and Mallett 2016). The goals of the Dublin regulations have failed because there is still substantial divergence in reception practices, procedures and qualification requirements. The goals have also failed because EU policies and the Dublin agreement did not recognize that other factors also influence and motivate the destination migrants select, such as language and existing social networks (see Brekke 2012) and, as Elias noted, coincidences. How the interconnectedness plays out at the local level and affects people's action must be examined through a multiscalar analysis connecting the various levels (Eriksen 2016).

The everyday border: arrival?

Applying for asylum in Norway is not the end of migrants' border-crossing practices. In cases where an asylum application is rejected, and the applicant is subsequently categorized as an irregular or illegal migrant and thus a potential candidate either for deportation or for assisted return, borders reappear in everyday life, at various meeting-points and events. The story of Amin, a Kurd from Iran, illustrates how borders surface within the nation-state as boundaries and shape migrants' movements and future plans.

Amin was twenty-six years old when I meet him in Oslo. He had spent three and a half years in Norway, and had converted to Christianity three years ago. His family in Iran was Sunni Muslim, his educated brothers had not been able to get jobs relevant to their training, and Amin had gotten in trouble with the government after initiating contact with his city's church: "they went further into interviewing the psychology police and then I knew that I am a danger due to different reasons so I had to escape from Iran." Amin did not go directly to Norway, but first fled to Spain. He explains:

> I didn't know where to go because it was not a situation in which I could decide. So I came to Spain, and from Spain that is when I heard the special info, because I had some people here in Norway and I was asking "what is the situation in Norway for refugees, for human rights?" And then I said "ok, that can be a good country to go [to]."

In Norway, Amin's asylum application was rejected, and he was living as an irregular migrant with an Iranian family in Oslo, working informally. His life in Norway was shaped by what he and other migrants called "the system": the asylum system and associated institutions as well as the need to be able to show documents in various places – something which made him nervous and uncertain. He had expected to feel relaxed and free in Norway, but instead felt scared in public places and restricted in his movement.

Compared to Iran, he believed he was more limited in his ability to participate in social activities, because he lacked a valid identity card:[17]

> like with the identity card that they give us – with that we cannot enter very many places. Like restaurant, some of the restaurants, some of the bars, some of the shops. So it's like you can easily feel the difference between you and other people.

In Norway, alcohol regulations give the licensee, manager and staff the right and duty to check the age of all customers wherever alcohol is served. Amin recalled situations in which he had enjoyed himself at a restaurant with friends when at some point in the evening the bouncer asked everyone to go out and then re-enter showing their ID card to verify their age. Since Amin had no valid ID he could not re-enter: "like, all of my friends, they were in, and I had to go back home. So that was like many, many things like this." Amin had medical problems for which he had visited a doctor. Because he was unable to sleep, he had asked for a meeting with a psychologist or a specialist. Amin recalls:

> they said no, because "you are illegal in Norway and that's not possible". (…). So I said what is the solution? The doctor said "with what has happened to you, the best thing to do is to go and run in the forest".

Amin laughed incredulously when telling me what the doctor had suggested.

Even if Amin had gained the freedom to express his opinions about politics and religion in Norway, he felt worse off now than in Iran:

> Like, in Persian we have a saying that when you don't have food to eat, you can forget about something like politics. The situation is like this in Norway. You are always trying for your primary rights, trying for a place to sleep, trying to eat and try to find something to wear.

Amin had previously had a relationship with a Norwegian woman, and her father had made an effort to help them get married, but failed. The process and situation had put a strain on their relationship, and they had gone their separate ways.

In Norway, as in other European countries, there has been a parallel process of liberalization for some migrants and the criminalization of others. The period from 1994 to 2010 was characterized by greater political resolve to manage migration through regulations that were to reduce irregular and unwanted migration, while opening up for migrants who were viewed favourably (Brekke 2012). While the labour market has been open to EU nationals and a limited number of high skilled migrants – moving policy in a more liberal direction (see Spencer 2003) – for asylum seekers and irregular migrants, access to rights such as health care, social benefits and the labour market has become more restrictive. Construing certain migrants as "productive" or "harmless" and asylum seekers as "unproductive" or "problematic", such policy responses feed into an increasingly strict environment for refugees and asylum seekers who have been subject to various processes of criminalization. This trend, which accelerated a shift from a focus on the rights of migrants to a focus on national interests and a more proactive immigration strategy, emerged around the year 2000 (Brekke 2012), arguably in response to the heightened mobility in and around the European continent.

Nation-state welfare regulations have become part of the internal border processes that create social boundaries for those living illegally in Norway (Bendixsen, Jacobsen, and

Søvig 2015). For generous and comprehensive welfare states, a central dilemma in the context of immigration is drawing the line between members and non-members (Faist 1996). Increasingly, the responsibility for making this distinction and thus for the boundary-making process has been scaled down to the "gatekeepers" of the welfare state who implement the laws and policies, such as local police, security guards at restaurants and receptionists at urgent care or medical offices (Bendixsen 2015). The right to social benefits, health care, housing (outside asylum reception centres) and education (after the age eighteen) is made conditional on residency status. Excluding irregular migrants from public services has become part of how the state seeks to discourage irregular migration. By reserving certain rights and welfare benefits to those whose presence within national borders is authorized by the state, such bordering practices are parts of welfare nationalism: "a place where the welfare state must be preserved and made sustainable for those on the inside by limiting access from the outside" (Barker 2013, 17; Aas 2014).

This is not particular to Norway: many countries curtail irregular migrants' access to public services (Faist 1996; Van Der Leun 2006). Such policies are founded on the belief of a particular interconnected world, namely that comprehensive welfare systems attract prospective (irregular) migrants and function as barriers when migrants consider returning to their home country (Bendixsen and Lidén 2017). Boundaries controlled by civil servants at the local scale are also part of the (re)construction of the external nation-state borders, and adds to the ongoing criminalization of migrants. When borders have the potential to emerge through everyday boundaries that are also often racialized, this also means that daily activities (working, being with friends, taking public transport) can be defined as criminal acts (De Genova 2002).

During my fieldwork, I noticed that some migrants were extremely focused on paying their bus ticket. I understood this both as an effort to position themselves as good citizens who are not breaking the law even if illegally in Norway (Bendixsen 2013), and as a precaution taken because the consequence of being caught without a ticket could be deportation. While deportation certainly will not happen to every irregularized person without a bus ticket and a valid ID, stories circulated in the grapevine about someone who had been taken into custody, transferred to a closed reception centre and later deported. The everyday fear of taking public transport without a ticket reflects the interchangeability and mutual reinforcement of criminal law and immigration law, described by some scholars as crimmigration law (Stumpf 2006). As Aas (2014, 525) has argued:

> [c]riminal law is applied not only to punish, but also to deport, while deportation is used not only for immigration purposes, but also because an individual is seen as a law and order problem (without necessarily needing to prove so with criminal law procedural means).

The folding of these two spheres emphasizes the centrality of citizenship or legal residency for the domestic penal order (Bosworth and Guild 2008; Aas 2014), and for the global mobility regime (Aas 2014). The increasingly strong connectedness between border security, boundary management, migration and crime in post-cold war Norway can be illustrated by the exponential growth in deportation based on criminal sentencing: from 190 decisions in 1991, the number of migrants deported from Norway on the basis of having been sentenced for a crime increased exponentially to nearly 2500 decision in 2014 (Aas and Mohn 2015).

Scholars have suggested that life as an irregular migrant in comprehensive welfare states with universal ambitions, such as the Nordic countries, is more difficult than elsewhere because there is limited available parallel (informal) structures for health care, housing and work (Khosravi 2010; Bendixsen 2015). Exclusionary mechanisms are legitimated by various imaginations, open social boundaries and by the signalling of a particular temporal frame. Politicians and public actors on the centre-right frequently argue that the generous welfare state is potentially at risk if unproductive persons (those not paying tax, or insufficiently so) are making "excessive" use of its services. Aas (2014) shows how Norwegian police officers talk about the country as a "honeypot" and themselves as its guardians. Another example is the ways in which healthcare regulations generally limit healthcare for irregular migrants to "emergencies" and "healthcare that cannot wait". These limitations are a consequence of the goal instituted in 2004 which stipulated that contact between public institutions and irregular migrants should be characterized by temporariness to indicate that these migrants' time in Norway should come to an end (Brekke 2008). Nation-state regulations and practices that provide or limit access to welfare rights and public spaces are linked to external border constructions because such regulations are intended to make Norway unattractive to potential asylum seekers and to induce irregular migrants to leave. One consequence of these forms of regulations were that irregular migrants waited too long before they sought health care assistance (Bendixsen 2015). One migrant had visited the Emergency unit with his hand bleeding due to a working accident, and the receptionist had quarrelled vehemently with him and his informal boss before granting him assistance because he lacked the required official personal number that all residents in Norway should have. Even if the doctors had asked him to return to have his stitches removed he had instead performed this act himself with instructions from youtube. As he saw it, since the receptionist had made so much hassle when he had been bleeding considerable, it was not worth going through a similar humiliating procedure again.

Return: the journey continued

"What will you do when you return to Afghanistan", I asked Khuram – a young man in his twenties who had signed up with International Organization for Migration (IOM) for assisted return to Afghanistan. He had been in Norway for six years, the last couple of years as an irregular migrant. "I don't know", he told me frankly. "I guess I will buy some potatoes cheap and sell them down the road," he added as to show the uncertain situation that awaited him upon return to Afghanistan and his lack of faith in any future there. Khuram had not been to Afghanistan since he was a young boy. Before leaving for Europe he had lived for several years with his family in Iran, where his parents were working. The difficult living situation for migrant workers in Iran had made his family decide to send him to Europe. However, his asylum application had been rejected and after several years of trying to change his asylum case and living as an irregular migrant he gave up waiting for policy changes or something to happen. His mother had died two years earlier, which had made him rethink his situation in Norway. His sister lived with her husband in Iran and had asked him to come live with them. "She says that they will help me find work in Teheran, and also that I should get married there", Khuram explained. Khuram felt that he was growing older and had not had the chance to marry, get an education or a satisfactory job. He talked about having grown tired of being in a liminal position, waiting for his desired future to start. However, signing up for assisted return did not represent a return in the sense of going back, but a continuous migration movement, where other border crossings would follow. He would be returned to Afghanistan, but was already planning continued movement to Iran.[18]

Norway has had no official regularization programmes for irregular migrants, in contrast to countries such as Italy, Sweden and France. Instead, the current system of assisted return has increasingly become an integral part of the asylum process, and a central part of the state's approach to asylum seekers and irregular migrants in Norway. Today, migrants are introduced to the Norwegian government programme of assisted return when they apply for asylum.[19] Assisted return programmes reflect the Norwegian government's explicit policy objective of encouraging as many rejected asylum seekers as possible to leave as soon as possible.

Assisted return helps reaffirm the idea that some migrant groups are socially, economically and politically unwelcome, potential threats to society, and "out of place" (Douglas 1966). Dealing with irregular migrants through assisted return programmes is meant to signal to the Norwegian population that the government is in control of those inside its borders, to signal to irregular migrants in Norway that assisted return is the only acceptable option and finally to signal to those who have not (yet) migrated that they should not undertake the journey to Norway (Bendixsen and Lidén 2017). By showing that they are dealing with "the problem" of irregular migration through assisted or forced return, the Norwegian government re-establishes sovereign power and re-inscribes borders, marking a distinction between those who belong and those who should leave the territory. The implementation of assisted return is strongly linked to the potential of forced return, in a circular argumentation: without assisted return, it becomes difficult to legitimize forced return, and without the latter, it becomes harder to implement the former. The government frequently presents assisted return programmes as a humanitarian option compared to forced returns, while the latter is legitimized by the argument that if irregular migrants "fail" to opt for assisted return, a forced return is the only option available to the government. One unintended effect of this policy in a world which is shrinking but where social inequality continues is the increase of migrant mobility: deportation tends not to construct sustainable return, but rather to continued migration.

The Norwegian government continues to implement agreements with relevant countries in order to facilitate forced returns. The implementation of such international arrangements and treaties positions return programmes as part of the concurrent externalization of migration control. From the point of view of the EU Member States, the current failure of the return system is thought to encourage irregular migration. The Commission argues that:

> smuggling networks often play on the fact that relatively few return decisions are enforced – only 39.2% of return decisions issued in 2013 were effectively enforced. To increase the enforcement rate, we first need to ensure that third countries fulfil their international obligation to take back their own nationals residing irregularly in Europe. (European Commission 2015, 9)

Such "remote control" initiatives in Europe and North America that extend border controls beyond a country's territory in order to regulate migrants' movements (Zaiotti 2016) are becoming increasingly common in European nation-states and in EU border constructions.

International return agreements effectively increase the deportability of any person belonging to a country with which Norway has such an agreement. It magnifies the distinction between those legally inside and those who can potentially be excluded. The local perception of these policies had consequences at the level of migrants' action. The migrants with whom I carried out fieldwork had a clear perception, accurate or not, of whether they were likely to be deported and this assessment informed their behaviour in urban space and their relation to public institutions, such as whether or not to visit the Emergency care unit and certain parts of the city at specific times of the day. Defining themselves as deportable shaped their movements, scope of action, and understanding of future prospects, albeit in different ways. While some migrants talked about fearing the police and public officials, others left to Sweden because it was perceived as easier to live there as irregular, and assess to informal work greater. Yet others would engage in political demonstrations. Nonetheless, being deportable is part of a governing process of drawing an ultimate line between members and non-members, and is "constitutive of citizenship" (De Genova 2010). Thus, while some migrants tried to constitute themselves through political mobilization in the public as already integrated in Norway, although without papers, by pointing to that they had paid tax in the past, or showing that they had adapted what is generally viewed as Norwegian values, and overall through public behaviour and speeches trying to adhere to the potentially "good" citizen, being deportable reaffirms the formal and normative boundaries of membership.

Whilst beyond the scope of this article, a fourth moment of the migrant's journey could have been added here, namely legal residence. This moment is not the end of border and boundary crossings, although the internal boundary practices becomes substantially more important in the migrant's everyday life than the external borders. Each immigration status entails different openings, limitations and consequences for access to work, health care and public services, education and the eventual possibility of gaining citizenship. Even when migrants have become citizens, in Norway border time still continues in that the second and third generation are viewed as "immigrants", citizens somehow foreign to the nation (Nyers 2015) and stigmatized (Anthias and Yuval-Davis 1992). Clearly, such boundary processes are not produced, implemented or created merely by state power, but also through various forms of differentiation, including cultural recognition, linguistic hierarchy and various forms of stereotyping that exclude (Balibar and Wallerstein 2011) as well as include differentially (Nyers 2015). It reminds us how boundaries may be invisible IOM to some while recognized and experienced by others (Cohen 1985).

Conclusion

The Japanese management theorist Kenichi Ohmae published the book *The Borderless World* in 1990. The book had a major impact on the debate on globalization and (the end of) borders in a period which in retrospect is associated with the fall of the Berlin Wall and of apartheid, the deregulation of global trade and the emergence of the internet and mobile phones. Today, we see that the "borderless world" has led to a multiplication of new borders (Mezzadra and Neilson 2013) which function selectively to allow some to move freely and others to stay stuck, and the production of border management has become part of various policy areas at different scales, including welfare, crime, security, marriage, etc.

AN OVERHEATED WORLD

In the current border crisis where mobility has become overheated (in terms of politics, mass media, numbers of people moving and actors engaged at different levels with that mobility), nation-states, supranational bodies as well as migrants' management of mobility create new forms of interconnectedness where actions at different scales have ramifications on local, national and global levels. By describing stages in informal migrant careers, and by distinguishing between physical borders and social boundaries, I have shown how borders are destabilized and restabilized through formal and informal techniques, regulations, policies, and policing, in complex interaction with migrants' movements and actions. Technological and material border constructions, legal structures, welfare and work policies, international return agreements, the creation of boundaries through the racialization of migrants and the culturalization of ethnic minorities, are important features of the reconfiguration of European nation-states' borders, making Europe legible as a social imaginary.

Recognizing and taking seriously these interconnections of borders, boundaries and actors at different scales mean that our focus on the power of the state must be modified. Indeed, borders do not always function the way the state intended. It calls for an ethnography of local perception and action that engages with multiscalar contextualization (Eriksen 2016). Further, mobility is regulated at various scales as a response to migrants and their movement and decision-making, rather than from an ideologically and politically motivated position. Policy and regulation practices in this field resemble high-stakes cat-and-mouse play rather than a political and civic engagement with global mobility and immobility resulting from different kinds of crises. The violation of international obligations, high human costs and migrants living constantly at the border are some of the consequences of the current border (mis)management in Norway, as in several other European countries.

An ethnographic lens on the reconfiguration of the border in the globalized world opens up the question of how we understand mobility and border crossings: where and when does a migrant cross a border, and where and when has he or she entered society? Borders are not only increasingly mobile and diffused throughout society, but are also complexly linking (through policies, laws and practices) actors whose activities take place at very different scales. By examining the increasingly multifaceted modalities of borders, how the bordering practices function political and socially (Paasi 2012, 2307) through boundary processes and their consequences for migrants' lives, as well as how migrants' acts inform the politics of the border, this article has sought to contribute to the continued denaturalization of borders necessary to make it possible to think beyond borders (Agnew 2008, 176). In this post-cold war world, when the formation of European borders is less concerned with politico-military struggles over territory (Walters 2009) and more with channelling flows of capital, goods and people, we need to better understand how border production configures the society in which we all live.

Notes

1. http://ec.europa.eu/dgs/home-affairs/what-is-new/news/news/2016/20160202_2_en.htm. Accessed February 2, 2016.
2. https://www.bundeskanzlerin.de/Content/EN/Artikel/2016/02_en/2016-02-29-merkel-annewill_en.html. Accessed March 6, 2016.

3. https://www.youtube.com/watch?v=nPm1ECl2-7U.
4. http://www.aljazeera.com/news/2016/02/turkey-open-border-syrian-refugees-160207113555928.html. Accessed February 2, 2016.
5. For an extensive overview of studies of borders, see Green (2013).
6. An agency which is only partly conscious and intent-driven.
7. The construction of the Schengen area was first integrated into the EU acquis with the signing of the Treaty of Amsterdam (1999), which obliged Member States to adopt legally binding instruments in asylum and immigration policies. Some years earlier, the Maastricht Treaty (1992) incorporated migration in the EU's "third pillar" of justice and home affairs.
8. According to Brekke (2012), the introduction of the Eurodac identification system in 2002 is viewed by people in the Norwegian Ministry as a key factor in bringing down the refugee numbers in Norway and the rest of Europe.
9. The Government's website containing the December 2015 bill describes it as consultation on a number of proposed measures to impose restrictions and make it less attractive to apply for asylum in Norway, see: https://www.regjeringen.no/no/dokumenter/horing--endringer-i-utlendingslovgivningen-innstramninger-ii/id2469054/. Accessed February 1, 2016.
10. The recent discussion, particularly in the UK, about the limitations on social benefits for non-national EU workers in UK may be indicative of such a direction.
11. The Hollywood movie from 2004 featuring Tom Hanks tells a story about Victor Navorski, who gets stuck for several months at JFK Airport. The movie is inspired by the true story of Iranian refugee Alfred Mehran (previously called Mehran Karimi Nasseri) who was stuck at Charles de Gaulle airport in Paris from 1988 to 2006.
12. In Dubai all foreigners must have a sponsor, also called a guarantor, and this might be an individual, a company or an institution.
13. People who for various reasons were unable to use legal routes have used what we today call smugglers as long as borders have existed. For example, in the 1920s Japanese migrants made use of smuggling expertise to get to Canada despite the restrictive measures targeting them. Movies have been made about well-known smugglers during the Second World War and those helping people cross the Berlin Wall (van Liempt and Sersli 2013).
14. http://www.thetimes.co.uk/tto/news/world/europe/article4678348.ece. Accessed February 25, 2016.
15. By introducing this definite responsibility of a particular Member State, the EU sought to avoid a situation of which refugees are in orbit, with multiple applications for asylum, avoid the duplication of Member States' resources, and reduce backlogs and delays in the examination of asylum applications.
16. The Dublin Convention replaced the Schengen provision on asylum. The Dublin system came to be viewed as neither fair nor efficient. The development of Dublin II and Dublin III aimed to reassess the responsibility-sharing procedures within the EU/EEA (Hurwitz 1999).
17. Asylum seekers are provided with an identity card that is only valid for a set number of months. If the card has expired and the asylum application is rejected, the card will not be renewed. While some irregular migrants told me that the police withdrew their expired card, others had managed to hold on to the card by arguing that it was the only form of identification they had, and in case something occurred to them, others would need to be able to identify them.
18. Schuster and Majidi (2013) found that 80% of the deportees from the UK to Afghanistan whom they interviewed left Afghanistan again within two years of their return.
19. If a migrant signs up for a voluntary return programme, they will be offered a lump sum (usually between 1200 and 2400 Euros) depending on the return destination and whether they are single or in a family – in addition to the other assistance (including a return flight). The amount of money provided also depends on the period of time that has elapsed after the asylum application was rejected and before the migrant applied for the programme.

Disclosure statement

No potential conflict of interest was reported by the author.

Funding

The writing of this article was made possible through the project "Denaturalizing difference: Challenging the production of global social inequality" at the University of Bergen, funded by the Research Council of Norway. Thomas Hylland Eriksen provided valuable comments on early drafts which were helpful in clarifying aspects of my argument.

References

Aas, Katja Franko. 2014. "Bordered Penality: Precarious Membership and Abnormal Justice." *Punishment & Society* 16 (5): 520–541.
Aas, Katja Franko, and Sigmund Book Mohn. 2015. "Utvisning som straff? Om grensesnittet mellom strafferett og utlendingskontroll." *Tidsskrift for Strafferett* 2: 153–176.
Agnew, John. 2008. "Borders on the Mind: Re-Framing Border Thinking." *Ethics & Global Politics* 1 (4): 175–191. doi:10.3402/egp.v1i4.1892.
Anderson, Malcolm. 1996. *Frontiers. Territory and State Formation in the Modern World*. Cambridge: Polity Press.
Andersson, Ruben. 2014. *Illegality, Inc: Clandestine Migration and the Business of Bordering Europe California Series in Public Anthropology*. Oakland: University of California Press.
Andreas, Peter. 2000. "Introduction: The Wall after the Wall." In *The Wall Around the West*, edited by Peter Andreas and Timothy Synder, 1–14. Oxford: Rowman and Littlefield.
Anthias, Floya, and Nira Yuval-Davis. 1992. *Racialized Boundaries*. London: Routledge.
Balibar, Etienne. 2002. *Politics and the Other Scene*. London: Verso.
Balibar, Etienne. 2009. *We, the People of Europe? Reflections on Transnational Citizenship*. Princeton, NJ: Princeton University Press.
Balibar, Etienne, and Immanuel Wallerstein. 2011. *Race Nation Class: Ambiguous Identities*. London: Verso.
Barker, Vanessa. 2013. "Nordic Exceptionalism Revisited: Explaining the Paradox of a Janusfaced Penal Regime." *Theoretical Criminology* 17 (1): 5–25.
Barth, Fredrik. 1969. "Introduction." In *Ethnic Groups and Boundaries*, edited by Fredrik Barth, 9–38. Oslo: Universitetsforlaget.
Bendixsen, Synnøve. 2013. "Becoming Members in the Community of Value: Ethiopian Irregular Migrants Enacting Citizenship in Norway." In *Migration Matters*, edited by A. Edelstein and M. Dugan, 3–22. Oxfordshire: Inter-Disciplinary Press.
Bendixsen, Synnøve. 2015. "Vilkårlige rettigheter? Irregulære migranters tillit, sosiale kapital og kreative taktikker." In *Eksepsjonell velferd? Irregulære migranter i det norske velferdssamfunnet*, edited by Synnøve Bendixsen, Christine Jacobsen and Karl Harald Søvig, 184–202. Oslo: Gyldendal.
Bendixsen, Synnøve, and Thomas Hylland Eriksen. 2017. "Timeless Time Among Irregular Migrants: The Slowness of Waiting in an Accelerated World." In *Ethnographies of Waiting: Doubt, Hope and Uncertainty*, edited by Manpreet K. Janeja and Andrea Bandak. London, NY: Bloomsbury.
Bendixsen, Synnøve, Christine Jacobsen, and Karl Harald Søvig, eds. 2015. *Eksepsjonell velferd? Irregulære migranter i det norske velferdssamfunnet*. Oslo: Gyldendal.
Bendixsen, Synnøve, and Hilde Lidén. 2017. "Return to Well-Being? Irregular Migrants and Assisted Return in Norway." In *Return Migration and Psychosocial Wellbeing*, edited by King Russell and Zanna Vathi. London: Routledge.
Bigo, Didier. 2002. "Security and Immigration: Toward a Critique of the Governmentality of Unease." *Alternatives: Global, Local, Political* 27 (1): 63–92.
Bigo, Didier, and Elspeth Guild, eds. 2005. *Controlling Frontiers: Free Movement Into and Within Europe*. Adelshot: Ashgate.
Bosworth, Mary, and Mhairi Guild. 2008. "Governing Through Migration Control: Security and Citizenship in Britain." *The British Journal of Criminology* 48 (6): 703–719.
Brekke, Jan-Paul. 2008. "Making the Unreturnable Return. The Role of the Welfare State in Promoting Return for Rejected Asylum Seekers in Norway." Paper presented at IAFSM conference in Cairo, Egypt, January.

Brekke, Jan-Paul. 2012. "Hvorfor kommer asylsøkere til Norge?" In *Asylsøker: i velferdsstatens venterom*, edited by Berit Berg and Marko Valenta, 59–81. Oslo: Universitetsforlaget.

Brown, Wendy. 2010. *Walled States, Waning Sovereignty*. New York: Zone Books.

Cohen, Anthony P. 1985. *The Symbolic Construction of Community*. London: Tavistock.

De Genova, Nicholas. 2002. "Migrant "Illegality" and Deportability in Everyday Life." *Annual Review of Anthropology* 31: 419–447.

De Genova, Nicholas. 2010. "The Deportation Regime: Sovereignty, Space and the Freedom of Movement." In *The Deportation Regime: Sovereignty, Space and Freedom of Movement*, edited by Nicholas de Genova and Nathalie Peutz, 33–65. Durham, NC: Duke University Press.

Diez, Thomas. 2006. "The Paradoxes of Europe's Borders." *Comparative European Politics* 4 (2/3): 235–252.

Douglas, Mary. 1966. *Purity and Danger: An Analysis of Concepts of Pollution and Taboo*. London: Routledge.

Eriksen, Thomas Hylland. 2016. "Overheating: The World Since 1991." *History and Anthropology* 27 (5): 1–19.

European Commission. 2015. *Communication from the Commission to the European Parliament, the Council, the European Economic and Social Committee and the Committee of the Regions, A European Agenda on Migration*. Brussels, COM (2015) 240.

Faist, Thomas. 1996. "Immigration, Integration and the Welfare State: Germany and the USA in comparative perspective." In *The Challenge of Diversity: Integration and Pluralism in Societies of Immigration*, edited by Rainer Bauböck, Agnes Heller, and Aristide Zolberg, 227–258. Aldershot: Avebury.

Fassin, Didier. 2011. "Policing Borders, Producing Boundaries. The Governmentality of Immigration in Dark Times." *Annual Review of Anthropology* 40: 213–226.

Green, Sarah. 2013. "Borders and the Relocation of Europe." *Annual Review of Anthropology* 42: 345–361.

Guild, Elspeth. 2006. "The Europeanisation of Europe's Asylum Policy." *International Journal of Refugee Law* 18 (3–4): 630–651.

Guiraudon, Virginie. 2001. "De-Nationalizing Control: Analyzing State Responses to Constraints on Migration Control." In *Controlling a New Migration World*, edited by Virginie Guiraudon and C. Joppke, 31–64. London: Routledge.

Guiraudon, Virginie, and Gallya Lahav. 2000. "Comparative Perspectives on Border Control: Away From the Border and Outside the State"." In *The Wall Around the West: State Borders and Immigration Controls in North America and Europe*, edited by P. Andreas and T. Snyder, 55–80. Lanham, MD: Rowman & Littlefield.

Hagen-Zanker, Jessica, and Richard Mallett. 2016. *Journeys to Europe. The Role of Policy in Migrant Decision-Making*. London: ODI insights.

Hurwitz, Agnès. 1999. "The 1990 Dublin Convention: A Comprehensive Assessment." *International Journal of Refugee Law* 11 (4): 646–677.

Johnson, Corey, Reece Jones, Anssi Paasi, Louise Amoore, Alison Mountz, Mark Salter, and Chris Rumford. 2011. "Interventions on Rethinking 'The Border' in Border Studies." *Political Geography* 30 (2): 61–69.

Kearney, Michael. 1991. "Borders and Boundaries of State and Self at the End of Empire." *Journal of Historical Sociology* 4 (1): 52–74.

Khosravi, Shahram. 2010. "An Ethnography of Migrant 'Illegality' in Sweden: Included yet Excepted?" *Journal of International Political Theory* 6 (1): 95–116.

van Liempt, Ilse, and Stephanie Sersli. 2013. "State Responses and Migrant Experiences with Human Smuggling: A Reality Check." *Antipode* 45 (4): 1029–1046.

Mezzadra, Sandro. 2004. "The Right to Escape." *Ephemera* 4 (3): 267–275.

Mezzadra, Sandro. 2015. "The Proliferation of Borders and the Right to Escape." In *The Irregularization of Migration in Contemporary Europe. Detention, Deportation, Drowning*, edited by Yolande Jansen, Robin Celikates, and Joost de Bloois, 121–135. London: Rowman & Littlefield.

Mezzadra, Sandro, and Bret Neilson. 2013. *Border as Method or, the Multiplication of Labor*. Durham, NC: Duke University Press.

Nyer, P. 2010. "No One is Illegal between City and Nation." *Studies in Social Justice* 4 (2): 127–143.

Nyers, Peter. 2015. "Migrant Citizenships and Autonomous Mobilities." *Migration, Mobility, & Displacement* 1 (1): 23–39.

Paasi, Anssi. 2012. "Border Studies Re-Animated: Going Beyond the Relational/Territorial Divide." *Environment and Planning A* 44 (10): 2303–2309.

Reeves, Madeleine. 2014. *Border Work: Spatial Lives of the State in Rural Central Asia*. Ithaca: Cornell University Press.

Rumford, Chris. 2006. "Theorizing Borders." *European Journal of Social Theory* 9 (2): 155–169.

Rumford, Chris. 2008. "Introduction: Citizens and Borderwork in Europe." *Space and Polity* 12 (1): 1–12.

Rumford, Chris. 2010. "Global Borders: An Introduction to the Special Issue." *Environment and Planning D: Society and Space* 28 (6): 951–956.

Schuster, Liza, and Nazzim Majidi. 2013. "What Happens Post-Deportation? The Experience of Deported Afghans." *Migration Studies* 1 (2): 221–240.

Spencer, Sarah, ed. 2003. *The Politics of Migration. Managing Opportunity, Conflict and Change*. Oxford: Blackwell.

Stumpf, Juliet. 2006. "The Crimmigration Crisis: Immigrants, Crime, and Sovereign Power." *American University Law Review* 56 (2): 367–419.

Van Der Leun, Joanne. 2006. "Excluding Illegal Migrants in The Netherlands: Between National Policies and Local Implementation." *West European Politics* 29 (2): 310–326. doi:10.1080/01402380500512650.

Walters, William. 2006. "Rethinking Borders Beyond the State." *Comparative European Politics* 4 (2/3): 141–159.

Walters, William. 2009. "Europe's Borders." In *Sage Handbook of European Studies*, edited by Chris Rumford, 485–505. London: Sage.

Wilson, Thomas. 2012. "The Europe of Regions and Borderlands." In *A Companion to the Anthropology of Europe*, edited by Ullrich Kockel, Máiréad Nic Craith, and Jonas Frykman, 163–180. Chichester: Wiley-Blackwell.

Wonders, Nancy A. 2006. "Global Flows, Semi-Permeable Borders and New Channels of Inequality: Border Crossers and Border Performativity." In *Borders, Mobility and Technologies of Control*, edited by Sharon Pickering and Leanne Weber, 45–62. Dordrecht: Springer.

Zaiotti, Ruben. 2007. "Revisiting Schengen: Europe and the Emergence of a New Culture of Border Control." *Perspectives on European Politics and Society* 8 (1): 31–54.

Zaiotti, Ruben, ed. 2016. *Externalizing Migration Management in Europe and North America*. New York: Routledge.

From coal to Ukip: the struggle over identity in post-industrial Doncaster

Cathrine Thorleifsson

ABSTRACT
The article explores the local history and set of conditions central for the rise of "coal nationalism" in the post-industrial town of Doncaster. Based on ethnography, interviews and archival research, the essay shows how Doncastrians were not merely victimized by the effects of neoliberal restructuring programmes and deindustrialization, but strived to cope with and give meaning to the changes affecting their lives. In the space left by the dissolution of industrialism, new competing scale-making projects over meaning, memory and future played out. Several social actors nostalgically invoked the industrial past to cope with existential insecurity. Some called upon the lost empire or the EU, while others turned to exclusionary Englishness as the solution to current hardship and grievances. United Kingdom Independence Party (Ukip), strategically locating their annual conference in 2015 in the white-majority working-class town, tapped into local anxieties and disillusionment, promising to secure future and security for British nationals in the extractive industries. Examining the tensions emerging out of the intersection of various scale-making projects, the essay suggests that the rising appeal of English nationalism cannot be reduced to neoliberal restructuring, nor just the legacies of industrialism, nor to the passage of transition or global migration. It is all of these, which in turn constitute the Ukip code.

Multiscalar overheating

They talk about statistic, about the price of coal, the price is our communities, dying on the dole.

From a song sung by Lancashire Women Against Pit Closures.

In May 2015, United Kingdom Independence Party (Ukip) got its breakthrough in the general elections on an anti-immigration, anti-EU and pro-coal platform. At Ukip's annual conference in Doncaster in September, strategically located in traditional Labour heartland, Ukips Energy spokesperson Roger Helmer promised "to keep the lights on", securing jobs in the extractive industries for another 200 years.

This essay explores the local history and set of conditions central for the rise of Ukip, appropriating nostalgia for "Fordist forms of feelings of stability and belonging" (Muehlebach and Shoshan 2012, 318) with exclusionary "coal nationalism". In the mid-1980s,

Doncaster, a white-majority working-class town in South Yorkshire, went from boom to bust when most of the coalmines shut during Thatcher's neoliberal restructuring programme.[1] Doncastrians were far from the accelerated growth in London and other urban regions, experiencing a crisis-laden cooling down of the economy with rising unemployment and precarization of labour (Standing 2014). At the same time, diversification processes intensified due to increased global migration. The three past decades, Donaster has thus been marked by a combination of social forms and ideals constructed at various scales of time and space. Taken together, the accelerated changes caused by neoliberal restructuring of the economy and global migration constitute an *overheating* effect (Eriksen 2016). The (un)-intended consequences of overheating, such as socio-economic inequality, have experienced varied growth at multiple geographical scales, from nation-states to regions and neighbourhoods (Sassen 2007; Standing 2014).

Recognizing the multiscalar and multitemporal character of neoliberal economic transition and diversification processes (Vertovec 2007), this essay explores the multiple tensions and contradictions emerging out of processes of overheating and cooling-off in Doncaster since the early 1990s. People in Doncaster were not merely victimized by neoliberal polices, but actively strived to cope with and give meaning to the changes affecting their lives. In the space left by the dissolution of industrialism, new competing scale-making projects over meaning, memory and future played out. Some actors engaged with the town's industrial past, nostalgically appropriating coal as source of national and regional identity. A few chose to align themselves with cosmopolitan globalism, celebrating the town's old and emerging diversity. Others embraced Ukip's anti-migration and anti-EU politics when faced with existential uncertainty. The essay suggests that the rising appeal of English nationalism cannot be reduced to neoliberal restructuring, nor just the legacies of industrialism, nor to the passage of transition or global migration. It is all of these, which in turn constitute the Ukip code.

A coal place

Gone – The darkness and the grime, the heat, the dirt, and the slime.
Gone – The laughter, the mates and the hot canteen, the showers, the lockers and the scrubbing clean.
Gone – The dust, the bile and the smell that makes you ill, the face, the gate, and the roof that can kill.
Gone – The union, the strikes, and the rage, the defeat, the humiliation, the wage
Gone – The Deputy, the Over-man, and the Boss, the union man, who was always at a loss.
Gone – The certainty, the dignity, and the grit, the friendship, the community, the Pit –

From the poem "Farewell Brodsworth Pit" by Brian Gray.

Several scholars have shown how long-term neoliberal restructuring of economics economies as well as short-term developments like the more recent economic recession-financial crisis (2008) have accelerated socio-economic inequalities at various scales (Carrier and Kalb 2015; Ekholm Friedman and Friedman 2008). The following section examines the effect of and responses to structural change and economic recession in Doncaster, taking the early 1980s as the point of departure. At this particular moment in time, industrialism was fundamental to British national identity. Like other towns in South Yorkshire, Doncaster was synonymous with the coal and mining industry. "Coal was king" and it was impossible to imagine a future when the bustling region would not depend or thrive because of it. In addition to jobs in the pits, thousands worked in the Coal Board's office and in firms that made mining equipment or provided support services to the men who went underground. Other major employers included the tractor maker Case, or International Harvester, as most people called it, and mega-factories such as Bridon Wire and Peglers that provided jobs for tens of thousands of skilled and semi-skilled manual workers.

In the mid-1980s, Doncaster went from boom to bust as a pit-closure programme went into full swing under the Thatcher Government. Thatcherism represented a particular aggressive programme of neoliberal restructuring, spearheading the policies that would become the dominant political and ideological form of capitalist globalization throughout the world. Faced with the declining profitability of traditional Fordist mass-production industries, states began to dismantle the basic institutional components of the post-war settlement and to mobilize a range of policies intended to extend marked discipline, competition and commodification throughout all sectors of society. Neoliberal doctrines were employed to justify the deregulation of state control over major industries, dismantling Fordist labour relations and Keynsian welfare programmes (Brenner, Theodore, and Jamie 2009; Ekholm Friedman and Friedman 2008).

In Doncaster, the neoliberal policy agenda had immediate and devastating effects. Several collieries shut and other major employers were "shedding jobs like confetti". Unemployment shot way above the national average and in pockets hit more than 40%. Resistance to the closing of the mines took form in the Miner's Strike of 1984–1985 that was a terrible struggle for communities across England (Tuffrey 2011, 122). The closing of the mines resulted in stagnation and deprivation, themes that were frequently covered by the local newspapers, *The Doncaster Star* and *The Doncaster Gazette*.

A survey amongst youngsters in former pit communities in Doncaster in 1993 showed that more than 40% would like to move somewhere (The Doncaster Star 1993). In 1997, the Coalfield Communities Campaign issued a manifesto to every MP at Westminster that said:

> No other industry in Britain or the rest of Europe has suffered such savage and sudden cutback. It has been an economic hammer blow. Pit closures have devastated not just miners and their families, but entire communities. But where is the help we deserve?

The campaign claimed that unemployment, poverty, ill health and spiralling crime were the direct result of the pit closures (Yorkshire Post 1997).

The poem "Farewell Brodwsworth Pit" by Brian Gray captures the existential uncertainty that arose with the closing of the mines. The miners, albeit in a Fordist compact of management–labour collaboration, had experienced job security, fully equipped with extensive social rights and organized in trade unions. Mining was a physically demanding and risky form of work that nevertheless created visions of camaraderie that extended from the workplace and into social life. Mining, like Fordism, was in short an "affect factory", organizing women, men and children into an "econometrics of feelings" (Muehlebach and Shoshan 2012). When the mining-related industries closed, families did not only lose their job, but also the very activities that gave locals a sense of "community, identity, certainty, dignity and friendship" as the poem goes.

The precarization of labour

Ten years after the Miner's Strike, in 1999, the EU recognized South Yorkshire as one of the most deprived areas in Europe, sparking investment in the region's regeneration. Despite the investment in new infrastructure, a new library, council hall, a lavish cultural centre and the Robin Hood Airport, growth was low. Unlike other towns in England such as Leeds and Sheffield that previously had relied on traditional industry for jobs, Doncaster saw little growth during the good times (Mollona 2010). New jobs were created in sales and customer service, leisure and sales, but not enough to curb the relative deprivation of the borough. The economic decline accelerated in the mid-2000s (Beresford 2013). One week before Christmas in 2006, more than 300 jobs were lost when McCormic tractors closed down its Doncaster manufacturing plant after seventy years, switching production to Italy (Tuffrey 2011).

If the labour conditions during the industrial era were rough and risky, the neoliberal and service-oriented economy has created even worse living conditions. According to the Office of National Statistics, Doncaster Central, a ward of around 18,000, has one of the highest youth unemployment and teenage pregnancies rates in the country, poor educational attainment, poor levels of health and pockets of high crime rates (ONS 2003).

Doncaster, and particularly those relying on the enterprise economy, was hard hit by the global financial crisis.[2] The numbers of job seekers' allowance claimants rose faster than the national average, reinforcing the relative deprivation of the town. John, a hairdresser in his mid-fifties, has run a salon in Doncaster for thirty years. Located at the Northern part of Highgate in a greyish 1970s box, he complained that his business was struggling. Before the recession, he had customers who would regularly come to colour and cut their hair. John noticed a sharp decrease in customers when the crisis hit in 2008:

> Women started to color their hair at home. And you could see more on telly these commercials for home dyeing products. We had to cut staff. It became very difficult to do business here. And I cannot say it has improved. Today you see shops opening and shops closing. Like during Christmas. You had these pop-up shops selling Christmas decorations for a few weeks and then shut. You see a lot of this now.

In an age of globalization and accelerated change, places that once were experienced stable have become uncertain and precarious (Bauman 1998; Storm 2014). Labour in globalising Doncaster had gone from being predictable, to insecure and vulnerable to marked fluctuations. The part of society recovering from its dependence on heavy industries, felt exposed and vulnerable under a new economic reality associated with casualization where they had to compete with cheap labour from elsewhere. Mining that once represented stability, now entailed highly uncertain future prospects, being vulnerable to forces beyond the reach of the community, such as the world market price for coal and EU environmental policies. In June 2015, during fieldwork Hatfield Colliery, England's last remaining privatized deep pit mine located in Doncaster, closed one year prematurely. The closure, resulting in the loss of some 500 jobs, brought to end almost a century of mining. The situation that already was liminal turned into yet another defeat.

The decline and marginalization of the mining communities have paralleled increased wealth concentration and growth in the metropolitan areas. The widening gap between an affluent London and deprived Doncaster can be analysed as a localized version of the Global North and the Global South divide, revealing the very logic of neoliberalism across geographical scales: its production of socio-economic inequality (Ekholm Friedman and Friedman 2008).

Nostalgia in an age of uncertainty

Turbulent times can lead to, as many scholars have noted, the proliferation of narratives about the past, the enforcement of cultural stereotypes, the rediscovery of religious identities and strengthening of ethnic nationalism. A typical response to radical social and economic change is nostalgia. Nostalgia can be approached as a form of social imagination that plays with the lateral possibilities and the longing for what might have been (Appadurai 1996) but is now unattainable because of the irreversibility of time (Pickering and Keightley 2006, 920). Particularly, in times of existential insecurity, nostalgia can function as a potent source of social reconnection and identity (Strathern 1995, 111).

In Doncaster, the tension between and idealized past and the discomfort with the present state of affairs surfaced as a frequent theme in the narratives of former miners, their children and grandchildren. Several informants valued experiences and practices constitutive of individual and collective forms of self-understanding during industrialism. Transition as progress or improvement of life as promoted by Thatcherism had a counterbalance in experiences with loss of status, resources and self-worth.

Lucy (forty-nine), working as a receptionist at a family-owned hostel, recalled with bitterness and emotion the devastating consequences the closing of the mines had for her family:

> We are still lying with our backs broken. My father, my uncles, cousins and brothers, they were all miners. I went down the pit with my father as a child. Mining was in their blood, and in mine. My husband Paul moved to different pits as each closed. We hoped the pits would be saved for the next generation, for our son. For Paul it was like this. He quit school on Friday and was working the pits by Monday. Like his grandfather and father had done. People don't realize the in our community, mining was all they ever known and done.

Responding to my interest in the local working men's club, Bob (seventy) showed me framed black and white photos of Doncaster. The widowed grandfather of three is working part-time in the club that for generations has played a central part in community cohesion for the working class.[3] Located in the Frenchgate Interchange (a 250 million pound structure and the 18th largest shopping centre in England), the club seemed out of place next to a selection of standardized chain stores like H&M, Tesco and Selfridges. Talking with nostalgia about the old days, Bob remembered his working life. He left school at the age of fourteen and began working in a local mine. A photo depicting Rossingly colliery appeared loaded with meaning. "It hurts, yes ... ", he says. Bob recalls in a low, but firm voice: "I had my last day at the pit 7th May 1993. I remember the time, 2:40. It was a tear-jerking moment. British coal put me on the scrap heap. That was it. Who would employ a forty-seven year old?"

A sunny Friday in June 2015 I meet with Stewart and Jennifer Jones at the Market Place, which has been the historical centre of Doncaster for centuries. Amongst fishmongers and fruit sellers, the couple in their late sixties spends time with their four-year-old granddaughter. Stewart and Jennifer who met in their teens returned to Doncaster from a six-year stay in Benidorm when their granddaughter was born. Their daughter and their son-in-law both have retail jobs, but cannot afford the cost of nursery. "I'm telling you, Britain has become an absolutely terrible place to live!" Jennifer says upsettingly. "It is a disgrace. Young, hard-working people who are struggling to pay their mortgage. Things have changed here, and I don't mean for the better". "Born and bred" in Doncaster, Jennifer remembers her childhood with affection. Her father worked at the Railway Plant, her mother was a housewife:

> Although I was the only child, my dad never spoilt me! I wished for a bicycle, but never got one. To my confirmation I got a gorgeous cocktail watch, but he never gave me that bike. I have tried to pass that one. I would walk an extra mile to save a pound. I like Doncaster, but things are changing here. We used to have the door open, now they are all locked. I would be careful to go into town at night with all the anti-social behavior and vandalism. Today who will take care of a neighbor that fell ill? Do you know the name of your neighbor? I love Doncaster and the community. I prefer Frenchgate to Meadowhall [shopping centre in nearby Sheffield]. But the community is rapidly disappearing. No, we won't get those days back. They are gone. If I could I would have remained in Spain. It was this one who wanted to go back, she said accusingly, pointing the finger at her Scottish husband.

Jennifer, smoking a cigarette, laughs towards her husband. Stewart, a self-declared Scottish nationalist, proudly reveals his tattoos, including a blue-faced Mel Gibson in the role as William Wallace, the thirteenth-century Scottish warrior who fought against King Edward 1 of England, a bagpipe and a purple thistle. A bit later, the upbeat and smiling man looks momentarily crestfallen:

> They may have tried to take away the pride and the hope in our communities, but we're still here. But I'm glad I will not be around in 100 years' time, because there is no future here! It is just getting worse. The richer are becoming richer and the poorer are becoming poorer. Before, you knew where your job was. You could take care of your family. But all that is gone now. I pray to God that I will die before my children.

Stewart and Jennifer morally evaluated the present through the lens of an idealized past (Herzfeld 1997, 109–138), expressing a sense of loss and nostalgia for "Fordist forms of feeling of stability and well-being" (Muehlebach and Shoshan 2012, 317).

Working in a local mine, Bob had experienced a long period of hard and dangerous labour, that also provide a sense of economic and social security. Now, in times of precarious labour, feelings of security and solidarity appeared lost or under threat. Their children's experience of great economic distress might have strengthened Jennifer's nostalgia and wish for a better life in Spain. A life outside England or even death was described as better options that witnessing the decline of the community and the uncertain future facing their children. However, more than just economic facts, Jennifer expressed an affective attachment to an era of security and modesty, values that she felt no longer existed in Doncaster. Through memory and longing for a return to Spain, she strived to cope with both a sense of structural entrapment and loss of self-worth.

Branding Doncaster into the future

The moral evaluation of the present through the lens of an idealized representation of the past can be a very practical form of action (Herzfeld 1997). The three past crisis-laden decades, various actors in Doncaster have appropriated the industrial era and icons to provide hope, inspiration and guidance in face of hardship and an uncertain future (Smith 1999, 263). Efforts to transform Doncaster into a distinctive and proud place have been heavily centred on the restoration and commemoration of its industrial past. At the early stages of economic transition, the City Council launched a campaign to attract more commerce, industries and tourists to the struggling borough, hoping that it would ease people off welfare into work. The leaflets and brochures invoked the region's coal-mining heritage, referring to Doncaster as "England's Northern Jewel". Rather than suggesting new routes into the future, the campaign invoked the source of historical wealth, power and energy that have shaped Doncaster. The local historiography narrated at an exhibition at the Museum and Art Gallery at Cusworth Hall also reflects a praise of the past. A poster commenting on where to go after industrial Doncaster reads the following text:

> The Railway came to Doncaster in 1849 and with it rapid industrial development. In the 19th century a wide variety of firms were established in Doncaster producing, taps, planes, cars, glass, nylon, mustard, motors, plastic pipes, metal ropes, tractors, clothes and lots of sweets. This was all on top on the railway Plant works and the coal mining. Most have now gone and Doncaster faces *a new future*. But it is a future that is not so very different. The town's excellent road and rail links will still play a *vital role in what comes next*.

The entire exhibition ends with a poster titled "The Ever-Changing Face of Doncaster":

> Over the last hundred years or so, there has been a whirlwind of demolition and development in Doncaster. Development was sparked off by the coming of the coalmines. Although the speed has slowed down, development has continued. Today the town is experiencing a revival as it emerges from the trauma caused by the closure of so many coalmines. The 1960s developments are already making way for something new.

The exhibition glorifies Doncaster's industrial past without specifying what the present entails. The present is defined by the trauma of the closing of the coalmines, a loss that the local communities are shaped by. The only certain aspect of the future is that it will "bring something new". The vague prediction for the future is that it might not be so different due to the very transport networks that brought modernity to Doncaster. The exhibition reveals how the industrial era is nostalgically commemorated as a golden age of security, whereas the present and future are narrated as uncertain.

Connections between the industrial past and present surfaced as powerful themes in local tourism. I meet with Colin Joy, the local tourist manager. We walk a stretch of the main road Highgate and he points to various historical buildings located between rival pound shops:

> While people in Liverpool would be pride and protective of their city when they meet outsiders like you, Doncastrians would not. If you say the town is bad they will moan in agreement. But there is a lot to be proud of in Doncaster! The town was the home to the confectionary firm that invented butterscotch! The most famous and fastest steam locomotives like the Flying Scotsman and Mallard were all built in Doncaster. We have the remains of an original Roman wall, and one of the few Roman shields ever found,[4] but this is not even taught in schools. When Ian Blaylock established a Brewery last year, I encouraged him to call it Doncaster Brewery. If Doncaster was celebrated as much as York celebrates itself, then Doncaster would definitely be the better of the two. We need to put Doncaster back on the map!

Like the council campaign of the 1990s and the museum exhibition, the local tourist strategy is invoking, although more enthusiastically, the industrial past to turn Doncaster into a new, distinctive place its residents can be proud of. The strategy has already materialized. Two recently constructed pubs are named after the two most famous steam locomotives built in Doncaster at the Railway Plant: the Mallard and the Flying Scotsman Tap. A local group wants to remain Doncaster Danuma, the name the Romans gave the area around the Don river as early as the first-century AD. Led by "Britain's longest serving head teacher", Tony Story, the group hope that by highlighting the town's Roman roots and pioneering role in the development of the railways can help to soften the town's rough reputation as an anti-social hotspot.

A group of three men I interview at the working men's club described a town that had lost its "old bubble and fizz" and turned proud when they talked about the mines. Still, they were upset with the name-changing proposal. "You can't shake off Doncaster's reputation simply by rebranding. It would put the town on a par with Sellafield", Paul (fifty-six) says, drawing parallels to the nuclear power site which was renamed from its original Windscale after Britain's worst nuclear accident. "You have these people who want to give Donny a trendy twenty-first century makeover. But new names and fancy hotels won't sort out the kind of problems we have in town".

The nostalgic invocation of the past reflects a town that is struggling with the transition from a place where the heavy industries, the coalmines in particular, are no longer major employers. The council campaign and icons, the museum exhibition from 2005 and the tourism strategy of 2015 can be seen as scale-making projects invoking various temporalities to reimagine Doncaster in a globalizing world. Moreover, these practices and social imaginaries resemble processes of "structural nostalgia" (Herzfeld 1997), in which time scales and events are collapsed into generic, imagined and stylized accounts of "the good old days". The temporal compressions found in memory work in Doncaster are evident in the multiple temporalities that are being invoked from the industrial era to the towns' Roman roots. The industrial past is nostalgically remembered as an era signalling stability, as opposed to the uncertainty, socio-economic decline and hardship of the present.

Cosmopolitan Doncaster and its discontents

While the industrial era is nostalgically remembered, there are social actors in Doncaster that promote alternative temporalities, allowing locals to believe that their future can be imagined according to logics that lie outside structural nostalgia for the industrial past or protectionist nationalism. Doncaster, while being a white-majority town, has always been multicultural. It has the largest Roma and Traveller population in the UK. In the 1990s and later 2000s, diversification processes intensified due to global migration. Since the EU enlargement and opening of borders, the biggest rise in new residents has come from Poland and Latvia. After English, Polish is the most spoken language in Doncaster Central followed by Kurdish, Urdu and Panjabi (localstats.co.uk). The names of stores and restaurants and the myriad of religious congregations reflect the town's diversity. Located in the centre of Doncaster is the "the Chinese, Indian and Oriental Supermarket" and "Polskie Delikatesy" (Polish delicatessen). In the context of the UK, the diversity is not extraordinary, but locals tell me that these are rather new developments in Doncaster.

Acknowledging the town's old and enveloping diversity, in May 2014, Warren Draper founded the magazine *Doncopolitan*, demonstrating a "cosmopolitan compentency" to ironize communitarian rhetoric of absolutism (Amit and Rapport 2012, 97–102). According to its editorial statement, the "magazine will big up anything which has the potential to add to Doncaster's metropolitan appeal" and counter all the moaning about Doncaster as a "cultural desert". The first issue of the magazine was titled *Fake it till You Make It*, promoting themes such as diversity, the green movement, gay-rights and anti-fascism.[5] The editorial ended with the sentence "We'll celebrate Doncaster's culture, arts, style, music, people, fashion, lifestyle, architecture and even *its coal black underbelly*" (Doncopolitan 2014). The editor's embrace of diversity accompanied by a somewhat jokingly invocation of coal reflects how the cosmopolitan is capable of inhabiting multiple worlds expressing attachment both to a valorized past and a fast changing present (Hannerz 1990, 24, 2005, 6). Particularly, the younger generation in Doncaster appeared less nostalgic and more prone to draw on global cultural and economic flows (Appadurai 1996) to assign meaning and value to their lives.

To Susan (twenty-two), a student of graphic design at the local college, whom I chat to at café Culture, envisioned a Doncaster modelled around cosmopolitanism and innovation, both of which she claimed Doncaster lacked:

> There are those people looking to the past for inspiration. But those days are gone. The coal belongs to the past. As does Maggie [Thatcher]. We need more innovation, something that the town does not portray at the present. I have many ideas of how the future can look like in Doncaster. My father's friend works at the Messe Düsseldorf convention centre. Imagine how many jobs a similar exhibition centre located next to the Robin Hood airport would generate! Why can't Doncaster be like Düsseldorf?

Invoking the entrepreneurial successes of a convention centre in Germany, Susan compared Doncaster's post-industrial struggling landscape to another European landscape. Moreover, in contrast to other informants supporting Ukip's call for a "Brexit", British withdrawal from the EU, Susan insisted that Britain's, England's and Doncaster's economic future were intimately linked to Europe. To Susan, the EU signalled a potential better life, for local Ukip voters, the EU, increased cross-border mobility and diversification processes were experienced as threatening to jobs, welfare and national identity.

Contrary to only framing migrants and minorities as dangerous and polluting others, the Ukip supporters I interviewed framed newcomers as competitors in a precarious labour market, a factor driving anti-immigration sentiment. "The immigrants are stealing our jobs" or "We are still unemployed; we can't afford housing while the newcomers get all state benefits" were common complaints.

A Sikh man named Aadi, in his mid-fifties, working in a local drug store, turned his own struggle for recognition into a rationale for supporting Ukip's anti-immigration politics. Aadi serves customers, wipes the counter and arranges adult magazines on the narrow shelf behind him, all while explaining his support for more restrictive immigration policies. Invoking kinship terminology to justify exclusion of new migrants, he states that:

> The house is full, and you can only have so many guests. I have worked very hard to get this job. I would wash; I took all kinds of jobs. I have served customers for 24 years. I have worked long, hard hours, seven days a week. I look at the people from Poland and Africa who enter my shop. Some would not have survived one week in India. You need to work and not only claim benefits. The United Kingdom used to be called Great Britain. What is it now? United States of Europe?

To Aadi, an imagined British home and work ethic is threatened by European and global integration. Aadi seemed to distance himself from the historical hardship he had endured by scaling globally to include an appreciation of historical Asian–British links and the British Raj. In order to deal with his fear of becoming redundant, he voted for Ukip, a party that scapegoats migrants through at times ultra-nationalist discourse while nurturing nostalgia for the grandiose days of the Empire.

Wrapped in St. George

Perhaps, the most controversial mobilization of popular nostalgia for an idealized past is that of Europe's political radical right. In many deprived European towns, a notable response to socio-economic decline and demographic change has been the heating of exclusionary identity politics and call for the reinforcement of symbolic and physical borders. Populist politicians such as Ukip's Nigel Farage, Fronts National's Marine Le Pen and the Republican Presidential Candidate for the President of the United State in the 2016 election, Donald Trump, mark migrants as the defining Other, warning against the internal or external strangers that are "invading" or threatening their national culture and security (Holmes 2000).

Underpinning processes of externalization is a popular emphasis on ideas about bio-social purity, culture and "roots" in a particular land (Gullestad 2006, 69). Douglas Holmes (2000) calls these territorially based essentializing ideas "integralism". The examination of integralist ideas promoted by the populist right reveals some of the ways in which nationhood is being reimagined (Anderson 2006) in times of economic and cultural dislocation.

I interview Ukip local politician Guy Aston (sixty-four) who stood for election in Don Valley. In May 2015, Ukip got its electoral breakthrough in Doncaster, obtaining 24.1% of the votes, an increase of 20% from the last General elections in 2010. The party became the second largest after Labour, on a heavily anti-EU, anti-immigration, pro-coal platform (BBC 2015).

It is a Tuesday afternoon, and Aston's household is all aflutter, with his wife Bernie Aston, hosting a Ukip dinner in the kitchen. Aston, a self-declared hobby historian, has decorated the living room walls with his historical heroes, amongst them Oliver Cromwell (1599–1658) and other seventeenth-century parliamentarians. The bookshelves are filled with military history. A talkative man, Aston compares Ukip's struggle for political power and the disappointing General Election results at the national level to the formation of battalions during war:

> Like the British army in 1940. We sharpen up and build our forces. In the beginning you saw an almost naïve enthusiasm, but it's gonna be along war in Donny [Doncaster] for my troops. We're like a season battalion, retreated, but not defeated.

Knowing that Ukip supporters are also far more likely than those of other parties to describe themselves as "English" rather than 'British" (Goodwin and Ford 2014), I ask about the difference between the two:

> I guess English these days means not being an immigrant. And being proud of that. Our local schools are swamped with people who can't speak English. As a Ukip politician I have to say I'm doing this for Britain, but I am also doing this for England. We need to wrap ourselves in the

flag of St. George! We have to fight for what is English. British socialists have long undermined any sense of nationalism. But people want to belong. If we can't have nationalism, what are we then besides some people living in the land? No, we need to be proud of England. We need to stand up to the champagne socialist elite in London and all their political correctness. People are tired of being bullied by the state.

The local Ukip code is playing on fear over migration and its impact on national identity and livelihoods. In Aston's populist narrative, a mythical way of British/English life is threatened from the outside, whether from the cosmopolitan London elites, the EU or migrants. With its emphasis on the protection of national identity and borders, Ukip increasingly appeals to the losers of globalization at the precarious edges of proper society, in particular the disillusioned working class.

New voice for the working man

In September 2014, Doncaster became part of a political field in which the struggle over values and identity got further enacted. The Party Leader of the Ukip, Nigel Farage, entered Doncaster St. Ledger Racehorse lane at Ukips annual conference, stating to enthusiastic applause "I will park on the lawn!" Scaling down to Doncaster, Ukip appealed to the neglected electorate in traditional Labour land, promising to challenge Ed Miliband – the Labour candidate for Prime Minister who is "no voice for the working man".

In September 2015, the ritualized political performance was repeated when the party conference was yet again held at the St. Ledger Racehorse lane, symbolically moving Doncaster from a stigmatized periphery to the foreground of national politics. With a VIP pass around my wrist, I was allowed full access to the conference venue. Flags and flowers in the Ukip colours purple and yellow are displayed outside the entrance. The hall is filled with souvenir stands selling Ukip teddy bears, stickers, rosettes, knitting patterns for an Ukip woolly jumper and anti-EU slush drinks in the party colours. A devoted kipper reveals a tattoo of Nigel Farage on her upper arm. To massive applause, Farage enters the stage to the 1986 single by the Swedish rock band Europe, "The Final Countdown", a soundtrack chosen to reflect the political message of the conference titled "Out of the EU and into the world".

Not surprisingly, the conference focused on migration as the central theme. Ukip's answer to the alleged threats posed by migration is to leave the EU, "take back the control of the borders and reinstate British territorial waters". Several of the talks consisted of scaremongering on the issue of the allegedly uncontrolled continuing arrival of non-indigenous people to the UK, stating that migrants were a drain on resources and threat to national security.

If migration is framed as threatening to reproduction, coal is framed as a sustainable source of energy. Ukip is in favour of reinvigorating the UK's coal industry. Roger Helmer, Ukip's spokesperson on industry and energy, is a fierce climate denier. The former conservative who is now a Ukip Euro MP is known for some of the most controversial remarks from Ukip members, on everything from climate change to same-sex marriage. Wearing a Ukip pin badge Helmer gives me a lecture in the pressroom about the "black propaganda from the green lobby in London":

> Our enemy number one is the ugly ghastly windmills. Our policy is to reopen the mines. We have at least enough coal reserved for 200 more years. We do not ... regard CO_2 as a pollutant. It is a natural trace gas in the atmosphere which is essential to life on earth. Coal is a cheap and reliable energy, so why not built more coal plants? The problem now is that steelworkers in Rotherham and miners in Doncaster will lose their work due to the damning taxations and emission restrictions imposed by Brussels and London. For every job created in the renewable sector, four jobs are destroyed elsewhere in the economy.

The author of Ukip's official energy report "Keeping the lights on" conveys not just opposition to UK's participation in the EU, but also a mixture of anti-environmentalism and disregard of scientific evidence (Ukip Daily 2012). Appropriating the plight of those affected by UK industrial decline, Helmer predicts an energy apocalypse at the hands of Brussels, climate scientists and wind power. Helmer constructs the image that British economy and cultural identity are depending on coal production and other extractive industries. Helmer's stance reflects how nostalgia can be applied as a powerful device in the quest for political power.

A nostalgic embrace of coal as the model for the future might appeal to parts of the struggling electorate in Doncaster where coal has occupied a proud position over generations and where the numbers of jobs provided by extractive industries have been dramatically reduced. The end of coal has reinforced "coal nationalism" where coal is turned into a key symbol of security and imagined Englishness in relation to threatening outsiders. In Doncaster, the end of coal has proved consequential for the fuelling of English nationalism.

Several of my informants in Doncaster, many of whom expressed nostalgia for the industrial past, discomfort with migration and neglected by Labour, were particularly receptive to the simple answers offered by Ukip. In a nation-wide referendum on Thursday, 23 June 2016, Britons voted for Brexit, the withdrawal of the UK from the EU, with large protest votes from deprived working-class areas. In Doncaster, 69% voted for Brexit, reflecting how the Ukip-led Brexit campaign has managed to position themselves as the new voice for the working man by mobilizing local disillusionment and discontent.

Conclusion

The industrial town of Doncaster was for decades emblematic of a golden industrial age. Up until the mid-1980s, the economic and cultural identity of Doncaster was connected to the mining industry that provided a sense of identity, security and future. In post-industrial Doncaster, neoliberal globalization coupled with the salience of accelerated immigration constituted an "overheating effect" that in turn have fuelled struggles over identity and belonging and rendered the town's meaning open for contestation. Doncastrians were not merely passive victims of changes beyond their control, but strived to cope with and give meaning to the neoliberal globalization processes in which their lives were entangled. In 2015, three decades after the privatization of the mines begun, my informants' social experience was partly formulated in terms of disillusionment with the present.

In response to existential insecurity, some residents created a local identity around a golden industrial age, appropriating the past in various place and identity-making projects. Others invoked the Doncaster's enveloping diversity, the lost British Empire, the

EU or other places beyond Britain's border to cope with social and economic decline. The interplay of the legacies of industrialism coupled with the precarization of labour and increased migration were key factors nurturing the rising appeal of Ukip's nationalism. Ukip taps into the anxieties of the working class disillusioned with the broken promises of modernity, economic transition and European integration. Thriving on a fearful working-class electorate, the party provides a future modelled around a proud history of extractive industries and protective nationalism. This appeared to be a powerful formula for the residents of Doncaster who expressed a pervasive sense of deprivation. The tensions emerging out of the intersection of the various scale-making projects in Doncaster partly constitute and make visible the struggle over identity and direction in globalizing England, between a society open to European integration and one that closes its borders on the path of rising English nationalism.

Notes

1. Doncaster is predominantly white working class and the "non-white" population make up around 4.4%, significantly lower than the number nationally at 12% (ONS 2003).
2. In 2009, the glass production at Polkingson in Kirk Sandall closed after 9 years of manufacturing. In 2010, more jobs were lost when the railway firm Jarvis closed and the City Council underwent restructuring.
3. https://issuu.com/robche/docs/working_mens_clubs.
4. Out of the extremely few (less than ten) Roman shields ever found, one was discovered at Doncaster in 1971 and is called the "Danum Shield".
5. Diversity in Doncaster is celebrated, *inter alia*, through the gay parade, first held in 2012 as well, but leading to protests such as the English Defence League's marches in Mexebourough.

Disclosure statement

No potential conflict of interest was reported by the authors.

Funding

This work was supported by European Research Council: [Grant Number 295843].

References

Amit, Vered and Nigel, Rapport. 2012. *Community, Cosmopolitanism and the Problem of Human Commonality*. London: Pluto Press.
Anderson, Benedict. 2006. *Imagined Communities: Reflections on the Origin and Spread of Nationalism*. London: Verso.
Appadurai, Arjun. 1996. *Modernity at Large: Cultural Dimensions of Globalization*. Minnesota: University of Minnesota Press.
Bauman, Zygmunt. 1998. *Globalization: The Human Consequences*. New York: Columbia University Press.
Beresford, Richard. 2013. "Coal, Coal Mining and the Enterprise Culture: A Study of Doncaster." PhD thesis, University of Warwick.
Brenner, Neil, Nik Theodore, and Peck Jamie. 2009. "Neoliberal Urbanism: Models, Moments, Mutations." *SAIS Review* 29 (1): 49–66.
Carrier, James G., and Don Kalb, eds. 2015. *Anthropologies of Class: Power, Practice and Inequality*. Cambridge: Cambridge University Press.

Ekholm Friedman, Kajsa, and Jonathan Friedman. 2008. *Historical Transformations: The Anthropology of Global Systems*. Lanham, MD: Rowman & Littlefield.

Eriksen, Thomas Hylland. 2016. *Overheating: Accelerated Change in a Globalised World*. London: Pluto.

Goodwin, Matthey, and Robert Ford. 2014. *Revolt on the Right: Explaining Support for the Radical Right in Britain*. London: Routledge.

Gullestad, Marianne. 2006. "Imagined Kinship: The Role of Descent in the Rearticulation of Norwegian Ethno-Nationalism. " In *Neo-Nationalism in Europe & Beyond: Perspectives from Social Anthropology*, edited by Andre Gingrich and Marcus Banks, 69–91. New York: Berghahn Books.

Hannerz, Ulf. 1990. "Cosmopolitans and Locals in World Culture." *Theory, Culture & Society* 7: 237–251.

Hannerz, Ulf. 2005. "Two Faces of Cosmopolitanism: Culture and Politics." *Statsvetenskaplig Tidskrift* 107 (3): 199–223.

Herzfeld, Michael. 1997. *Cultural Intimacy: Social Poetics in the Nation-state*. 2nd ed. New York: Routledge. December, 2004, 280 pp.

Holmes, Douglas. 2000. *Integral Europe: Fast-capitalism, Multiculturalism, Neofascism*. Princeton, NJ: Princeton University Press.

Mollona, Massimiliano. 2010. *Made in Sheffield: An Ethnography of Industrial Work and Politics*. London: Berghan Books.

Muehlebach, Andrea, and Nitzan Shoshan. 2012. "Post-Fordist Affect: Introduction." *Anthropological Quarterly* 85 (2): 317–343.

ONS (Office for National Statistics). 2003. *Local Authority Profiles & Population Pyramids: Yorkshire and the Humber*. Census 2001. http://www.ons.gov.uk/ons/rel/census/census-2001-local-authority-profiles/local-authority-profiles/index.html.

Pickering, Michael, and Emily Keightley. 2006. "The Modalities of Nostalgia." *Current Sociology* 54 (6): 919–941.

Sassen, Saskia. 2007. *Deciphering the Global: Its Spaces, Scales and Subjects*. New York: Routledge.

Smith, Anthony. 1999. *Myths and Memories of the Nation*. Oxford: Oxford University Press.

Standing, Guy. 2014. *The Precariat: The New Dangerous Class*. London: Bloomsbury.

Storm, Anna. 2014. *Post-industrial Landscape Scars*. New York: Palgrave McMillan.

Strathern, Marilyn. 1995. "Nostalgia and the New Genetics." In *Rhetorics of Self-making*, edited by D. Battaglia, 77–96. Berkeley: University of California Press.

Tuffrey, Peter. 2011. *Doncaster's Collieries*. Gloucestershire: Amberley Publishing.

Vertovec, Stephen. 2007. "Super-Diversity and Its Implications." *Ethnic and Racial Studies* 30 (6): 1024–1054.

Newspapers
Doncopolitan, Issue 1, May 2014.
Yorkshire Post, 6 March 1997.

Online sources:
BBC, http://www.bbc.com/news/politics/constituencies/E14000668.
Ukip Daily, http://www.ukipdaily.com/keeping-the-lights-on/.
http://localstats.co.uk/census-demographics/england/yorkshire-and-the-humber/doncaster.

Dreams of growth and fear of water crisis: the ambivalence of "progress" in the Majes-Siguas Irrigation Project, Peru

Astrid B. Stensrud

ABSTRACT
The boom in extractivist industries since the 1990s has resulted in a concomitant increase in socio-environmental conflicts in Peru. In the southern region of Arequipa, the Majes Irrigation Project has transformed 15,000 hectares of desert to fertile land and has become a hub for economic opportunities. In the planned second phase of the project, a new dam will be built to extend the amount of irrigated land and foster large-scale export-oriented agribusiness. Contrary to the government's promises about progress, modernity and employment, the planned extension triggers anxiety among the local farmers who fear privatization, corporate dominance and a neo-colonial return of foreign big estates. This article examines four different stories – both overlapping and contradicting – about Majes. The first story envisions expectations of growth and modernity, while the second focuses on hard work and sacrifice. The other side of the coin appears in the third story about debt, loss and vulnerability following from neoliberal deregulations. The final story concerns the lack of benefits for the local farmers and the growing inequalities, resulting in struggles for land rights and water justice. The stories reflect clashing local and global scales and tensions between private and public ownership and between individual and collective solutions. The farmers in the highlands are ambivalent about the project because in spite of dreams about progress, they have long-standing concerns with large-scale corporate dominance and lack of local autonomy.

Introduction

On 23 March 2011, the municipality of Caylloma province, Arequipa region, southern Peru, sponsored two buses full of people from Colca Valley who went to participate in a march to support a large-scale infrastructural project: the Angostura Dam and the Majes-Siguas II irrigation project. Trade unions, civil associations and the municipalities of Arequipa and Caylloma mobilized thousands of people who filled the streets and the main plaza in the city of Arequipa. The people from Caylloma shouted: "Where is the water born? In Caylloma! Who owns the water? Caylloma! What do we want? Angostura!" The dam would be constructed in the Pusa Pusa area in Caylloma, and the *cayllominos* wished for jobs and economic opportunities. In their opinion, the water belongs to them since the

Majes-Colca basin originates in their territory, and therefore, they feel entitled to take part in the economic development that the irrigation project is supposed to engender. However, when I returned to Caylloma in 2013–2014, most people seemed worried because a private Spanish–Peruvian consortium had obtained the concession for the project and they were concerned that the local population would not benefit from it.

This article will look at some of the contradictions in today's overheated neoliberal economy, which also in Peru started to accelerate in the 1990s, with economic "shock treatment", deregulation and the boom in extractivist industries. The Majes-Siguas II project is pushed ahead despite the chronic tension between economic development and environmental sustainability, as well as the conflict between universalizing forces of modernity and desires for local autonomy (Eriksen 2016). These tensions are consistent with recent analyses of new forms of resource extraction and their neo-colonial impacts (Boyer 2014; Howe 2014; Argenti and Knight 2015; Howe and Boyer 2016). Research related to "extractivism" in Latin America has grown massively over the last decade, yet it has mainly focused on the extraction of oil and minerals, and the environmental and social conflicts that these mining activities have caused (Bebbington 2015). Other forms of growing extractivist industries are agribusiness and renewable energy programmes, where power and value is extracted from wind, sun and water. Argenti and Knight (2015) have shown how renewable energy projects are starting to be seen as new forms of extractive economy, harnessing local natural resources for the benefit of foreign corporations. In today's Greece, they argue, harnessing the wind and the sun is perceived to be a colonial programme of economic extraction as much as a sustainable energy initiative, heralding a return to a time of foreign occupation. Likewise, Howe and Boyer (2016) argue that large-scale renewable energy projects in southern Mexico tend to prioritize the interests of international investors and federal officials over local concerns about cultural and environmental impact, and could result in deepening geopolitical inequalities. Hence, there is a real danger that projects legitimized as green capitalist renewable energy initiatives will emerge as new modes of resource exploitation.

The Majes Irrigation Project is an example of a form of extractivism that is growing in importance in Peru: the extraction of economic value from water in infrastructural mega-projects that are meant to enable large-scale export-oriented agriculture. In the second phase of the Majes-Siguas Irrigation Project, the consortium Angostura-Siguas will build the Angostura Dam, which will have a capacity of 1140 million cubic metres (MMC) at 4220 metres of altitude, and a canal to transfer the water to the existing Majes Canal. The amount of water running through the Majes Canal will be doubled and enable the construction of two hydropower stations in Lluta and Llucta, in addition to the irrigation of 38,500 hectares of arid land in the pampa of Siguas, next to the already irrigated pampa of Majes. This project was planned decades ago, but has been delayed for various reasons. Since 2009, farmers in Espinar province, in the neighbouring region of Cusco, have protested against the dam contending that it will leave them without water. In 2011, the constitutional court stopped the project and ordered a new environmental impact assessment and water balance report. In 2013, after the new report concluded that there is enough water for both regions, the court allowed the 550 million USD project to proceed as planned. The concession was awarded to the Consortium Angostura-Siguas, made up of Cobra Instalaciones y Servicios S.A. (Spain) and Cosapi S.A. (Peru). When the second phase of Majes-Siguas II was symbolically inaugurated on 6 February 2014 in the arid pampa of Siguas, president Ollanta Humala promised "a modern agriculture, an agriculture that can be exported and which will generate 200000 work places". But problems were not over, and in late 2015 the Angostura-Siguas consortium and the Regional Government of Arequipa were still negotiating compensation and the monetary value of land owned by farmers in Pusa Pusa. On the negotiating table were not only economic compensation, but also the possibility of receiving land in Majes. The claims from the farmers in Espinar and Pusa Pusa have also inspired the people in Callalli – the district where the Condoroma Dam is located – to initiate a struggle to obtain the legal property rights to 400 hectares of land in Majes and to get infrastructure and water to irrigate and produce on this land. They claim this right because they have not received any benefits from the dam, and they will no longer silently accept that agribusiness companies make profit on the water from their territory while they suffer from drought. If their project is not accepted, they are willing to start what they call "a water war".

At the same time, the farmers who started cultivating land in the 1980s as part of the first phase of the Majes Irrigation Project are worried about the crumbling concrete in the 30-year-old Majes Canal, which is in need of maintenance. Life in Majes totally depends on the water from this canal, and it has already broken a couple of times because of earthquakes, leaving the Majes population in a state of crisis for shorter periods. In October 2015, a video showing cracks and fissures in the Majes Canal was published online by a local news channel. They interviewed the leader of the water users' organization in the pampa of Majes, who stated: "I don't understand how they expect to make Majes II and transfer 34 cubic metres of water in this same canal… we could say that it is really an ignorance; that those who favour this project ignore this… " He planned to speak about the bad shape of the canal in a meeting with congress members and regional governors: "I hope they will take it seriously, because if they don't, as I have said, God not willing, any eventuality will happen and we could be transforming Majes into a desert" (Agencia AZB Noticias 2015). Adding to the sense of water insecurity, the drought periods in the highlands have become more frequent in the past decade because of climate change. In 2014, the water levels in the Condoroma Dam had sunk to 60% of its maximum capacity of 285 MMC. In January 2016, an Emergency Coordination Committee was established in Majes and in agreement with the National Water Authority, it was decided that the discharge from Condoroma should be reduced from 9.5 m^3/s (cubic metres per second) to 6 m^3/s from 1 February 2016. The farmers needed to reduce their crops according to the available water.

This unbearable situation is the result of processes of accelerated change in the global economy as well as the global climate. People's ambivalent attitudes towards Majes-Siguas II come from a desperate hope in that the expected economic growth will generate employment and benefit all, yet the prospective of a dominant and exploitative corporate agro-industry, in addition to the overhanging threat of a water crisis, create widespread anxiety. In spite of a firm optimism invested in the idea of progress, the unequal distribution of poverty, environmental vulnerability and access to water, land and markets nurture feelings of injustice and motivate struggles for rights to land and water. In this article, I look into the various historical processes leading up to today's state of the Majes-Sigaus project. I argue that the current tensions in southern Peru are caused by the past decades' accelerated changes that seem to have gotten out of control, especially concerning water management.

In Peru, globalization, exploitation of natural resources and social inequality are not new phenomena. The Spanish colonizers grabbed and exploited land territories, including the water resources, minerals and human labour in these territories. Nevertheless, in the past four decades, significant events have dramatically changed the country and its international relations; land reform, massive rural–urban migration, economic crisis, a war between guerrillas and the military, massive privatization, deregulation, extractivism and free trade agreements. The Majes Irrigation Project was constructed during the 1970s and developed in the 1980s and 1990s, amidst these sweeping social and economic changes. The neoliberal policies took off with the Fujimori regime, starting with the anti-inflation shock treatment called "Fuji-shock" in 1990 and the new currency "Nuevo Sol" in 1991.

I will describe how personal and collective stories have unfolded, and scrutinize how neoliberal ideology, policies and practices have impacted on the management of land, water, infrastructure and people. Wolf (1982) advocated a systemic look at world history, and to take seriously the stories of the people who are often excluded, seeing how they connect with the stories of the privileged. History – like geography – is not one, but multiple, and histories – like landscapes – are differentiated. History-making and place-making are tied together, yet different (hi)stories emphasize different things. In this article, I bundle the different versions of the history of Majes into four main narratives, or stories. The first story is about the dreams and hopes of progress, growth and modernity. The second story focuses on hard work, sacrifice, personal and collective effort, and accomplishment. The other side of the coin appears in the third story about the bust after the boom, deregulation, vulnerability, debt and despair. Finally, the fourth story concerns the struggle for water justice; claims about ownership and compensation. All the stories are connected, overlapping and contradicting at the same time, and they all reflect clashing local and global scales, as well as long-standing concerns with foreign dominance and lack of local autonomy.

First story: a dream about progress

> The Special Project Majes-Siguas, today Majes District, generous and friendly land of singular beauty because of her soil, earlier desert and today green savannah, the enviable climate that makes her own [people] and strangers consider it a greenhouse, land considered as the promised land where milk and honey flow, thanks to the arrival of the water and the effort of the first settlers who came to these pampas, until it came to be considered today as the leading milk basin of the south region of the country and leader in agro-exports. (Zamalloa 2013, 1)

These words open the book *Reseña histórica del Distrito de Majes*, a local history of Majes, written by Edgar Zamalloa. The author is an engineer by profession and came to Majes to work in the construction of the irrigation project in 1985, a couple of years after the water and the first farmers had arrived. The book tells the story of how the Majes Irrigation Project came into being. Illustrated with photographs and maps, the book describes the engineers' dreams and plans, the farmers' work, the international agreements, the local politics, the public ceremonies and institutions. It also presents details about irrigation systems, soil, seeds, infrastructure, buildings and urban planning. "This was a dream from many years ago; to irrigate these pampas by derivating water from the highlands of Arequipa", an engineer working in AUTODEMA told me. AUTODEMA (*Autoridad Autónoma de Majes*) is the state entity in charge of the irrigation project, which was transferred from the national to the regional government in 2004. Engineers and their dreams play an important part of this history. The first engineer that took the dream seriously was Charles W. Sutton, a North American who acquired Peruvian nationality and became known as Carlos. He was asked by the Leguía government to do research for irrigation projects already in 1908, and in 1912 he was the first who made detailed studies of water availability and land in Colca and Majes. In 1946, he made a concrete project that considered the use of water from the Colca River to irrigate the pampas of Majes and Siguas (Zamalloa 2013). These were vast areas of arid, barren land on the coastal line between the Andean Mountains in the northeast and the Pacific Ocean in the southwest, and between the narrow valleys of Majes River and Siguas River. The desert land with no human population was imagined as waiting for water in order to become fertile and spur life, economic growth and progress for Peru.

The practice of engineering, aiming to control the environment by constructing infrastructure, is backed by a vision of development and modern statecraft. Civil engineering expertise in Peru was central to the rise of the modern state, not only in relation to the technical infrastructures – like roads, bridges, dams and canals – through which territorial integrity was imagined and materialized but also for the ways in which a sense of public benefit was consolidated around these arenas of state practice (Harvey and Knox 2015). The enthusiasm that infrastructural projects all over the world have been met with during the past century, can be explained by the imagination that "infrastructures simultaneously shape and are shaped by – in other words, co-construct – the condition of modernity" (Edwards 2003, 186). Larkin (2013) points out that infrastructure has its conceptual roots in the Enlightenment idea of a world in movement and open to change where the free circulation of goods, ideas and people created the possibility of progress. This mode of thought is why the provision of infrastructures is so intimately caught up with the sense of shaping modern society and realizing the future: the belief that by promoting circulation, infrastructures bring about change, and through change they enact progress, and through progress we gain freedom (Larkin 2013).

Several Peruvian governments made studies and plans for Majes-Siguas. In 1960, the Italian firm Electroconsul of Milán made the project design, and the first Belaúnde government secured the financial part in 1967 by signing a contract with the General Mining and Finance Corporation Ltd Robert Construction of South Africa. It was, however, the military government of Juan Velasco Alvarado (1968–1975) that in 1971 started the execution of the "Special Project Majes-Siguas" by taking up loans and creating the state entity DEPEMA (Dirección Ejecutiva del Proyecto Majes), which in 1982 would change name to AUTODEMA. In the 1970s, this was considered "the world's most expensive irrigation project" (CIP 2013, 42). The total investment was 630 million USD; 35% of which was financed by the Peruvian state, and 65% from international finances (Zamalloa 2013, 38). In 1974, the government signed the financial and construction contracts for the first phase of the project with the International Consortium MACON, which consisted of five companies from five countries: Sweden, England, South Africa, Canada and Spain. MACON built the Condoroma Dam, situated 4158 metres above sea level and with a storage capacity of 285 MMC, from which water is released downriver to the water intake in Tuti, where it is led into the system of 88 kilometres of tunnels through the mountains and 13 kilometres of open canal. In Querque, the water flows into Siguas River and down to the intake in Pitay, where it is led into the network of irrigation canals crisscrossing the pampa of Majes. Situated at 1000 m.a.s.l., Majes provides a stable and warm climate all year round that secure good conditions for agriculture (Zamalloa 2013).

The project was part of Velasco's reformist government's endeavour of bringing Peru out of feudalism and poverty and into an era of equality and progress. The government passed a water law that nationalized water (del Castillo 1994), and the 1969 land reform dramatically changed property relations in Peru by ending the dominant power of the large estate owners in the highlands (Collier 1978). However, similar to the situation of the peasantry in pre-socialist Hungary (Hann 2016), the break-up of estates together with continued rural poverty generated migration and proletarianization. The new agrarian cooperatives and associative enterprises, which were largely managed by public-sector technocrats and bureaucrats, encountered huge problems, such as corruption, clientelistic relationships and internal conflicts (Hunefeldt 1997). Lack of planning, technical support and training were some of the reasons that the reform mainly failed (Rénique 1991). Instead of stopping rural–urban migration, the shortcomings of the reform, in addition to rural poverty and expectations of a better life in the cities, led to a massive increase in migration from the highlands to the urban coast, where informal settlements and the informal economy flourished.

The Majes irrigation project aimed to create employment and economic activities based on agricultural and industrial production, and to spur development for the whole region. When the water arrived to the pampa of Majes on 24 November 1982, the first settlers (*colonos*) started to work on their land. In the first group there were 592 *colonos* who had been selected by draw according to the different categories they had signed up for: smallholding farmers, landless peasants, agricultural workers and professionals (mostly agronomists, but also doctors, lawyers and engineers). Each *colono* got to buy 5 hectares of land, which was considered a standard family unit, with a subsidized loan from the state owned Agrarian Bank (Zamalloa 2013). Today, there are 2600 farms in the total area of 15,800 hectares that have been irrigated in the first phase of the project. All of these *colonos* have stories to tell about the hard work and suffering involved in the transformation of the desert into fertile soil.

Second story: hard work and sacrifice

> The dream has already turned into reality, it didn't matter to leave the comfort of living in advanced cities surrounded by family and the comfortable society, what was of basic interest was to achieve mastery over these uncultivated lands, it turned into the hope for a more appropriate life, with a more secure future for the family, with the possession of a property (a parcel), because of that we have changed many years of youth, effort, dedication, total devotion, vacations have not been considered, there is no free time, there is no trips for pleasure or rest, the dedication is the work, like in a family where a child is taken care of with extreme attention day and night.

> How can we forget the first time we arrived to see the parcel […], many of us were disappointed when we found the terrain's surface full of stones of all sizes […] I took out a bottle of wine from Churunga, drank to courage and with the *tinka* of wine [libation to the earthmother] which I did with my husband, I screamed to the earth and to the four winds

that from her virgin entrails one day we would pull out the nectar which we toasted with her (the wine); today this dream has also become reality in our parcel [...] Don Carlos' vineyard and wine cellar was established, it is true; the vineyard is a dream, it becomes reality when one puts in desire, enthusiasm, force, will and God's blessing. (Zamalloa 2013, 71)

Señora Adby Corrales, who came to Majes from the city of Arequipa, told her story to Edgar Zamalloa, who has collected testimonies and anecdotes from some of the first settlers in his book on the history of Majes. Her testimony reflects a narrative that I heard from all the settlers and their children that I talked to; a shared story about stones, dust, wind, labour, suffering, effort and dedication to make the land produce. The settlers are seen as pioneers and frontier men, and are praised for their hard work and sacrifice in speeches, poems, songs and monuments. The monument of the settler, *el Monumento al Colono*, has a central place in the urban centre of Majes, Villa El Pedregal, and the picture of the monument is printed at the front page of Zamalloa's book.

Juan was the very first settler to arrive in Majes. He was 74 years old when I interviewed him in 2014, and he told me about how he came to his property in "section A" on 28 October 1982, two months before the water came; "when there was nothing here and we had to bring supplies". Together with his son and several hired workers, he prepared the land by removing stones, levelling and preparing the subsoil, before he sowed alfalfa. After seven months, when the Peruvian president Belaúnde came to visit on 28 May 1983, his fields were already green with alfalfa. All the settlers started by sowing alfalfa, a plant that nourishes the land with nitrate and is used as cattle fodder. Juan talked about how they started working at 5 am every day. After taking a break from 10 am to 2 pm because of the strong winds, they worked again from 2 pm until nightfall. In the first months, they also got foreign help; engineers from Israel brought irrigation equipment and came to teach them about agrarian techniques and technologies: how to clean the terrain with horses, how to throw the fertilizers, how to sow and how to irrigate. Each family farm installed systems of sprinklers or drip irrigation, and connected to the grid of water canals and pipes. As the first settler, Juan took initiative to create the first Irrigation Committee named after their irrigation channel "2R La Colina" on 18 December 1984. According to 1979 regulations, all water users had to be organized in committees, commissions and boards, according to different irrigation districts, and these were dependent on the National Water Directory of the Ministry of Agriculture. These regulations were supplementing the 1969 Water Law, in which water management was centralized and brought under state control (Oré and Rap 2009, 36)

When the first school was built in 1984, Juan's wife came with the rest of his seven children, six of whom still live in Majes. The sons and daughters of the *colonos* who have grown up in Majes have first-hand experience of the hard work and sufferings families went through to make farms and lives in Majes. They have seen their parents going out in the field at 3 am to put out the sprinklers, and they have helped with milking the cows. José, who came to Majes as an 11-year-old in 1983 as the son of a *colono*, also learnt to work hard and got used to wake up at 4 am to herd the cattle.[1] When I accompanied him to a family reunion to meet his father, uncles, aunts and the 102-year-old grandfather, they talked about how life had been. When they lived in the highlands, José's family had been the poorest in the village. His grandparents only had a tiny piece of land and a couple of cows, and they had to work as labourers for others in order to provide for their nine children. When the Majes project opened, all of these children – who were adults by then – registered, and four of the brothers got farms in "section A". José says that they were all dreaming about coming here and changing their lives. The brothers' farms were not next to each other, but they helped each other in the work. Instead of hiring help like others did, they joined forces and worked together in all of their fields; "like in *ayni*", which is a reciprocal form of work exchange in the Andes.

The establishment of the family farms on 5-hectare parcels in Majes coincided with a change towards privatization of land and the dismantling of the associative enterprises from the agrarian reform. The turn toward neoliberal policies began with the military government of Morales Bermúdez (1975–1980), which after pressure from the United States and IMF, started reducing the role of the state and enhancing that of the market (Klarén 2000, 359). This policy was strengthened under the second presidency of Fernando Belaúnde Terry (1980–1985), who, backed by a team with backgrounds from the University of Chicago, implemented the free-market doctrines of Milton Friedman, removed tariff protection and encouraged private foreign investment (Klarén 2000, 374; see also Kesküla 2016). A new approach of "agrarian developmentalism" implied that state subsidies were eliminated and the policy-makers' focus changed from land distribution and social justice to a concern with efficiency and higher output rates. Following a worldwide trend, liberal technocrats believed that the only way to increase productivity was through private ownership (Hunefeldt 1997, 112–113).

In the period 1984–1992, the farmers of "section A" in the Majes Irrigation Project were supported by the EEC (European Economic Community), and received financial help, technical assistance, technology, equipment and machinery, reproductive animals and training (Zamalloa 2013, 57). Among the technical solutions were artificial inseminations of cattle and a factory for production of concentrated cattle fodder. Settlers that I interviewed often emphasized the external funding and technology that they received, and talked with pride about the modern irrigation technology from Israel, and the genetically improved cows from Holland and Germany. The plan was to develop an industrial export-oriented agriculture, yet the majority of the farmers continue to rely on alfalfa and cattle, and work hard to maintain their livelihood of dairy production. Majes has changed a lot during the past 30 years, however, as we will see below. Juan told me that he is overall satisfied with what he has done in Majes, and that the place "has developed". Yet his predictions for the future are quite gloomy, because of his experience of boom and bust in the past decade. Juan has seen many of his fellow farmers lose their land: "Of the first group of settlers, now there is only half of them left."

Third story: the boom and bust of a neoliberal economy

> The future will be according to the agreements that are made. The price of the water will increase; the corporations will dominate. There will be no market [for farmers], and the prices [of their products] will not increase. […] The prices always fall, when everyone sow potatoes, the prices fall […] In 2009, there was a good harvest of aji paprika; the price fell from 2,80 USD per kilo to 0,80 cents. The same happened with the onions […] There is more risk now than 30 years ago; now there is free market. Earlier we had stable prices, but Fujimori made free market. […] The financial institutions that give loans take a lot of interests; 18 percent and until 30 percent! Some get indebted because the intermediaries don't pay the products that they have bought and taken away. (Juan interview, 17 February 2014)

AN OVERHEATED WORLD

The broad availability of credits and loans in combination with the fluctuating product prices on the "free market", as well as a lack of coordinated planning and subsidies in the agrarian sector, have led to a situation in which most farmers in Majes describe agriculture as a lottery where you can either win or lose everything. This shows the other side of the coin of modernity and progress: lack of control, debt, dispossession and despair. The news about the Majes Canal that is cracking up because of lack of maintenance, and the explosive increase in water demand because of population growth, add new dimensions to the farmers' sense of vulnerability. Several processes from the late 1980s led up to this chaotic situation: civil war, financial crisis, cuts in public spending, privatization and deregulation. These processes are all part of the overheating on a global scale; change triggered by the tendency in the global economy to generate crises and unintended consequences.

Towards the end of Alan García's first government (1985–1990), Peru underwent a deep economic and social crisis in which inflation soared to almost 7000% and the following devaluation resulted in rising unemployment, food shortage and malnutrition (Klarén 2000). In 1990, the government of Alberto Fujimori implemented austerity measures and a shock treatment that included higher interest rates and taxes, as well as a slashing of price subsidies and social spending. As a result, food prices rose 500% and gasoline prices soared 3000%. This "Fuji-shock" was followed by massive privatization and deregulation, tax and tariff reform, and investment incentives. After the dissolution of the Congress in 1992, Fujimori ruled as dictator until 2000, continuing the neoliberal deregulation of the economy and opening the market to free trade and international investment (Klarén 2000). In agrarian policy, the neoliberal restructuring and reduction of the state entailed a total reversal of the agrarian reform; the closing of the agrarian bank, the cancellation of all forms of subsidies and special credit to farmers, the shutting down of the bureau responsible for peasant communities and the dismantling of the state apparatus that had dealt with agrarian reform and rural development. The last vestiges of protectionist agrarian laws were removed, allowing unlimited private property. Land was to be freely bought and sold without any top limits (Mayer 2009). This policy also had consequences for Majes, where the increment in demand for land has recently caused the price of a 5-hectare parcel to increase from 100,000 to 400,000 USD. Peasants can no longer afford to buy land and are reduced to rural proletarians working for landowners and the large-scale agribusiness that was welcomed in Majes in the 1990s. After new irrigation infrastructure had been installed in an area called Pampa Baja, a land property of 1288 hectares was sold to a private company in a public auction in 1998. Today, the Pampa Baja Group has employed 2000 workers and produces avocado, grapes, mandarin and pomegranate for export to Europe, United States, Mexico, Canada and Asia (http://www.pampabaja.com/eng/main.php).

In water management, the neoliberal policies started in 1989 with the supreme decree 037-89-AG, which implied that the functions of the state institutions in operation, maintenance and administration of the irrigation infrastructure were handed over to the boards of the water user organizations (*Juntas de Usuarios*). To finance this work the *Juntas* could charge a tariff and increase it in order to have financial autonomy from the state. However, the implications were not felt until large numbers of state functionaries in the water administration were fired in the Fujimori period (Oré and Rap 2009, 46–47). The decree is seen as the first step towards privatization of water, and one of the promoters behind it was Absalón Vásquez, who was the vice-minister of agriculture in 1989. Three years later, he became minister of agriculture in the Fujimori government. During the 1990s, the minister Vásquez made several attempts at passing a new water law that would privatize water and create a water marked, inspired by the Chilean Water Code, which was actively promoted by the World Bank and the Interamerican Development Bank. However, the Fujimori government failed to privatize water due to strong opposition from the irrigation organizations (Oré and Rap 2009; Oré et al. 2009, 52–53). Nevertheless, several legal decrees aimed to give the irrigation organizations a more "modern optic and business bias" (Cupe Burga 2001, 1).

In his second government, Alan García continued on the neoliberal road. In his speech delivered during the launching of the social programme "Water for everyone" (*Agua para todos*), García warned poor people that they should not expect the state to intervene and solve their problems and that they should not be begging for help: "Stop stretching out your hand to see if it rains. Stop asking for [things] because that is what only parasites do" (Perú21 2007). When he signed the Free Trade Agreement with the USA on 14 December 2007, he declared: "It is a great day for democracy and social justice, and freedom. On the contrary it is a bad day for authoritarianism and those who are against democracy and free trade." In 2007, the García government adapted the water law to the Free Trade Agreement (del Castillo 2011, 94–95), and in 2009 García succeeded in passing the new law on water resources (ANA 2010). This law, although water is still explicitly acknowledged as state property, has been adapted to a neoliberal project that induces the state to downplay its role in economic and social politics. The state has therefore given ample space for private companies to intervene and invest in water management (del Castillo 2011).

The hope is now that the investment of the Angostura-Siguas consortium will stimulate growth, jobs and progress, and that the availability of new irrigated lands will attract agribusiness that will finally make the dream come true; not the dreams of the small and middle-sized farmers, but the dream of engineers and governments about growth on a regional and national scale. The original plan of the Majes Project was to develop an industrial export-oriented agriculture, but many – especially engineers and politicians – complain that this has not happened. Some blame the farmers:

> It was supposed to be an agro-industrial project. The alfalfa was just to prepare the terrain; it was transitory. But the farmers have gotten used to it and they have continued with alfalfa. And who benefits from milk production? Gloria! And the farmers? Instead of taking risks and orienting the crop to exports, they continue with alfalfa and cattle, and they are satisfied with what Gloria pays for the milk every two weeks. (Engineer who has worked in Majes for 30 years, 6 February 2014)

Today, most of the farmers still have alfalfa fields and cattle: 70% of the crops are cattle fodder. Most of the cattle farmers sell milk to the Gloria plant, which is owned by the Gloria Group, one of the largest companies in Peru, whose owners are among the few Peruvian billionaires on the Forbes lists. Since the start of the company in 1941, it has expanded with centres for fresh milk collection and production plants on various sites all over the country. Today, Gloria produces a range of milk products like evaporated and sweet condensed milk, yoghurt, butter and cheese for the national market, and exports evaporated milk to 40 countries in the Caribbean, Latin America, Middle East and West Africa (Gloria 2016). In Majes, 800,000 litres of milk is produced on a daily basis, and most farmers deliver milk to Gloria. However, the idea that farmers are satisfied with Gloria is not completely true; they have organized several protests against the Gloria Group's monopoly and low payments. There were big protests in 1992 and 2008, where one man died. Another protest was organized on 27 March 2015, when the farmers spilled 5000 litres of milk outside the Gloria plant. Yet, although the cattle farmers complain about the low price of milk, they see it as a stable and reliable income. A few farmers sell their milk to the smaller competitor Laive, or to one of the five Milk Centres called CAL (*Centros de Acopio de Leche*) run by small associative milk enterprises that were created through a project funded by EU in the 1990s (Zamalloa 2013, 7). The goal of supporting such enterprises was to achieve a "change in attitude and mentality of the settler: that they stop working in a traditional way and transform themselves into entrepreneurs (*empresario*)" (Zamalloa 2013, 343).

Most crops are sold to middlemen or to one of the agro-export factories in Majes: the Peruvian company Open World Export and the Danish–Peruvian company DANPER, which produce canned artichokes and red peppers for export. The prices of crops vary according to the supply and demand in the market, and farmers describe it as a lottery where you can either win or lose. Many farmers lost their land because they were unable to pay their debts after the bust of the paprika boom in 2009. Today, the farmers are in the middle of the quinoa boom, and it seems that those who are sowing quinoa hope to get as much out of the high prices as they can before the bust eventually comes. To minimize risk, however, some farmers organize themselves in business associations, and there is much talk about the importance of "associativeness" (*asociatividad*), especially in small and micro enterprises.

The second phase of the irrigation project was inaugurated on the pampa of Siguas on 6 February 2014. In his inauguration speech, president Ollanta Humala said that this project is important for "the country's development", and he was keen to promise work for everyone:

> It would be a shame that this project, which has cost so much effort by different regional governments, different governments, our congresists, our mayors, would not go to the Peruvians. So shortly, all the productive forces in Arequipa should dive into Majes-Siguas II, to make a modern agriculture, an agriculture that can be exported and that generate 200.000 work places, because it is estimated that Majes-Siguas II will generate this. And it will benefit 300.000 families who will live of our agriculture, of our export agriculture.

However, the 38,500 hectares of new irrigated land in the pampa of Siguas will be sold in units of 200, 500 and 1000 hectares each, and therefore, the farmers in Majes fear the dominance of foreign agro-corporations. Nelson Martínez, the leader of the water users' organization in the pampa of Majes was sceptical about the benefits for farmers:

> With Majes-Siguas II it will be hard for the small farmers to get access to land. It will not benefit us. If it fosters more jobs, it would be good. But it will harm us because we will have to pay the same for the water as the big firms; the tariff will increase.

AUTODEMA is financed from the public budget, and the government spends annually 33 million USD (8 million for infrastructure insurance, 22 million for staff). This amount is in marked contrast to the negligible public expenditure on most Andean irrigation systems, the costs of which are mainly borne by the local water users (Vera Delgado and Zwarteveen 2008, 17–18). The current irrigation tariffs paid by the farmers in Majes do not cover the cost of maintenance of the Majes Canal, and they fear that when the Angostura-Siguas corporation get the concession to administer the canal for 20 years, they will increase the tariff to recover their investments. The leader of the water users' organization in Colca Valley said that Majes-Siguas II will not benefit Caylloma province, but that people are afraid that if they protest like they did in Espinar, the company will not give work to the local population. Others, however, admire the people in Espinar for their courage and for gaining attention to their problems and demands.

Fourth story: the struggle for water justice

> This is the social vindication of the highlands. The Majes Project I was a Project for integration of the high part, the middle part and the lower part [of the basin]. The project has broken this principle … The middle part [Colca Valley] has certainly been given water, but the high part has absolutely been abandoned from the project. […] Therefore we as proprietaries of the water, as owners of the water, owners of the earth, owners as *arequipeños* and as *cayllominos* – who we are because these lands belong to Caylloma – we have taken this democratic and legal option in order to be able to take on this project with the regional government […]. We have not come to beg for charity from anyone; on the contrary, we come to contribute; we want to invest here. (Victor, interview, 2 February 2014)

Victor was the leader of a group of 300 families from the district of Callalli, where the Condoroma Dam is located, and the project he was talking about in the quotation above was a collective claim for property rights to 400 hectares of land in Majes. Their goal is to grow fodder and other crops with the water that comes from their home district. The engineers who designed and implemented the Majes Irrigation Project in the 1970s did not consider the indigenous peasants in Colca Valley, whose local forms of water management were seen as "backward" (Vera Delgado and Zwarteveen 2008, 118). However, after the construction of the Condoroma Dam and the Majes Canal, the communities in Colca Valley demanded access to the water flowing in the canal. They were not heard until a group of peasants from Cabanaconde – the "eleven heroes" as they were later called – used dynamite to blow a hole in the canal in 1983 (Gelles 2000). Today, the canal has 26 valves from which the communities in Colca receive regulated amounts of irrigation water. However, the people in Callalli have not seen any benefits from the Majes Project. There is a profound feeling of structural injustice because of the uneven distribution of climate vulnerability, money and economic opportunities between the headwaters and the Majes Irrigation Project (Stensrud 2016). Most people in Callalli make a living on alpaca pastoralism in a harsh and extremely climate-sensitive mountain environment, where glaciers have disappeared and springs and pastures are drying up as a consequence of climate change. Peasant farmers in the southern highlands are among the poorest in Peru, and as their livelihood is increasingly difficult to maintain because of free-market policies and climate change, the migration to the coastal cities is steadily growing. In Majes, many of the recently arrived migrants join squatter groups (*grupos de invasores*) to occupy desert land. The situation was often described to me as chaotic because of illegal land trafficking, corruption and violent conflicts. The sense of ownership that the population in Callalli and other parts of the Caylloma highlands have towards the water emerging from their local springs, make the basis for claiming the benefits that they feel entitled to. In one of the meetings that the Callalli group had about their land claim, Victor told the others what he had said when he met one of the engineers working for AUTODEMA:

> I said to his face: "Why do you drive around in the 4x4 Toyota Hilux van? Because of your abilities? No! Because of my water!" Why does the security guard in AUTODEMA earn 2500 soles? Why? Because AUTODEMA produce something? AUTODEMA does not produce anything! Just because of the water do they earn like that! They shelter 300 employees. What should be our proposal? That 50 percent of the workers in AUTODEMA should be our people! But nothing ... [...] Because we are not well organized.

In 2012, the group of 300 families from Callalli organized to claim their rights by formally presenting a project proposal to AUTODEMA and the regional government. They were inspired by their "brothers" in Espinar, who have fought for compensation for the water that they will lose to the Angostura Dam. The Callalli group claims that they have the right to land and water in Majes because the water that enable the Majes economy originates in their home territory. While waiting for a formal recognition and title deeds, they have started making ownership to the land by planting trees. By organizing themselves in smaller groups, they take turns to travel by bus from Callalli every Saturday night, and on Sunday morning they arrive to the outskirts of Majes where they water their plants. Victor says that if they do not get this project through, they will make "a water war". They gave all for free to the first settlers who arrived in Majes, he says, but "we are the owners of the water!" Despite the revolutionary rhetoric, however, the claim is not very radical. What they are asking for is legitimate access to invest, work and produce. The deputy mayor of Callalli District said that the rearing of alpacas in Callalli and the cultivation of fodder in Majes are complementary activities. They are not all going to move to Majes if they get this project going. They will send a few family members while the rest stay in Callalli. When there is scarcity of water and grass in the highlands, they can send fodder from the fields of Majes. In this way, the project aims to practice the vertical way of organizing production in different ecological niches as it has been done in Andes for centuries (Murra 2002).

In July 2015, the second phase of the Majes-Siguas Project was inaugurated once again – this time in Pusa Pusa, the area where the Angostura Dam will be constructed. The municipality of Caylloma province announced on their Facebook page on 16 July 2015 that the regional governor of Arequipa had participated in the celebrations of the much-desired project and promised that the local farmers would get a "fair price" for their land properties. The mayor of the province demanded that labour should be contracted locally in the construction of the project, in which the regional government will invest US$78,417,384, the central government will contribute with a loan of US $203,862,616 from the Development Bank of Latin America CAF (*Corporación Andina de Fomento*), and the Angostura-Siguas consortium will invest US$268,121,572. However, two months later, the issues of compensation and labour were still uncertain although the construction work had started. On 2 September, the 20 district mayors of Caylloma province gathered to present collective claims to the consortium and the regional government: employment of at least 300 workers and immediate payments to the landowners. One of the mayors called for solidarity with the people from Pusa Pusa who will "sacrifice their lives, sacrifice their land, and it is not reasonable that they go bankrupt in exchange for the country's development".

Conclusion

> We are a pilot centre of economic development [...] The monthly movement here is 30 million US dollars. This place has the highest economic growth rate on a national level. Or maybe in the whole world? (Elard Hurtado, mayor of Majes 2011–2014, interview 13 February 2014)

The urban centre and infrastructure of Majes was designed for 40,000 inhabitants, yet today's population is already three times as big with an estimated number of 120,000 people that are spreading out in the desert, where there is no access to safe drinking water. Majes is a bustling and chaotic place of farming, engineering, industry and business; it is called a "place of opportunities" and attracts new people every day who come in search for work and business. As a product of accelerated change in global markets and regulatory politics during the past three decades, Majes has become an overheated place. However, there are different stories about the Majes Irrigation Project: stories of how it was made, of what Majes is today, and what it will become. Different experiences make different accounts of the past as well as different expectations and anticipations for the future. Although all agree that Majes is changing at an accelerated speed, there are different views on how to interpret the unintended consequences of the project. Jensen and Morita (2016) argue that infrastructures hold the potential capacity to do such diverse things as making new forms of sociality, remaking landscapes, defining novel forms of politics, reorienting agency, and reconfiguring subjects and objects, possibly all at once. As emergent and experimental systems, however, they also generate unplanned and unforeseen effects (Jensen and Morita 2016).

The farmers who came to start a new life in Majes brought big dreams and a desire to work; they made sacrifices to transform the desert into fertile soil and to make a livelihood and a future for their families. The migrants who have come in recent years have left their homes in the highlands and hope for new opportunities to make money: many work as day labourers in the fields, while others make money on informal business, street vending or find employment in agribusiness companies, small-scale industry or in the service sector. These farmers, workers, vendors and entrepreneurs have one thing in common with engineers and politicians: great expectations of modernity and progress (cf. Ferguson 1999). However, these expectations have been followed by disappointments because of the future that never came as imagined and a ubiquitous fear of a future water crisis because of drought in the highlands, lack of maintenance of the infrastructure, and more expensive tariffs following the privatization of the canal. Another concern is the dispossession and precarization following unpaid debt, foreclosure, lost farms and prospects of ending up as the labour force for agribusiness.

The future of the Majes-Siguas II is anticipated with strong ambivalence. On the one hand, most people desire economic growth and employment for themselves and their children. On the other hand, many fear the exploitation and humiliation from the big agro-corporations that most certainly will buy most of the land and that seem to indicate a return to the times before the land reform. To the extent people oppose the project, it is because they see that the harnessing of water to extract value and profit will benefit foreign corporations rather than local populations. However, the opposition is weak due to people's fear of being left out, run over and ignored. At the heart of these concerns are the tensions between individual and collective – private or public – solutions. Neoliberal ideology and practice focus on the individual entrepreneur and transform issues of responsibility and justice from being a question of collective solidarity to a question of individual ability, whether it is in water management, environmental adaptation or economic distribution. Yet, people in the highlands refuse to sit quietly and watch how corporations make money on their water, and they organize to confront injustice and find solutions. Making accusations of water grabbing, demanding compensations and fair payments, and threatening with a water war, are forms of politics from below that can only be done collectively. These demands are not about being excluded or included in "progress", but about taking part in the making of change.

Note

1. Names of persons are anonymised. Exceptions are persons holding public offices.

Disclosure statement

No potential conflict of interest was reported by the author.

Funding

This work was supported by European Research Council [295843] and Norges Forskningsråd [222783].

References

Agencia AZB Noticias. 2015. *Canal madre en Achoma se deteriora más y así soportará caudal de Angostura*. October 28, 2015. Accessed February 1, 2016. https://www.youtube.com/watch?v=24Kum3UHij4.
ANA (Autoridad Nacional del Agua). 2010. *Ley de recursos hídricos y su reglamento*. Ley No 29338. LIMA: Ministerio de Agricultura.
Argenti, Nicolas, and Daniel M. Knight. 2015. "Sun, Wind, and the Rebirth of Extractive Economies: Renewable Energy Investment and Metanarratives of Crisis in Greece." *Journal of the Royal Anthropological Institute* 21: 781–802.
Bebbington, Anthony. 2015. "Political Ecologies of Resource Extraction: Agendas Pendientes." *European Review of Latin American and Caribbean Studies* 100: 85–98.
Boyer, Dominic. 2014. "Energopower: An Introduction." *Anthropological Quarterly* 87 (2): 309–334.
del Castillo, Laureano. 1994. "Lo bueno, lo malo y lo feo de la legislación de aguas." *Debate Agrario* 18: 1–20.
del Castillo, Laureano. 2011. "Ley de Recursos Hídricos: Necesaria pero no suficiente." *Debate Agrario* 45: 91–118.
CIP (Colegio de Ingenieros del Perú). 2013. "Ambicioso y esperado proyecto multipropósito Majes-Siguas II." *Ingeniería Nacional. Revista Oficial del Colegio de Ingenieros del Perú, Consejo Nacional* 3 (12): 40–42.
Collier, David. 1978. *Barriadas y élites: de Odría a Velasco*. Lima: IEP.
Cupe Burga, Javier, ed. 2001. *Programa de Fortalecimiento de Organizaciones de Usuarios. Legislacion para Juntas de Usuarios y Comisiones de Regantes*, JNUDRP (Junta Nacional de Usuarios de los Distritos de Riego del Perú) y PSI (Proyecto Subsectorial del Irrigacion). Lima: Rolling Impresores S.A.
Edwards, Paul N. 2003. "Infrastructure and Modernity: Force, Time and Social Organization in the History of Sociotechnical Systems." In *Modernity and Technology*, edited by Thomas J. Misa, Philip Brey, and Andrew Feenberg, 185–225. Cambridge: MIT Press.
Eriksen, Thomas Hylland. 2016. "Overheating: The World Since 1991." *History and Anthropology*, this issue.

Ferguson, James. 1999. *Expectations of Modernity. Myths and Meanings of Urban Life on the Zambian Copperbelt*. Berkeley: University of California Press.
Gelles, Paul H. 2000. *Water and Power in Highland Peru: The Cultural Politics of Irrigation and Development*. New Brunswick, NJ: Rutgers University Press.
Gloria, S. A. 2016. "Exports." Accessed February 1, 2016. http://www.grupogloria.com/gloriaEXPORTACIONESE.html.
Hann, Chris. 2016. "Overheated Underdogs: Civilizational Analysis and Migration on the Danube-Tisza Interfluve." *History and Anthropology*, this issue.
Harvey, Penny, and Hannah Knox. 2015. *Roads. An Anthropology of Infrastructure and Expertise*. Ithaca: Cornell University Press.
Howe, Cymene. 2014. "Anthropocenic Ecoauthority: The Winds of Oaxaca." *Anthropological Quarterly* 87 (2): 381–404.
Howe, Cymene, and Dominic Boyer. 2016. "Aeolian Extractivism and Community Wind in Southern Mexico." *Public Culture* 28 (2): 215–235.
Hunefeldt, Christine. 1997. "The Rural Landscape and Changing Political Awareness. Enterprises, Agrarian Producers, and Peasant Communities, 1969–1994." Chap. 4 in *The Peruvian Labyrinth: Polity, Society, Economy*, edited by Maxwell A. Cameron and Philip Mauceri, 107–133. University Park: The Pennsylvania State University Press.
Jensen, Casper Bruun, and Atsuro Morita. 2016. "Infrastructures as Ontological Experiments." *Ethnos*. doi:10.1080/00141844.2015.1107607.
Keskülä, Eeva. 2016. "Temporalities, Time and the Everyday: New Technology as a Marker of Change in an Estonian Mine." *History and Anthropology*, this issue.
Klarén, Peter F. 2000. *Peru: Society and Nationhood in the Andes*. New York: Oxford University Press.
Larkin, Brian. 2013. "The Politics and Poetics of Infrastructure." *Annual Review of Anthropology* 42: 327–343.
Mayer, Enrique. 2009. *Ugly Stories of the Peruvian Agrarian Reform*. Durham, NC: Duke University Press.
Murra, John V. 2002. *El Mundo Andino: población, medio ambiente y economía*. Lima: IEP/Pontificia Universidad Católica del Perú.
Oré, María T., Laureano del Castillo, Saskia Van Orsel, and Jeroen Vos. 2009. *El Agua, ante nuevos desafíos: Actores e iniciativas en Ecuador, Perú y Bolivia, Agua y Sociedad*. Lima: Instituto de Estudios Peruanos.
Oré, María Teresa, and Edwin Rap. 2009. "Políticas neoliberals de agua en el Perú. Antecedentes y entretelones de la ley de recursos hídricos." *Debates en Sociología* 34: 32–66.
Perú21. 2007. "García pide a sectores pobres no ser 'parásitos.'" *Perú21*, February 23. http://peru21.pe/noticia/11436/garcia-pide-sectores-pobres-no-parasitos.
Rénique, José Luis. 1991. *Los sueños de la sierra. Cusco en el siglo XX*. Lima: CEPES.
Stensrud, Astrid B. 2016. "Harvesting Water for the Future: Reciprocity and Environmental Justice in the Politics of Climate Change in Peru." *Latin American Perspectives* 43 (4): 56–72.
Vera Delgado, Juana, and Margreet Zwarteveen. 2008. "Modernity, Exclusion and Resistance: Water and Indigenous Struggles in Peru." *Development* 51: 114–120.
Wolf, Eric R. 1982. *Europe and the People Without History*. Berkeley: University of California Press.
Zamalloa, Ing, and Edgar Bravo. 2013. *Reseña Histórica del Distrito de Majes*. Lima: Corporación Grafical.

Creating and dissolving social groups from New Guinea to New York: on the overheating of bounded corporate entities in contemporary global capitalism

Adam Leaver and Keir Martin

ABSTRACT

Attempts to create and fix the boundaries of various social entities have always been central features of modern capitalism. Such entities have always had the potential for either instability, on the one hand, or a lack of flexibility that is experienced by many as threatening, on the other. Such tensions have reached a point of intensification with the overheating of contemporary global capitalism. In this paper, we compare two examples of the changing and problematic nature of attempts to redraw the boundaries of such entities in an attempt to shape changing economic circumstances. The first is based upon research in Papua New Guinea, where attempts to create ever more bounded land holding groups with increasingly exclusive rights to parcels of land have exploded since the 1990s. The second is the changing nature of the corporation, perhaps the most significant entity in the history of global capitalism, whose boundaries have become increasingly unclear and permeable with the rise of finance capital. Whilst the move towards bounded landholder groups might seem to fit a narrative that would predict that a move towards capitalist modernity would entail the creation of ever more fixed and bounded social groups, the latter trend suggests that contemporary capitalist accumulation tends to simultaneously both fix and deconstruct the boundaries of such entities in different contexts. Contemporary overheated capitalism brings both tendencies to a head in a manner that makes the ever-present tension between them increasingly difficult to successfully manage or control.

Introduction

The emergence and global spread of the corporation as a social entity has been one of the major motors for social changes in the past 150 years of world history.

Micklethwait and Wooldridge, for example, in their 2003 book, *The Company,* argue that the establishment of the corporate form in the latter half of the nineteenth century was the basis for the explosion of economic productivity and the spread of global capitalism that has characterized the period since. The evidence from Papua New Guinea (PNG) and similar examples from other parts of the postcolonial world in recent decades might lead us to believe that the intensification of commodity exchange and capital accumulation leads inherently to the global replication of this trend for the creation of ever bigger and more fixed and stable group-entities, as the corporate form distributes itself across the world, alongside other products originating in industrial capitalism's original Western heartlands, such as coke bottles and David Beckham T-shirts. But this would only be half the story. Simultaneous with these trends, the overheating of contemporary globalized capitalism has also led to a situation in which the corporate form established as "the basic unit of modern society" (Mickelthwait and Wooldridge) is often no longer able to hold the flows of debt and exchange obligation in a relatively fixed and stable form as was its original intended justification. In this paper, we explore what anthropological perspectives on the nature of social groups might tell us about the emergence and dissolution of corporations as particular kinds of social entities. We take this as the basis for an exploration of three case studies that illustrate the ways in which changes in the nature of debt have led to an overheating of a tension between fixity and fluidity in the corporate form, a consequent greater inability of the corporate form to hold shifting obligations in a relatively fixed state for the purposes of investment and accumulation, and an intensification of contests over the performative power of naming practices to fix the limits of obligation and the consequent boundaries of the social group-entity. In particular, we argue that in contrast to an expectation that capitalist modernity involves a relentless speeding up of time, that the corporation, as the major social entity associated with its spread, can be seen as a mechanism whose (not always successful) aim is to freeze or slow down the pace at which social entities can be brought in and out of being.

What is a social group?

Understanding the origins and effects of different kinds of social groups has been central to the anthropological project from its inception. Throughout much of the twentieth century, groups such as kinship lineages were seen as the basis of non-Western life and posited as the alternative to such institutions as the state, courts or corporations as the basis for the organization of society by writers across the theoretical range from functionalists to Marxists. In the final quarter of the century, the functions, origins and even the existence of such groups were increasingly thrown into question, however. In Melanesia in particular, the importation of social group models based upon African lineage groupings was subjected to a critique that led to a general questioning of the epistemological status of "social groups" in anthropological theory. In particular, Wagner's (1974) paper, *Are there Social Groups in the New Guinea Highlands?*, opened up a tradition that tended to argue that the assumption of entities called "social groups" as the basis for organizing social life was a particularly Western way of viewing and organizing social relations that, Westerners, such as colonial patrol officers and anthropologists, "felt a strong obligation to discover" (Wagner 1974, 112), and hence tended to impose upon non-Western people who did not necessarily share that starting point.[1] Wagner's insight has been built upon by other anthropologists in the region, many of whom have tended to nuance Wagner's stark contrast between a Western belief in fixed social groups that precede naming and Melanesian naming practices that elicit temporary collections of persons that tend to be misapprehended by Westerners as fixed social groups.[2] The shift from an assumption of entities called social groups as the foundation of social life to an assumption that the main work of ethnographic analysis in Melanesia is the study of their elicitation or constitution is well summarized by Merlan and Rumsey's (1991, 40–41) claim that,

> "Groups" in general, and "corporate" ones in particular, should not be taken as preconstituted entities, but as contested ones, which are more or less problematically instantiated or reproduced in social action...

Under Western eyes? Nation states and corporations as perspectives for the freezing of time

For all its undoubted influence, Wagner's depiction of Melanesia as a place where social groups did not exist as entities pre-existing the naming relations that elicited them seemed potentially to implicitly assume that such groups or group-entities might really exist in such a manner in the "West". Yet, as scholarship in the years since Wagner's (1974, 103) paper has emphasized, "[n]ations, societies and groups" as, "the *social* form or manifestation of the reliance on order, organization and consistency that pervades our whole approach to collective doing and understanding ... " are just as much,

> hard won social constructions, which, if they are to exist at all, must exist at least in part as more or less contested "representations". (Merlan and Rumsey 1991, 56)

in the "Western" world as they might be in New Guinea or anywhere else. Anderson (1983) detailed the way in which nations had to be carefully constructed as and indeed elicited as "imagined communities" by the careful construction of perspectives from which such collectivities came to appear as natural. Likewise, the sovereign power often vested in nation states that was frequently a major foundation for the construction of such imagined community has also come under similar critical scrutiny, with scholars exploring how this group-entity has to be carefully and painstakingly constructed globally (e.g. Benton 2010; Hansen and Stepputat 2005; Lombard 2012; Martin 2014a) and in Melanesia in particular (e.g. Rutherford 2012).

Likewise, the most powerful economic group-entities in the (Western) world, namely corporations, are also elicited from a mass of potential relations by creating a legal perspective from which certain potential relations are recognized and others are discounted, most crucially relations of potential debt obligation whose limitations are at the heart of the construction of the corporation as a collective person in US and UK law, both globally (e.g. Martin 2012, 2014b), and in Melanesia in particular (e.g. Golub 2014). Wagner explains how the use of the word "Para" draws particular distinctions and thus evokes or even calls into being a particular collectivity at a particular moment rather than describing a pre-existing social entity. Similarly, we might argue, particular linguistic performances (whether spoken in court or written in legal documents) draw particular distinctions and evoke a collective entity called "Rio Tinto Zinc" (or whatever) at a particular moment. Western social groups and group-entities are just as much performatively constituted effects of particular social perspectives as their Melanesian counterparts.

If there is a difference between the elicitation of a "Para" and a "Rio Tinto" it lies in the degree of permanence that the elicitation is designed to create. The legal elicitation of corporations and nation states is intended to create a group with a degree of longevity that will form the basis upon which future relations and transactions can be organized and conducted, whereas "Para", in Wagner's description, is momentary. The main difference then is the amount of time that the naming is intended to fix the boundaries of the group for. We are familiar with the idea that capitalist modernity involves a dizzying speeding up of temporal rhythms. Indeed, time is one of the things that we might consider to have become increasingly heated up in global capitalism and increasingly "overheated" by the global intensification of capitalist commodity circulation over the past quarter of a century. But this overheated speeded up time when viewed from one perspective can be viewed as a freezing or slowing down of time when viewed from others. When it comes to the ways in which names call collectivities into being, Daribi time operates at a dizzying pace, with the same name constantly calling ever-changing shifting collectivities in and out of being, whereas the time rhythm of capitalist modernity is deliberately slowed and frozen with legal mechanisms being manipulated in order to freeze a particular moment of elicitation into a perspective that allows the social form thus created to act as the basis for particular kinds of social action. Indeed, the slowing of time when viewed from this perspective is one of the bases upon which the speeding up of time is conducted, as the nation states and corporations whose longevity is enabled by this freezing of elicitation act as the basis for the commonly noted experience of the ever-intensifying speeding up of capitalist modernity. *The speeding up of time is not therefore a one-way process but relies precisely upon the slowing down of time in other contexts or when viewed from other perspectives and capitalist modernity therefore slows down time as much as it speeds it up, although this aspect is less widely noticed or commented upon.* Hence, a temporally rapid coming in and out of being of collectivities in the moment is the flipside of what might appear to be the slow, relaxed and repetitive way of life of the Daribi, as described by Wagner, whilst the temporally slow freezing of the elicitation of particular social or corporate entities is the flipside of the bewilderingly rapid way of life that is often said to characterize capitalist modernity.

Here, time rhythms are revealed to be at the heart of capitalist modernity much as Thompson (1967) observes to be the case in a different context. The difference is that the time-discipline described by Thompson is something imposed by the capitalist class upon the working class as a central part of the process by which the latter are forged out of pre-capitalist artisan labour into a working class capable of meeting the needs of capital accumulation in a system of industrial production. The time-regularization described here is one that is organized by entrepreneurs and lawyers in order to construct the entities that conduct capitalist enterprises and transactions (including the imposition of Thompson's version of time-discipline upon those whose labour they purchase).

Even this distinction between elicitations that are allowed to come and go and those that are deliberately frozen is not best described as a Western/Melanesian contrast, however. Temporary elicitations of the kind described by Wagner happen all the time in Western Europe, as anyone who has observed the processes of in- and out-groups being formed amongst high school students, for example, could testify to. More to the point, despite their degree of fixity relative to more momentary elicitations such as "Para", corporations go out of being or change their boundaries subject to new legal-linguistic performances subsequent to their initial incorporation, such as mergers, divestments or winding up proceedings. *Social life inherently entails moves in both directions—towards greater fixity and greater fluidity of social forms, whether in New Guinea or in*

AN OVERHEATED WORLD

New York. The condition of overheated twenty-first century global capitalism can be read at least in part as one in which these necessarily complementary double movements, in which the creation of fixity at one point presupposes and encourages fluidity at others and vice versa, now oscillate at such a speed that they increasingly remove solid ground from which people can thrive and act in the world.

There are social groups in the New Guinea highlands

Ever since Wagner, Papua New Guinea has provided the basis for a body of anthropological work that has stressed the relative fluidity of social forms as an ideal type basis for Melanesian sociality in opposition to an ideal type fixity of forms that are described as forming the basis for Western "society". Yet, simultaneously with this narrative that could be characterized as attempting to itself freeze time in order to keep ideal type Melanesia intact as the basis for a particular type of Western anthropological thought experiment (cf. Fabian 1983), another narrative emerged that stressed the ways in which different kinds of actors attempted to introduce greater social fixity in a variety of different contexts. Filer (2007, 139), for example, describes what he refers to as, "Melanesian heavy industry" as being a, "creature with four legs": oil/gas, mining, logging and oil palm. Although the dynamics differ in all four industries, they tend to involve a move towards the creation of more stable fixed groups that are able to negotiate the relationship between locals, who become reconfigured as members of groups, and outside interests who are interested in extracting or developing resources from or on their land (e.g. Filer 2014, 77). Much of the impetus for this comes from relatively powerful actors who are perceived as being external in origin, such as the state that encourages the creation of such groups through legislation such as the 1996 Land Act (Filer 2014) or multinational corporations who want to have clearly defined groups of people to negotiate and deal with. However, as Filer (2007, 142) observes, although the process of group "incorporation" is pushed heavily by the nation-state of Papua New Guinea and by industries, it is also a process in which local people themselves take a leading role in order to secure particular positions within global flows of wealth. Hence,

> [i]f nowadays we find a cult of incorporation amongst the Landowners themselves, this suggests that the ideology of landownership is not the property of any one party to the social relations of resource compensation, but is a form of the relationship itself. (Filer 2007, 165)

This process can be clearly seen in legal moves to create incorporated land groups (ILGs) under the provisions of various land and forestry acts since the 1970s in response to the threats and opportunities presented by large-scale resource extraction. The moments at which groups are brought into being through legal ritual sometimes attract great attention. One report mentions 25,000 people attending the official unveiling of a certificate of group incorporation in an area of the Eastern Highlands where it was thought that oil had been discovered (*Post Courier* 27 January 2005). But the process of introducing increasing fixity to social relations so that entities that look more and more like groups emerges in response to perceived economic opportunities goes beyond official land group incorporation and has been observed now for several decades. In the 1990s, observers such as Jorgenson (1997) detail a process later described by Ernst (1999) as "entification"; namely how shifting social collectivities rapidly became re-described as fixed social units in response to the hope of royalty payments from predicted resource extraction projects as potential beneficiaries attempted to limit potential overlapping claims. The process was one in which people,

> who were familiar with government notions of landholding, began talking of traditional cognatic descent categories *(tenum miit)* as "clans", complete with patrilineal descent' (Jorgenson 1997, 611).

Likewise, Filer (2007, 160–166) describes how rapidly the idea of a clan as a fixed social group has been adopted by many Papua New Guineans in the past two decades, as part of a process in which entities such as ILGs are created out of flexible contextually elicited social groups which are then retrospectively re-envisioned as fixed social groups that become seen as the basis for the incorporated groups that they themselves are in fact modelled upon. Less dramatically but equally significantly, the few areas of PNG where local people have a long history of making significant money from cash cropping on their own customary land have seen moves towards a greater fixity in the boundaries of clans that begin to look a little bit more like the social groups that Wagner warned us against taking for granted. The Gazelle Peninsula of East New Britain Province, for example, has one of the lowest number of legally registered ILGs in the country, but nonetheless has a long history of a process of gradually increasing fixity in social relations that make those relations look more "groupy", as Wagner (1974, 101) might have it (see Martin 2013, 30–99).

What is clear is that recent years have seen a rapid acceleration and overheating of this previously gradual tendency. For example, Filer (2014, 77) claims that between 2003 and 2011, when the PNG government called a temporary halt to the process, fully 11% of PNG's customary land was subject to de facto alienation through the issuance of "Special Agricultural and Business Leases" in the forestry sector alone. Given that 97% of PNGs land surface is commonly (if perhaps inaccurately) reckoned to be customary, this amounts to at least 10% of the land surface of PNG and this does not take into account land also subject to de facto alienation by virtue of other legal mechanisms in oil, gas and mineral mining. This is a significant trend, with 80% of this alienation occurring in the two years before the government called a halt to proceedings. These processes and others like them rely upon the legal incorporation of groups and it is no accident that this process has been subjected to an almost unimaginable overheating in the recent years. Between the passage of the Land Groups Incorporation Act in 1974 and 1992, only eight groups had been established in the entire country. By 1995, this had risen to 700, and by 2014, Filer (2014, 84) estimates somewhere in the region of 18,000.

This explosion can be seen largely as a response to the intensification of logging, oil palm cultivation and extractive industries in PNG over recent years, itself a phenomenon driven at least in part by the overheating of the global economy in the years since 1991. Although these groups may appear fuzzy around the edges when subject to close examination compared to an ideal type of a perfectly bounded group, they do introduce a relatively greater fixity and "groupiness" into social relations in response to the needs of intensifying capital accumulation. And as we shall see, the same is true for other kinds of group-entities set up for similar purposes in capitalism's traditional heartlands. Although the particular nature of the fuzziness of the groups has a particular Melanesian character, the fuzziness itself in general is in no way a distinctively Melanesian or non-Western trait. The groups and group-entities established to enable relations of capital accumulation are always works in progress with the potential for some relations to exceed the bounds of the form, albeit that the particular form that that potential may take will vary in different contexts. What the explosion of group forming tendencies in Papua New Guinea might suggest to us, however, is that contemporary overheated capitalism leads to an expansion of a general tendency in capitalism to create relatively fixed stable groups as a "form" for the management of the relations of capital accumulation. Whilst this would appear to be true in the case of land groups and clans in contemporary PNG, it might be a mistake to generalize too far in this direction. *Just as social groups rely upon the simultaneous speeding up and slowing down of time, so capital accumulation always tends towards a simultaneous fixing and dissolution of social groups and forms. What overheated capitalism does is to intensify the oscillation between these two tendencies to a point that seems to increasingly create a dangerous lack of secure ground from which to experience and act in the world.*

Are there corporate groups in the capitalist heartlands?

Case study one: Liverpool football club and Kop Investment LLC

In the first half of this paper, we have suggested that social life everywhere inevitably involves simultaneous moves towards greater fixity and fluidity of social group-entities, even if the details of that dynamic might vary wildly in different contexts. One key problem of contemporary overheated global capitalism is that the oscillation between these two tendencies has intensified as a result of bewilderingly complex reconfigurations of debt obligations that mean that the corporate form, established to ensure a degree of relative fixity from which investment can be planned, is often no longer able to fulfil that undertaking. One good example would be recent takeovers in the UK football sector, where supporters' groups have expressed a sense of bewilderment, disorientation and anger—not only at the substance and form of the takeovers where private equity style leveraged buyouts hampered club development, but at the way in which such takeovers have forced a re-evaluation of the moral purpose or essence of the club.

Arguably, the most acrimonious of the takeovers in the English Premier League was the takeover of Liverpool Football Club by private equity partners Tom Hicks and George Gillett in February 2007 for £220 m from the previous shareholder David Moores. LFC represented an easy "buy and build" opportunity in private equity terms—it had weak matchday revenues relative to rivals with a stadium that needed updating and enlarging; a loyal, international fanbase that had yet to be fully "levered" and potential sponsorship and commercial revenue streams that had not yet been capitalized upon. The pair, however, did not want to risk any of their own money in the deal and financed the buyout entirely with borrowed money, which they hoped to service using the club's strong cashflows, with the deal seemingly representing a number of secure "outs" should the broader "buy and build" strategy fail. That might include the selling of property, land and other assets belonging to the club or the sale of star players to clear debt; or alternatively to pay cash directly to the owners through dividends, emoluments or the charging of consultancy fees to related parties.

The buyout involved a restructuring of the club into a tier of discrete limited liability companies, each treated as separate legal persons in the eyes of the law and each with individual responsibilities for their liability obligations. The operating entity (i.e. the actual club) was called Liverpool Football Club and Athletics Ground—a wholly owned subsidiary of Kop Football Ltd, which in turn was a wholly owned subsidiary of Kop Football (Holdings) Ltd—and so on (see Figure 1). This tiered structure created a variety of spaces to facilitate fluid profit maximizing or cash extraction strategies around the operating entity. This might classically involve the use of transfer pricing, intercompany loans and other such accounting devices for tax efficiency reasons (Palan 2006; Shaxson 2012; Sikka and Willmott 2013) or it might involve dividend recapitalizations to extract cash (see Erturk et al. 2008 for examples).

The figure below outlines the fluid refinancing activity in a little over two years at Liverpool FC. Both fluidity and confusion were built into the model through the use of tax havens and multiple refinancings which moved debt around the corporate structure, making it difficult to trace what was going on where and most crucially which corporate entity held responsibility to meet those debt obligations in the final instance. In terms of the tiering, there were at least three holding companies traceable from the company accounts, spanning at least three domiciles: the UK and the tax havens of the Cayman Islands and Delaware in the USA, whose limited reporting rules added further obfuscation.

These corporate forms were legally established as fixed points through which a series of fluid financial arrangements were instituted. In February 2007, Hicks and Gillete's UK-based company Kop Football (Holdings) Ltd established a £296.5 m facility with Royal Bank of Scotland (RBS) from which £202.6 m was drawn down at LIBOR[3] + 1.5% to finance the buyout. In January 2008, RBS opened another £350.5 m facility, from which Kop Football Limited (Kop Football (Holding) Ltd's subsidiary) drew down £245 m at LIBOR +3.5%, repaying the debt originally drawn down by Kop Football (Holding) Ltd in February 2007; the operating entity—Liverpool Football Club and Athletic Ground—also drew down £14.4 m from a separate facility. At the same time, intercompany debt[4] cascaded down the corporate network as Kop Football (Cayman) Ltd lent its subsidiary Kop Football (Holdings) Ltd first £43.5 m in Jan 2008, then £144.4 m in July 2009 at an interest rate of 10%. The principal effect was to depress taxable post-interest profits in the UK and to suck interest income back up the corporate structure into the low-tax domicile of the Caymans, where extraction might also be easier. A third refinancing package was then advanced in July 2009, with £297 m lent to Kop Football Ltd on the proviso that the owners issued personal guarantees of £110 m and committed to a sale of part or all of the club (Blitz and Sakoui 2010).

The reliance on floating, short-term debt was ultimately to prove disastrous in a post-Lehman world as LIBOR rates spiralled: in the 2009/2010 accounts, interest payments reached 116.4% of operating profit at the operating entity, Liverpool Football Club and Athletic Ground's. By May 2010, RBS viewed the club as a solvency risk and Hicks and Gillett's willingness to improve the club's debt position was questioned, so the bank used their right as senior creditors under the terms of the loan to introduce board changes to protect their investment. Martin Broughton was installed as chairman of Kop Football Ltd and the articles of association were rewritten so that he had sole ability to appoint or dismiss board members (Conn 2010). On 5 October 2010, Broughton sanctioned the

AN OVERHEATED WORLD

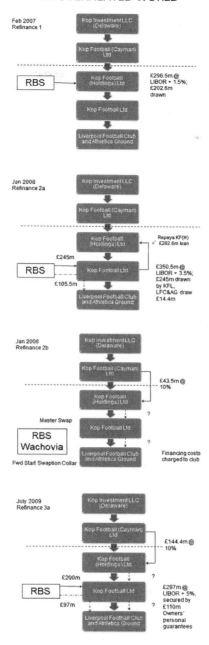

Figure 1. The multiple refinancing arrangements at Liverpool Football Club.
Source: authors' own diagrams derived from hard copy company accounts.

sale of the club to New England Sports Ventures (later Fenway Sports Group). This was to raise fundamental questions about boundaries and obligations.

The attempted sale was initially frustrated because the elicitation of different groups formed as part of the original takeover resulted in confusion about multiple issues:

which company had precedence in the hierarchy, which set of actors were able to do what to whom, which legal entity held responsibility for which liabilities and which jurisdiction's laws prevailed in the final instance. Broughton's sanctioning of the sale to New England Sports Ventured prompted an attempt by Hicks and Gillett to sack Broughton and other members of the Kop Football Ltd board, claiming that this was their right as directors of this subsidiary's parents—Kop Football (Cayman) Ltd and Kop Investment LLC (Delaware). RBS responded by bringing an injunction against Hicks and Gillett in an English court preventing the sacking of Broughton and other board members so that the sale could be completed—only for this to be met by a counter-injunction by the owners in a Texan court to prevent the sale. The US-based injunction was eventually overturned and the sale did go through on 15 October 2010, but this did not prevent Hicks and Gillett from suing for $1.6bn of damages in a Dallas court—an act met by an anti-suit injunction in the UK preventing their search for damages in a non-UK court (Reade 2011). The claim for damages was eventually dropped in January 2013.

All of this serves to illustrate a central tension or paradox at the heart of an overheating capitalism: that at the micro level, capital seeks an ever more detailed refinement of liability obligations in ever more elaborate corporate structures; but as a direct consequence of this tendency, responsibility has never been so contested, ambiguous and diffuse at the aggregate. The corporation was supposed to create a fixed point and a collective legal person through the limitation of debt obligations; and that legal person or social entity was then empowered to act in the world, to invest in new technologies and enterprises with all of the positive economic benefits for the wider society claimed by advocates such as Micklethwait and Wooldridge. But the current era represents a rather different reality—it is one where the creation of a multiplicity of fixed points makes it harder to identify where obligations begin and end. The growing complexity of the corporate form through subsidiarization creates further tensions when corporate debt obligations increase, as they did through much of the 2000s (Greenwood and Scharfstein 2013): at a time when responsibility to meet those growing obligations increases, the growing complexity of corporate arrangements makes that responsibility less clear and open to legal challenge. The result is not increased security and an incentive to invest for the social good, but a confusion of responsibility and greater corporate fragility, with dubious social benefits.

Case study two: Barclays Bank and Protium Hedge Fund
Whilst the purpose of the limited liability corporation was to establish groupings that were both defined by, and able to establish the fixing of, clear liabilities, the current era of overheated financialization has created possibilities for the more temporary creation of fluid elicitations whose liabilities are increasingly unclear. Amongst other factors, this development is immutably linked to an increasingly mobile and globally connected elite who, through access to accounting and law expertise, employ a variety of flexible strategies to exploit these legal forms or the gaps between these elicitations for personal reward. These elite strategies involve a kind of bricolage which has continued unhindered after the crisis through deals between insiders of different firms who may both derive benefit. One example of this is the way in which Barclays drew on ex-employees in a hedge fund to improve its balance sheet which was beneficial for the ex-employees following the credit crunch.

AN OVERHEATED WORLD

In 2009, Barclays sold $12.3bn of mainly monoline insured[5] toxic assets to a hedge fund called "Protium". The purported aim of the exercise was to limit Barclays' balance sheet exposure to monoline bankruptcy at a time when many of those insurers were suffering from the collapsing sub prime mortgage-backed securities market. However, despite the fact that Barclays and Protium were separate companies, there was much to connect the two. C12, the US asset management company that owned Protium, was run mainly by ex-Barclays employees and they received an annual management fee of $40 m for administering those toxic assets (Croft 2009). Similarly, Protium funded the purchase of the $12.3bn of toxic assets from Barclays using $12.6bn of debt provided by Barclays themselves plus $450 m investment from the ex-employees and other outside investors (Aldrick 2011). Crucially, the interest payment on the Barclays loan taken out by Protium was subordinated to the $40 m management fee and distributions to Protium partners (Croft and Jones 2009), meaning that the traditional hierarchy of claims on an income stream had been inverted: the ex-Barclays investors in, and mangers of, C12 and Protium were paid before any other claimants, including the senior creditor, Barclays.

Despite the formal separation of Barclays and Protium, practically, this did not change Barclays' real exposure to the risk of the underlying assets that it previously owned. If those assets did blow up completely, then Protium would default on its loan from Barclays, leaving Barclays as a senior creditor on a fund whose assets had just disintegrated. This was recognized as much in February 2011 when Barclays marked its loan to Protium to the fair value of the underlying collateral—the toxic assets sold to Protium, undermining the key rationale for the deal (Aldrick 2011). Barclays as an organization lost an estimated $1bn on the deal, but its ex-employees fared much better as Protium received an additional $83 m in performance fees on top of all the previous income and fees received (Pratley 2011).

This was represented at the time of the deal in 2009 as an egregious case of regulatory arbitrage[6] which seemed to change little in the way of Barclay's risk exposure, but did handsomely reward a few financial actors who happened to be ex-employees of that bank. But as is commonplace in finance, these apparently maverick acts become the unspectacular standard for the next generation. By 2014, activity like this was so commonplace that it had been given a title – "blind pool transactions", leading to situations where, for example, 2500 companies that borrowed more than €11bn from the German bank Nord/LB had the main risk of their loans transferred to Christofferson Robb, a US-based hedge fund (Arnold 2014). None of these companies were aware of this transfer, neither were Norrd/LBs staff who were overseeing these loans—despite representing 10% of their total loan book. Far from being a marginal, exceptional or unconventional kind of transaction, it is estimated that hundreds of billions of Euros have been transferred into the shadow banking sector in this manner since 2009 (Arnold 2014).

All of this points to a kind of overflowing of the corporate form that has always been potentially present, but has begun to intensify in a manner that threatens one of the core raisons d'etre of the limited liability corporation. The corporate form was always represented as a social collectivity elicited by legal naming practices in order to hold and manage investments and debt obligations (for the purpose of investing these into productive and entrepreneurial activities), but this case illustrates how these obligations travel across firm boundaries through other social relations. This is not to suggest wrongdoing in the case of Barclays and Protium; rather, it is instructive as an example of how the corporation is increasingly unable to fully contain economic activity. And these practices are arguably intensifying as capitalism overheats and elite connectivity increases. Practices that were seen as marginal or unthinkable have rapidly become mainstream, leading to a situation where the corporation is often increasingly unable to act as an entity that holds obligations but has a more porous form that fulfils a very different role; and in more extreme cases—takes the form of a conduit for elites who wish to benefit at the expense of the corporations in which they are embedded.

Case study 3: SIVs and CDOs
One of the more striking features of the financial crisis of 2008 was the way in which the boundaries of distinct and discrete legal entities collapsed suddenly into one another. The crisis revealed how many banks used off-balance sheet structured investment vehicles or "SIV[7]"s to conduct many of their more speculative derivatives investments (Gorton and Souleles 2007). SIVs were particularly involved in the sub prime mortgage-backed securities and collateralized debt obligation markets, funding their investments in these long-dated securities using short-term dated asset-backed commercial paper (Crotty 2009; Tett, Davies, and Cohen 2007). These SIVs differed materially from other Special Purpose Vehicles insofar as they were wholly or partly sponsored by their parent banks. That effectively meant that if these SIVs were unable to sell their asset-backed commercial paper, parent banks would be contractually obliged to extend a credit line, rather than cut the vehicles loose (Tavakoli 2008). When the crisis hit, no one wanted to buy the SIVs commercial paper which was backed by risky sub prime loans and so these toxic assets were then subsumed onto the balance sheet of the mainstream banks, creating liquidity and solvency problems when these asset values were written down (Engelen et al. 2011). As Roubini (2008) noted at the time, these assets were always de facto on balance sheet items even if they were *de jure* off-balance sheet. As with the previous cases, formally legally separated entities could easily be viewed as aspects of a singular grouping when viewed from different angles or at different times, particularly at moments when an intensification of debt obligations, that had previously been hidden by an economic bubble and innovative re-structuring and re-packaging of debt, led to the linkages between the entities becoming so apparent and important that they appeared more as aspects of a unified group.

Although the collapse was ultimately due to the poor quality of the assets held and the sudden drying up of their short-term financing, the constructed corporate forms—the elicitation of particular groups—used to carry out these trades reflected a desire on the part of the sponsoring banks to game Basel capital adequacy ratios (Sakoui and Tett 2008). By using off-balance sheet SIVs that were technically legally separate from themselves, banks appeared to be less exposed to risky assets and therefore did not have to hold back as much capital as a buffer against future defaults or writedowns, freeing up funds to speculate with.

By 2008, the value of gross off-balance sheet derivatives contracts outstanding was $672 trillion (Levinson 2016) and the crisis spurred the US Congress to address this problem of risky off-balance sheet derivatives exposures through the Dodd Frank Wall Street Reform Act. The act sought to introduce new reporting and transparency rules so that investors (and regulators) might have a better insight as to the risk exposures of large banks. This was coupled with new trading rules designed to bring derivatives trading onto an exchange, as part of the "Clearing and Trading Requirements" of that Act. This posed a considerable threat to bank business interests because most derivatives were sold "over the counter" and so were not exposed to the competitive price pressures that open trading on an exchange would bring. Exchange traded derivatives would also likely bring new competitors into the market and would reduce fees.

The industry response was predictable: lobby regulators heavily and employ an army of lawyers to find loopholes. The sticking point for the banks was a small but significant insert in Dodd Frank which stated that the act would apply to all those activities that had "a direct and significant connection with activities in, or effect on, commerce of the United States". In effect, that meant that US bank overseas subsidiaries would come under the act's remit, which was a problem when London-based operations were a major source of derivatives and swaps activity. It was an attempt to force a legal recognition that the creation of separate entities that were so closely linked by debt obligations that flowed between them that the boundaries between them often appeared blurred or even practically non-existent was problematic. In response, the banking sector's lawyers focused on a small definitional distinction in the Act—that it would apply to those overseas entities with a parent-subsidiary "guarantee". Digging further the lawyers found the definition of "guarantee" as one where there is an "explicit" promise of financial support (Levinson 2016). The banks response was to simply strip out any reference to a guarantee in their swaps and derivatives contracts, thus evading its "explicit" expression.

This small loophole did not radically change the activity—US banks continued to bet heavily in those derivatives and swaps markets, but it did change the formal groupings within which that activity took place. US banks moved quickly to book their trades through London affiliates without any credit guarantees linking them back to the USA: a prospect much more risky than the previous situation. Yet, despite that apparent risk, the market does not appear to have been put off and swap trades continue unabated. The key point here is that this provides a good example of the performative power of names in a process of capitalist "entification". The re-classification of loose gatherings as fixed entities meant that the naming process became an organizing device for those with the influence and desire to do so to financially clip and alter the flow of a particular revenue stream.

Conclusions

The emergence, first of the modern corporation in the UK and the USA in the late nineteenth century, and then subsequently of other forms of entification such as incorporated land groups (ILGs) in PNG in the early twenty-first century, might lead one to expect that an opposition between fluid elicitations of shifting collectivities and the establishment of more permanent entities was a fundamental feature of an opposition between Western and non-Western societies (as posited by Wagner in his 1974 paper for example) or that the move from the former to the latter was a feature of spreading Western modernization. However, what an examination of the modern corporation suggests is that a tension between fluidity and fixity has always been at the core of its creation and maintenance, and that this tension has been exacerbated by recent developments that introduce incentives for radically destabilizing fluidity in which more sub-entities become partially fixed for shorter periods of time, changing the nature and capacities of the corporation as an entity. The intensification of this tension that the corporation was able to largely contain within its constitution during periods of seemingly stable growth could be seen as a major manifestation, simultaneously both symptom and cause, of the current state of overheating in which contradictions that were inherent in capitalist modernity from the start reach a new and dangerous level.

And similar tensions existing have always existed in the elicitation of social groups in PNG.[8] So, for example, Martin (2013) observes that a distinction between the ways in which names can be seen as either eliciting social groups or describing pre-existing separations between already discrete entities among Tolai people in PNG. Disputes among Tolai people over the boundaries an entity that holds exclusive rights to land or other assets, for example, often centre around the extent to which a name can elicit a difference between groups or act as a description of a pre-existing difference, much as the naming processes around the degree of separation between an SIV and its parent bank can also act as means of fighting over the ownership of valued (or toxic) assets and the boundaries of the group that might claim such ownership. The tension between these two principles is not an example of the expression of two different cultural orders but is rather constitutive of an enduring tension in human relations, much as Mauss' (1970) distinction between the logic of the gift and the logic of commerce was not ultimately intended as the description of the underlying cultural difference between the West and its Others, but as a fundamental tension to be balanced in all societies, including the Western Europe of the early twentieth century.

Just as this tension appears to be intensifying in financial trades between commercial banks and corporations listed in New York and London, so also the competition over the boundaries of the corporate form appears to be intensifying in PNG, albeit it is a contest commencing from a different base line and evolving for the time being often along different contours. A.L. Epstein who worked with the Tolai community of Matupit, in the late 1950s nearly half a century before Martin's fieldwork in the 2000s, describes how the local word describing a matrlineage; "vunatarai" contained, "a fertile language for controversy" of which the best illustration was the custom of "turguvuai", in which two lineages that had apparently originally been separate had stood together in alliance so long that they had come to be universally thought of as a single group. They would act in unison at gift exchange ceremonies with other *vunatarai*, for example, for so many years or generations that they had become in the eyes of their own members and others a single entity; a clear example of the ways in which it is participation in exchange and debt obligations shape the boundaries of the entities that engage in them as much as it is the nature of the entities that shapes the flow of the exchange. Epstein describes how at times a controversy or a dispute would lead to the emergence of a claim that a *vunatarai* that had universally been considered unitary was in fact two *vunatarai* united by *turguvuai*, a process that I myself (Martin) observed in 2004 when a land dispute following the death of a *vunatarai* elder led to such claims by some parties that a singular *vunatarai* was in fact no such thing. For Epstein, this led to the, "apparently odd result … that persons who in one context are recognised as belonging to a single *vunatarai* may not be so regarded in others", a result perhaps no more odd than the ways in which a business seen as a singular entity when viewed from the perspective of the chains of debt obligation that tie it together internally and tie it to other businesses externally, may be viewed as multiple separate corporate entities when viewed from other legal perspectives.

These kinds of tensions over the limits and boundaries of social groups have long been a part of the ethnographic record for Tolai people, but there is little doubt that they have intensified over the past half-century as a population explosion and a growing tendency to view land as a productive asset from which money can be made have had an effect. Although the particular dynamics might vary in both the Tolai case and the case of global financial markets, in both cases, the tension is constitutive of a battle between tendencies towards more permanent fixing social groups, on the one hand, and being more tolerant of more temporary elicitations that sub-divide and merge such entities, on the other. In both cases, this enduring tension appears to be overheating as intensification in the nature, technologies, scale and reach of networks of debt obligation and capital accumulation reach previously unimaginable levels.

Notes

1. Wagner's argument was to a large degree foreshadowed by Barnes' (1962) critique of the application of African models of patrilineal descent groups to the New Guinea Highlands, but it is Wagner's work that has gone on to have the most far-reaching influence in anthropological theory, perhaps due to its more sweeping general critique of the necessity of the assumption of the existence of social groups per se. Wagner's work of the early 1970s went on to be a major influence on the so-called New Melanesian Ethnography of the late 1980s, for example.
2. For example, Lederman (1986) and Merlan and Rumsey (1991) both in their different ways explore a shifting dialectic between moments of apparent fixity and fluidity in the ways in which names create or relate to entities that could be described as social groups in the New Guinea Highlands.
3. The "London Interbank Offered Rate" is an average rate based upon what leading commercial banks in London would supposedly pay if borrowing from other banks. It is the main base interest rate upon which loans between commercial banks and other large financial institutes are calculated and is a fundamental part of the infrastructure underpinning global finance.
4. An intercompany loan is one from parent to subsidiary or subsidiary to parent within the same corporate network.
5. A monoline insurance company is one that provides guarantees and other credit enhancements to issuers of particular securities. They were principally involved in the insurance of municipal bonds in the USA but became embroiled in the sub prime crisis after providing credit enhancements for mortgage-backed securities and collateralized debt obligations in the 2000s. As these assets were written down, many monoline insurers were unable to meet their obligations and went into liquidation, leaving the assets they insured almost worthless.
6. That is a form of gaming the system by taking advantage of legal loopholes and technicalities.
7. A SIV is an investment vehicle, often sponsored by a bank, that invests in long-dated securities financed by short-term borrowing, often through the issuance of commercial paper. They make a profit traditionally through the credit spread between the lower interest rates on short-term debt and the higher returns on their long-term investments.
8. As, previously noted, both Lederman and Merlan and Rumsey have observed.

Disclosure statement

No potential conflict of interest was reported by the authors.

References

Aldrick, Philip. 2011. "Barclays Takes £500 m Hit as It Quits Toxic Protium Deal." February 16, sec. Finance. http://www.telegraph.co.uk/finance/newsbysector/banksandfinance/8326510/Barclays-takes-500m-hit-as-it-quits-toxic-Protium-deal.html.

Anderson, B. 1983. *Imagined Communities: Reflections on the Origins and the Spread of Nationalism*. London: Verso.

Arnold, Martin. 2014. "Banks Unload Risk into Blind Pools." *Financial Times*, June 17. http://www.ft.com/cms/s/0/c5c33f20-e051-11e3-b341-00144feabdc0.html#axzz40yBucf4m.

Barnes, J. 1962. "African Models in the New Guinea Highlands." *Man* 62 (1): 5–9.

Benton, L. 2010. *A Search for Sovereignty: Law and Geography in European Empires*. Cambridge: Cambridge University Press, 1400–1900.

Blitz, Roger, and Anousha Sakoui. 2010. "Chairman on the Offensive in Liverpool Clash." *Financial Times*, October 6. http://www.ft.com/cms/s/0/071ff6e0-d154-11df-8422-00144feabdc0.html#axzz41Sf30sa8.

Conn, David. 2010. "Liverpool Sale: How Martin Broughton and RBS Won Control of Club's Future." *The Guardian*, October 7, sec. Sport. http://www.theguardian.com/sport/blog/2010/oct/07/liverpool-takeover-martin-broughton-rbs.

Croft, Jane. 2009. "'Curious' Case of Barclays Assets Sale." *Financial Times*, September 17. http://www.ft.com/cms/s/0/56b8afa8-a3ba-11de-9fed-00144feabdc0.html#axzz41Sf30sa8.

Croft, Jane, and Sam Jones. 2009. "Barclays de-Risk Deal Leaves Analysts Puzzled." *Financial Times*, September 16. http://www.ft.com/cms/s/0/72e03676-a2ff-11de-ba74-00144feabdc0.html#axzz41Sf30sa8.

Crotty, James. 2009. "Structural Causes of the Global Financial Crisis: A Critical Assessment of the 'New Financial Architecture'." *Cambridge Journal of Economics* 33 (4): 563–580. doi:10.1093/cje/bep023.

Engelen, Ewald, Ismail Ertürk, Julie Froud, Sukhdev Johal, Adam Leaver, Mick Moran, Adriana Nilsson, and Karel Williams. 2011. *After the Great Complacence: Financial Crisis and the Politics of Reform: Oxford University Press*. Oxford: Oxford University Press.

Ernst, T. 1999. "Land, Stories and Resources: Discourse and Entification in Onabasulu Modernity." *American Anthropologist* 101 (1): 88–97.

Fabian, J. 1983. *Time and the Other: How Anthropology Makes Its Object*. New York: Columbia University Press.

Filer, C. 2007. "Local Custom and the Art of Land Group Boundary Maintenance in Papua New Guinea." In *Customary Land Tenure and Registration in Australia and Papua New Guinea Anthropological Perspectives*, edited by J. Weiner, and K. Glaskin, 135–173. Canberra: ANU Press.

Filer, C. 2014. "The Double Movement of Immovable Property Rights in Papua New Guinea." *The Journal of Pacific History* 49 (1): 76–94.

Erturk, I., J. Froud, S. Johal, A. Leaver, and K. Williams. 2010. "Ownership Matters: Private Equity and the Political Division of Ownership." *Organization* 17 (5): 543–561.

Golub, A. 2014. *Leviathans at the Gold Mine: Creating Indigenous and Corporate Actors in Papua New Guinea*. Durham: Duke University Press.

Gorton, Gary, and Nicholas Souleles. 2007. "Special Purpose Vehicles and Securitization." In *The Risks of Financial Institutions*, edited by Mark Carey, and Rene Stulz, 549–602. Chicago: University of Chicago Press.

Greenwood, Robin, and David Scharfstein. 2013. "The Growth of Finance." *The Journal of Economic Perspectives* 27 (2): 3–28.

Hansen, T., and F. Stepputat. 2005. "Introduction." In *Sovereign Bodies: Citizens, Migrants and States in the Postcolonial World*, edited by T. Hansen, and F. Stepputat, 1–38. Princeton, NJ: Princeton University Press.

Jorgenson, D. 1997. "Who or What is a Landowner? Mythology and Marking the Ground in a Papua New Guinea Mining Project." *Anthropological Forum* 7 (4): 599–627.

Lederman, R. 1986. *What Gifts Engender: Social Relations and Politics in Mendi, Highland Papua New Guinea*. Cambridge: Cambridge University Press.
Levinson, Charles. 2016. "Why U.S. Banks Hid Billions in Derivatives Trades from the CFTC." *Reuters*. Accessed March 7. http://www.reuters.com/investigates/special-report/usa-swaps/.
Lombard, L. 2012. "Raiding Sovereignty in Central African Borderlands." PhD thesis., Duke University.
Martin, K. 2012. "Big Men and Business: Morality, Debt and the Corporation." *Social Anthropology* 20 (4): 482–485.
Martin, K. 2013. *The Death of the Big Men and the Rise of the Big Shots: Custom and Conflict in East New Britain*. New York: Berghahn Books.
Martin, K. 2014a. "Sovereignty and Freedom in West Papua and Beyond." *Oceania* 84 (3): 342–348.
Martin, K. 2014b. "Knotwork Not Networks: Or Anti-Anti-Anti Fetishism and the ANTi-politics Machine." *Hau* 4 (3): 99–115.
Mauss, M. 1970. *The Gft: Forms and Functions of Exchange in Primitive Societies*. London: Cohen and West.
Merlan, F., and A. Rumsey. 1991. *Ku Waru: Language and Segmentary Politics in the Western Nebliyer Valley, Papua New Guinea*. Cambridge: Cambridge University Press.
Micklethwait and Wooldridge. 2003. *The Company: A Short History of a Revolutionary Idea*. New York: The Modern Library.
Palan, Ronen. 2006. *The Offshore World: Sovereign Markets, Virtual Places, and Nomad Millionaires*. Ithaca, NY: Cornell University Press.
Pratley, Nils. 2011. "Barclays and the C12 Jackpot." *The Guardian*, April 27, sec. Business. http://www.theguardian.com/business/2011/apr/27/viewpoint-barclays-and-protium.
Reade, Brian. 2011. *An Epic Swindle: 44 Months with a Pair of Cowboys*. London: Quercus.
Roubini, Nouriel. 2008. "How Will Financial Institutions Make Money Now That the Securitization Food Chain Is Broken?" *Roubini*, May 19. https://www.roubini.com/analysis/how-will-financial-institutions-make-money-now-that-the-securitization-food-chain-is-broken.
Rutherford, D. 2012. *Laughing at Leviathan: Sovereignty and Audience in West Papua*. Chicago, IL: University of Chicago Press.
Sakoui, Anousha, and Gillian Tett. 2008. "A Ray of Light for Shadow Banking." *Financial Times*, June 18. http://www.ft.com/cms/s/0/4a72cace-3ccf-11dd-b958-0000779fd2ac.html#axzz40kvqYMFV.
Shaxson, Nicholas. 2012. *Treasure Islands: Tax Havens and the Men Who Stole the World*. London: Vintage.
Sikka, Prem, and Hugh Willmott. 2013. "The Tax Avoidance Industry: Accountancy Firms on the Make." *Critical Perspectives on International Business* 9 (4): 415–443. doi:10.1108/cpoib-06-2013-0019.
Tavakoli, Janet M. 2008. *Structured Finance and Collateralized Debt Obligations: New Developments in Cash and Synthetic Securitization*. 2nd ed. Hoboken, NJ: John Wiley.
Tett, Gillian, Paul J. Davies, and Norma Cohen. 2007. "Structured Investment Vehicles' Role in Crisis." *Financial Times*, August 12. http://www.ft.com/cms/s/0/8eebf016-48fd-11dc-b326-0000779fd2ac.html#axzz40kvqYMFV.
Thompson, E. P. 1967. "Time, Work-discipline and Industrial Capitalism." *Past and Present* 38: 56–97.
Wagner, R. 1974. "Are there Social Groups in the New Guinea Highlands?" In *Frontiers of Anthropology – An Introduction to Anthropological Thinking*, edited by M. Leaf, 95–122. New York: Nostrand.

Overheated Underdogs: Civilizational Analysis and Migration on the Danube-Tisza Interfluve

Chris Hann

ABSTRACT
Drawing on four decades of field research on the Danube-Tisza interfluve, the Western zone of the Great Hungarian Plain, this paper places the "overheating" of the post-Cold War era in a *longue durée* perspective. The first section traces a millennium of history in terms of multi-directional migrations and civilizational encounters of various kinds: between sedentary agriculturalists and pastoral nomads, between Christian and Muslim agrarian orders, and between capitalist and socialist industrial orders. The Hungarian variant of Marxism-Leninism (unlike most other variants) relied considerably on material incentives to households. It attached high priority to transforming the countryside, which experienced an effervescent involution or "overheating" in the last decades of socialism. Since 1991, however, the market socialist synthesis has given way to a peripheral variant of Western market capitalism. Overheating is no longer a phenomenon of the rural economy, which has lost the dynamism of the socialist decades and experiences deprivation in absolute as well as relative forms. Rather, overheating is to be observed in the symbolic dimension of political legitimation, as populist political parties vie with each other in nationalist rhetoric. This overheating was evident in negative attitudes towards strangers seeking to transit this part of Hungary in the summer of 2015, a migratory process which provided a challenge to the whole of the European Union. It is argued that these attitudes in rural Hungary can be explained in terms of the *ressentiments* of a population which has been palpably thrown back into an underdog position on the margins of Western capitalism.

Introduction

For an ethnographer whose first studies in a particular location are focused emphatically on the present and near past, it seems a natural progression in later research to take a closer interest in the more distant past (Hann 1980, 2015a). Even if the present is always full of dramatic transformations and the ethnographer continues to visit regularly to document them, as I have done since the 1970s for the Hungarian village of Tázlár, the buzz of the contemporary fades as the years go by, while the puzzles and seductions of the more remote past become more salient, both in making sense of the ongoing changes and in their own right. In my case, this tendency has been encouraged by changes in temporal consciousness among villagers themselves. Very much oriented to the future in their household accumulation strategies in the last decades of socialism, most rural residents have few such options available to them nowadays. I argue that this renders them susceptible to neo-nationalism, which builds on earlier forms of populism dating back to pre-socialist generations.

In this paper I place the rural–urban divide, the narrowing of which was a major accomplishment of the socialist decades, in a much longer temporal framework. Drawing on civilizational analysis (Arnason 2003; Schlanger 2006), I link localized history to larger patterns of migration and political economy. On this occasion, I take not the community of Tázlár but the wider region of the Danube-Tisza interfluve as my spatial unit. Although close to Budapest, from the point of view of power holders in Istanbul and the West alike, for centuries, this space was an underdeveloped "frontier zone". This frontier was gradually conquered by peasant colonists of diverse origins who remained on the periphery of European capitalism. Their life-worlds were transformed under socialism but the years since the end of the Cold War, in particular the period since accession to the European Union in 2004, have ushered in new forms of peripherality. This configuration makes the Danube-Tisza interfluve an instructive location in which to investigate the themes of Thomas Hylland Eriksen's "Overheating" project, the focus of this Special Issue. I shall argue that in the period with which this project is concerned the heat has been transferred from the rural economy, which boomed under socialism, to identity politics and symbolic legitimation. In the final section, this argument will be illustrated with a brief analysis of the Hungarian stance in the European "migrant crisis" of 2015, in which this region played a prominent role.

Civilizational Encounters and Migrations Through the Centuries

The Carpathian Basin is an ill-defined geographical construction that has little recognition outside Hungary. For the Hungarians (*Magyarok*, in their own language), it has signified a homeland ever since their arrival as immigrants from the East at the end of the ninth century. Nowadays, this era is elaborately commemorated at a history theme park located (somewhat arbitrarily – see Hann 2015b) between the rivers Danube and Tisza at the village of Ópusztaszer. The state consolidated under King Stephen and his successors included large sections of the Carpathians which nowadays belong to Slovakia, Ukraine and Romania. Magyar settlement also extended west of the Danube, in territories that had once formed the Roman frontier province of Pannonia. East of the Danube the land is overwhelmingly flat. The zone between the Danube and the Tisza, the second major river of the country, is characterized by sandy soils, with dunes that impede cultivation and make agriculture altogether impossible in some districts. Some areas of the interfluve, however, are as fertile as the rest of the Great Plain to the east of the Tisza. Villages were established in these fertile spots even before the arrival of the first Hungarians. The latter followed their predecessors in combining animal husbandry with the cultivation of crops. Following Stephen's conversion, they became Christian. Their villages were vulnerable to non-Christian invaders from the East, notably the Mongols, who swept away most settlements in 1241, and then later the Ottoman Turks, whose victory at Mohács in 1526 had similar consequences for the established rural population.

AN OVERHEATED WORLD

The early civilizational encounters (Arnason 2003) can be theorized in the familiar terms of a clash between marauding nomadic pastoralists and sedentary cultivators. The Ottomans, however, constituted a powerful agrarian empire. Although the network of villages was destroyed after the Battle of Mohács, market towns such as Kecskemét and Szeged flourished during the Turkish occupation of the Danube-Tisza interfluve. The local population cultivated fields in the vicinity of the towns and rented the lands of remote settlements such as Tázlár as pasture, which they visited in the summer months only.

After a century and a half the Ottoman Turks were repelled and the Habsburgs, the victorious Western power, initiated a systematic resettlement of the Great Plain. Immigrants were recruited primarily from territories that nowadays form parts of southern Germany and Slovakia. The resettlement was top-down and the Empress Maria-Theresia herself played a key role. But the re-establishment of Christian feudalism in the eighteenth century did not entail the reconstruction of the medieval settlement network. Locations like Tázlár remained *puszta*, that is, uninhabited, serving only as summer pasture. Such regions had a reputation for banditry, beyond the civilized pale of the urban settlements.

Towards the end of the nineteenth century, following the abolition of serfdom, the conquest of Hungary's "internal frontier" (Den Hollander 1960–1961) entered a new phase. With the break-up of noble estates, land gradually became a commodity like any other. Capitalist social relations spread unevenly. Although promoted in 1867 to the role of junior partner in the administration of the Habsburg Empire, Hungarian elites devoted more energy to the assimilation of the minorities they governed than to processes of urbanization and industrialization. In the absence of such opportunities, the expanding rural population was faced with difficult choices. In the last decades of the Habsburg Empire, hundreds of thousands migrated to North America. But in the same period, many undertook the shorter journey to the internal frontier of the interfluve, where farmland was parcelled out by banks. The pioneers of the 1870s were able to build their farmhouses (*tanyák*) in fertile locations. Some succeeded in establishing large and relatively productive enterprises. Many others found themselves struggling on infertile soils to produce enough grain even for the subsistence needs of the household. Latecomers stemmed primarily from the lower strata of society in Szeged and other regions to the east. Many had little experience of family farming, and acquiring a few acres of sand dunes did little to change their status as rural proletarians. They survived by working as day-labourers for wealthier neighbours, and by sending their children to work as farm servants. These trends continued through the inter-war period of the twentieth century. Poverty levels peaked in the early 1930s when hundreds of residents received food aid in return for working for the community. At this point two small hamlets housed a few public buildings (administration, schools, churches and mills) but the great majority of inhabitants lived on more or less isolated farmsteads. The "tanya world" was a byword for backwardness. It featured prominently in populist political campaigning for radical reform of rural social and political relations. The inhabitants of these scattered farms approximated sociologist Teodor Shanin's general type of a "peasant" society, which highlights the "family farm as the basic, multi-dimensional unit of social organization", "land husbandry as the main means of livelihood" and "the 'underdog' position – the domination of peasantry by outsiders".[1]

AN OVERHEATED WORLD

The history of the pre-socialist era can be theorized in terms of economic backwardness and the "development of underdevelopment". While other parts of Hungary experienced the impact of capitalism differently (for example, in many parts of Transdanubia large estates persisted down to the 1940s), the resettlement of the interfluve exemplified atomizing trends as a response to demographic and economic pressures. But instead of leading to "healthy" processes of accumulation and innovation, the "civilization" of capitalism was associated with increased stratification and economic stagnation. Only in their vineyards did some immigrants introduce new technologies (the sandy soils were well suited to the production of basic table wine, for which demand was strong after *phylloxera* destroyed most of the country's historic vineyards in the 1890s). The need for casual labour in this sector was crucial to the survival of many poor families. But a high price was paid because alcohol abuse (in addition to wine production, the climate and soils of the interfluve were conducive to fruit trees, the harvest of which was partly used to distil brandy) wreaked havoc in this society, especially among the poor.

In the absence of economic prosperity, the main solace of the rural population in the inter-war decades (apart from alcohol) was found in nationalism. The demise of the Austro-Hungarian Empire was followed by the Treaty of Trianon (1920), which reduced the size of the country by two-thirds and left many ethnic Magyars outside its new borders. This "historic injustice" was rejected by all shades of political opinion. Following the swift suppression of the "Republic of Councils" in 1919, power was monopolized by right-wing groupings, culminating in the Nazi Arrow Cross party which capitulated to the Red Army in 1945.

There followed an experiment lasting less than half a century with an alternative variant of an industrial social order, a "socialist civilization" which did more to develop and transform Hungarian rural society in just a few decades than capitalism had been able to accomplish in the preceding century. On the interfluve as across the country the 1950s opened with an onslaught on the property rights and market relations of the old capitalist order. Coercive socialist interventions had disastrous economic consequences. They intensified the suspicion of the great majority of rural residents (not just the rich peasants classified as the "class enemy") towards left-wing power holders. Other measures of the late 1950s and 1960s, however, laid solid foundations for rural community development, in particular, of material infrastructure. In the microcosm of Tázlár, the lower hamlet was designated as the nuclear centre and *tanya* residents were encouraged to build new homes here. Incentives included the availability of electricity and piped water, new public buildings (both secular and religious), and cooperative shops and taverns. Many inhabitants left agriculture for jobs in new industrial factories such as the steelworks of Csepel, south of Budapest. But because resources did not allow urbanization to keep pace with industrialization, many industrial workers continued to reside in the countryside, where they were able to produce a significant proportion of their food supply and maintain continuities with previous patterns of household farming.

The last decades of socialism witnessed a remarkable transformation of material and social relations across the Danube-Tisza interfluve. Developments in this region exemplified the successful synthesis of household and large-scale (collective) production in the agricultural sector nationwide. In turn, the relative success of Hungarian agriculture can be taken as emblematic of Hungarian "market socialism" in general (Swain 1985). The key institutional innovation in this region was the "specialist cooperative" (*szakszövetkezet*), a much looser form of collective farm than the Soviet *kolkhoz* or its Hungarian equivalent. Joining such a cooperative signified a weakening of property rights and some obligation to share resources, including one's labour power. But property rights were vulnerable anyway, as the first repressive years of socialism had made clear. The imposition of mass collectivization in the years around 1960 was eased on the interfluve by the provision that members of the new specialist cooperatives could, in practice, carry on farming their existing plots, with only a very modest obligation to work for the collective sector. The theory was that, in the long run, this form of cooperative should develop into something like the *kolkhoz*, with highly qualified farm leaders organizing an increasingly industrialized productive system. But the distinctive ecology of the interfluve made it necessary to postpone this ideal socialist solution to a remote future, since to establish large mechanized farms would have meant eliminating the patchwork of vineyards and orchards which was the enduring legacy of the *tanya* settlement pattern. As a result, the specialist cooperatives of the 1960s remained small, with limited machinery at their disposal, under the leadership of local peasants.

Things had moved on by the time of my fieldwork in 1976–1977. With decentralization and increased use of market signals following introduction of the New Economic Mechanism in 1968, Hungarian agricultural production boomed. It did so thanks to a happy combination of increasingly efficient production on large farms organized according to socialist principles (both collectives and state farms) and exploitation of the established strengths of household farming, particularly in labour-intensive branches. The Danube-Tisza interfluve was a stronghold of the latter. In the grape/wine sector, the state planted large new vineyards and built wineries for processing. At the same time, it helped individuals to maximize output in their private vineyards and to find a market for their product after the harvest.

The symbiosis of socialist and peasant agriculture was even more potent in the hog-raising sector, which was less ecologically specific to the interfluve. Peasants accustomed to raising two or three animals per year, one of which they would slaughter in winter and process for their own consumption, were now able to obtain cheap feed through their cooperative (either grown locally using new mechanized methods or imported from other, more productive regions of the country). The cooperative also helped with veterinary services and guaranteed purchase of the animals when they reached a specified weight. The peasant household was responsible for all the dirty work in the sties, which was often carried out by the elderly, or by the wives of men who commuted to factory jobs. I was struck by how hard people worked, but the incentives were obvious. Consumer markets expanded greatly in the last decades of socialism, allowing villagers to build lavish new houses or, more modestly, to add bathrooms and "white goods" to existing accommodation, and to buy cars.

Social inequalities increased and I detected a renewal of phenomena critiqued by populists in the past, notably the prevalence of exploitative day-labouring in the vineyard sector. But this was a price which socialist power holders were now willing to pay. By the early 1980s, the ideologically determined goal of transforming the specialist cooperative into a more conventional form of collective farm had been abandoned. Instead, with an expansion of material incentives throughout the economy, more conventional socialist institutions such as the *kolkhoz* were increasingly modified to resemble the specialist cooperative (Hann 1993). The Danube-Tisza interfluve exemplified these developments, which was made possible by the political conjuncture (a distinctive regional ecology alone would not have been enough). In the 1960s, these flexible institutions were fostered at the highest level in Budapest by Ferenc Erdei, a left-wing populist who had analysed the atrocious social conditions of his home region in the 1930s and whose dedication to socialist ideology was matched only by his determination to improve the lot of the peasantry from which he came. In the county town of Kecskemét, the market socialist path in the rural sector was astutely promoted in the 1970s by Pál Romány, the First Secretary of the Party. As with the institutionalization of the specialist cooperative across the interfluve, the appointment of an agrarian expert to lead this large county reflected a pragmatic determination of the Hungarian Socialist Workers' Party to put the maximization of output and incomes ahead of economic and political dogmas.

Two further points need to be made. First, although most peasant households profited from these measures, which allowed many to reach a higher standard of living than that of urban workers, this prosperity did not entail any moral approval of socialist principles. They attributed their successes to their own hard work, while continuing to resent socialist property policies and bureaucratic inefficiencies. Second, the intensification of existing peasant farms did not, in the majority of cases, lead to *productive* investment. A few took advantage of opportunities to purchase tractors and other equipment when this was authorized in the 1980s, but most of the income earned through household production was spent on consumption.

The acceleration of consumer spending had far-reaching social consequences. Hungarian meat consumption rose to be the highest in Europe, but so did suicide levels and alcohol abuse. Large sums were given away at increasingly lavish wedding parties to endow the new couple (Hann 2014). The pressures of status emulation became significant. Virtually no one had time for holidays, since animals had to be looked after and there was always some urgent task to be done around the house/farm. In short, the changes of the late socialist period were experienced by many villagers as a phenomenon analogous to Eriksen's "overheating". The pattern might be compared to involution in Java, as analysed by Geertz (1963). Agricultural production was intensified but the peasant farmers who made a critical contribution did not alter their basic production techniques. The difference to Indonesia is that, in this socialist modernization drive, a strong state promoted not "shared poverty" but an increasingly differentiated countryside. The countryside was no longer the backward peasant (*paraszt*) "other" of urban civilization, but a world in which those now classified as "small producers" (*kistermelők*) could match or exceed the income levels of the town thanks to their intimate symbiosis with socialist farms that produced on a much larger scale using industrial methods.

Collapse and Migration Westwards

According to some analysts, Hungarian market socialism was a contradiction from the beginning. Critics argued that the limited successes achieved after 1968 had already proven unsustainable long before 1990 (see Swain 1993). This makes intuitive sense in the case of agriculture: why would new generations of rural residents be willing to endure punishing routines of hard and dirty labour? Surely the *kistermelők* would want in due course to emulate urban workers and enjoy more leisure time? I noticed such aspirations in Tázlár in the 1980s, especially among young people of both genders and older women. But this would only have been feasible if the old household sector were to be replaced by capitalized private farms. In the end, the symbiosis of the socialist years was broken up not by its alleged internal contradictions but by the "system change" (*rendszerváltás*) of the early 1990s. This brought the privatization of virtually all socialist farms and the land itself, and confronted the new owners with radically altered market conditions. With the loss of secure outlets in the USSR and Eastern Germany, the producers of wine now had great difficulty in adapting to increasingly global competition.

Although the Danube-Tisza interfluve has lost the agrarian dynamism of the later socialist decades, it is still by no means as severely handicapped as many regions of northern and eastern Hungary. The county town of Kecskemét has enjoyed significant growth, thanks above all to the proximity of the country's principal north-south highway. The prestige investment is a Mercedes car factory, which exemplifies the capitalist rationale to invest where skilled labour is cheaply available. This factory now employs more workers than the old canning factories which reflect the food-based industries of the socialist past. Some Mercedes employees commute from villages as far away as Tázlár (a journey which takes the best part of an hour). But such investments are insufficient to compensate for the jobs lost in agriculture (Swain 2011). Levels of rural deprivation rose dramatically after 2010 under a government whose principal electoral base lies in the villages and small towns (Keller et al. forthcoming). The explanation for this paradox is the resilience of the ideology of agrarian populism (Hann and Kürti 2015).

Government workfare schemes to alleviate unemployment have been intensified since 2010. Even so, hundreds of thousands of rural Hungarians have felt that they have little alternative but to emigrate westwards in search of a job. This began in the 1990s and became legal following accession to the European Union in 2004. Cheap flights have made travel back and fore much easier over the years, but the dispersion of family members has led to a withering of kin ties and of the forms of intense sociality characteristic of villages in the late socialist period (cf. Creed 2011). Weddings and childbearing are postponed, celebrations have become modest restaurant affairs. Pigs are no longer slaughtered because it makes no economic sense to raise them in the old way when pork is more cheaply available in a nearby German-owned supermarket (Vidacs 2015). In the socialist era, house-building in villages such as Tázlár was a major occasion for mutual aid. Nowadays, few new houses are constructed and many are up for sale for extremely low prices. Housing prices are perhaps the most obvious statistical indicator of the gulf that has widened between countryside and town in the postsocialist years. Budapest is a special case, but even county capitals such as Kecskemét and Szeged are out of reach financially for most village residents. The smaller market towns of the interfluve have also experienced economic decline, but even here, property prices are still far above village levels.

One of the couples I know best in Tázlár was proud to buck the trend in the 1970s. While others were spending the proceeds of their household farming on house-building, Zsolt and Kati were the first to take a holiday abroad (a package tour to Italy). They were content to bring up their two children in social housing in the village centre, to which Zsolt was entitled when he served as Secretary of the Communist Youth League. Eventually, his job was phased out and he was obliged to take up alternative employment in the specialist cooperative, and to build a family home on a plot belonging to Kati's family on the outskirts of the village. Their eldest son studied forestry and found a job in another village of the interfluve, less than an hour's drive away. Their daughter qualified as a kindergarten teacher and had no trouble in finding an appropriate position in the village, where she has married. Zsolt and Kati are happy to be able to see their grandchildren regularly and to look after them for extended periods in the school holidays. They had a third child shortly before the end of the socialist era, a bright boy with good computing skills who graduated from a technical college after leaving the village school. But unlike his elder siblings, Balázs was unable to find a job in Hungary. Instead he followed friends to London, where he has worked for many years at Heathrow Airport's Hilton Hotel. His long-time girlfriend also works there; but they have not married and it is hard for them to think about planning a family together. This troubles his parents, but it is the price this family pays for the new freedoms.

Changes in domestic institutions and inter-household relations have been accompanied by radical changes in the political landscape. As noted above, policies conducing to a high measure of continuity with the peasant farming of yore were never sufficient to reconcile villagers with socialist power holders. The exceptional continuities of smallholding on the interfluve made it a stronghold of the Independent Smallholders' Party, the strongest political party of the pre-war era, which was re-established in 1989. The Smallholders campaigned strongly for the restoration of pre-socialist property relations, regardless of whether the fragmentation of modern enterprises and fields made any economic sense. After a decade of colourful controversy, following the elections of 1998, this party was out-manoeuvred by Viktor Orbán's Alliance of Young Democrats (Fidesz) and disappeared from the political landscape. Fidesz has a virtual monopoly nowadays on the interfluve, triumphing in all three elections of 2014 (at European, national and local levels). Only in a few enclaves (the most notable being the city of Szeged) have charismatic individuals succeeded in defeating the Fidesz candidate. The dominance of the governing party resembles that of the Hungarian Socialist Workers' party in the era when other parties were formally proscribed.

The new "agrarian populism" bears some affinity to the local political climate of the inter-war period. Those decades were characterized by a sharp cleavage (also prominent in literature and the arts in general) between the populists and their "other", primarily cosmopolitan (non-Magyar) elites in Budapest. The antipathy for everything which smacked of the *urbánus* was a product of the unbalanced development of the pre-socialist era, described above. Four decades of implementing a very different model of industrialization changed a great deal in Hungarian society. But when the key material props of the socialist system were suddenly withdrawn in the early 1990s, the old cultural ideologies demonstrated their resilience. It is instructive to look more closely at this long-term continuity in assessing state-society relations in Hungary a quarter of a century after the *rendszerváltás*.

Although I did not know them personally, I read some of the literature produced by Hungarian dissident intellectuals in the 1970s and 1980s. I had some sympathy with their critique of the Hungarian Socialist Workers' Party, much of it written from a leftist perspective. But my fear around 1990 was that the political party to which most of these dissidents gravitated, the Alliance of Free Democrats, would yield to that variant of liberalism which stressed "civil society" and the necessity of opening up even more fully to the market and strengthening private property. To my way of thinking, such an emulation of Thatcher and Reagan was likely to increase inequalities enormously and undo the very significant achievements of the later socialist period, not least in the rural sector. I was therefore more sympathetic to the other oppositionist grouping of the transition years, which emphasized not Western-style free markets but rather the softer variants of Magyar populist nationalism. The Hungarian Democratic Forum won the first free elections in 1990 and dominated the government until 1994, when the ex-communists (now known as the Hungarian Socialist Party) returned to power. In-fighting and incompetence weakened the Forum in much the same way that the Independent Smallholders' Party self-destructed, eventually allowing Viktor Orbán to supplant them by shifting the focus of his own party, previously positioned at the liberal (even libertarian) end of the spectrum, towards increasingly nationalist, conservative agendas.

The resort to cultural nationalism in times of economic decline and multi-dimensional "dispossession" (Creed 2011; Kalb and Halmai 2011) is by no means limited to Hungary. It is found in both town and countryside (the examples explored in Kalb and Halmai 2011 are primarily urban workers). But I argue that it acquires particular force in predominantly rural regions such as the interfluve, where the roots of agrarian populism were nourished in subterranean fashion during the socialist period and where the decline from socialist prosperity to capitalist marginality has been particularly sharp (Hann 2015a). The new populist messages are disseminated in many media, from Duna television to revisionist school textbooks. Many Western critics have condemned Orbán's efforts since 2010 to muzzle judges and journalists. It is impossible to overlook the increased salience of national rituals and symbolism. The interfluve contains two of the major heritage sites cultivated to reinforce national identity through school visiting parties and tourism. One is the National Historical Memorial Park at Ópusztaszer, noted above, where demonstrations of horsemanship complement nostalgic reconstructions of pre-industrial peasant communities and the patriotism that was interrupted by socialism.[2] The other is the *puszta* of Bugac, south of Kecskemét, another major site for enacting Hungary's shamanic traditions and the ethnic traits which render the Magyars so different from all their neighbours (Kürti 2015).

It follows from this summary analysis that contemporary Hungary is far from the model of Hayekian market economy that was my worry 25 years ago (Hann 1990). Fidesz governments since 2010 have not hesitated to intervene in the economy whenever it suits their political purposes. Land and enterprises have been re-nationalized for political reasons. The massive expansion of Workfare schemes (launched rather cautiously by the preceding socialist government) distorts labour markets in ways that Hayek would certainly not have endorsed. Some anthropologists have theorized such schemes as the disciplinary or punitive side of neoliberalism (Wacquant 2012). Such analyses may have much to commend them in urban settings, but in the countryside, there is a lot of support for these initiatives. In Tázlár, the opportunity to work for the locality in this way is greatly preferred to dependence on day-labour, even if Workfare income comes out significantly lower when calculated on a daily basis. The problems start when there are not enough slots available for all those who would like to take advantage, and the Mayor's discretionary power comes into play. It is the same at higher levels, with government concessions or bank credits dependent on who one knows in Fidesz and allied groupings. The cronyism extends to Orbán's own family and entourage. A new generation of dissidents (including a few survivors of the socialist oppositional movement) have compared the present postsocialist state to that of President Putin's Russia and theorized it in terms of "mafia" (Magyar 2016).

Some of the features commonly bundled under the term neoliberalism can, of course, be found in Hungary today. There are elective affinities between national conservatism, an interventionist state, and the cultivation of neoliberal values such as personal responsibility and more individualist forms of "self-making" (see Harmes 2012). In Hungary, as elsewhere in postsocialist Eastern Europe, banks have greatly increased their profile in the course of expanding "everyday financialization". Yet when tens of thousands of Hungarians found themselves with negative equity following the surge of the Swiss Franc in which they had taken out their mortgages, the government intervened to negotiate compromise solutions. This particular reaction followed agitated campaigns by irate citizens. It is tempting to label them "overheated" but overall this metaphor seems less appropriate in the economic dimension today than it was in the 1970s and 1980s, when there was no unemployment, and when many people worked long hours outside their jobs because they had market-like incentives to do so, while still managing to socialize more intensively with wider circles of friends than is common in the more stratified society of today. The inhabitants of the Danube-Tisza interfluve, peasant underdogs in the pre-socialist era, were exceptional under socialism in the sense that many of them managed to avoid full incorporation into the new labour hierarchies. They prospered privately as a result of an "overheating" built on self-exploitation. Today, however, they are again underdogs in the wider configurations of global capitalism, and they have a consciousness of having lost ground in the national context. In this context, it is hardly surprising that many have become overheated in a different dimension, that of identity. As in the past, when things are not going well in the domains of politics and economics, the tendency to turn to the dimension of identity and to blame perceived enemies within (Jews and Roma) as well as without (nowadays primarily Brussels) is hard to resist.

Closing Down: Reactions to the Migrant Crisis of 2015

In the summer of 2015, Hungarians found a new "other" to blame for their relative deprivation in the form of large streams of migrants making their way through the country on their way to Germany or Sweden. Viktor Orbán was in the news for weeks on end, competing with the German Chancellor Angela Merkel for the mantle of "defender of Christian European values".[3] By coincidence, my regular late summer visit to Tázlár coincided with dramatic scenes at the Hungarian-Serbian border (particularly at the crossing of Röszke, near Szeged) and at the Keleti station in Budapest (Hann 2015c). The topic dominated the media throughout Europe and I found it instructive to compare foreign coverage with what I could read and hear inside Hungary. In the village (population nowadays around 1750) and in the nearby town of Kiskunhalas (population around 30,000), the great majority was highly critical of the stream of *migránsok* (this was the term generally used, rather than *menekültek*, refugees). The proximity of the frontier somehow brought the matter close to home. No migrants were visible in the village or the town, but everyone knew that several hundred were temporarily accommodated in a disused barracks just outside Kiskunhalas. It was asserted that taxis carrying the foreigners northwards to Budapest regularly used the minor roads of the Danube-Tisza interfluve in order to avoid police controls on the major highways, passing through villages such as Tázlár at the dead of night. The taxi drivers were thereby committing a criminal offence, but for many villagers, the migrants themselves were also tantamount to criminals, since they had entered the country illegally. They were certainly not wanted in Hungary. Viktor Orbán's construction of a fence to keep them out met with general approval. The general view was that a country that was exporting so much labour to more prosperous members of the European Union had no obligation to provide any help at all for new immigrants from the East.

In private conversations, a few villagers took a more generous line towards the refugees, suggesting that they deserved help rather than the scornful rejection which appeared to be driving the government's response. I think that, in some cases, this more tolerant opinion might well have been articulated because they knew I live in Germany and suspected that I would sympathize with Western criticisms of Viktor Orbán's nationalist rhetoric and fence construction. Negative Western reporting is a constant cause for complaint in much of the Hungarian media. I had no opportunity to conduct systematic surveys but I had the impression that unorthodox opinions on the *migránsok* were more likely to be voiced by persons who belonged to a minority of some sort, for example, the Lutheran religious minority, or the dwindling minority of villagers who had formerly sympathized with the Hungarian Socialist Workers' Party.

Of course, all human beings belong to minorities of one sort or another. Most of the contemporary population of Tázlár can trace their descent to the migrants who built their scattered farmsteads (*tanyák*) a century ago. Many had *sváb* (German) or *tóth* (Slovak) family names and these languages were still spoken here in the first half of the twentieth century. Only in a final massive wave of Magyarization during the Second World War did almost all of these families adopt Hungarian-sounding surnames (this was not enough to save many individuals from deportation and death in Siberia following the victory of the Red Army). In the socialist decades, when the nuclear centre grew dramatically and hundreds of isolated *tanyák* were abandoned, Tázlár became a modern Hungarian village. After the change of regime, there was a modest revival of interest in ethnic minorities in neighbouring settlements, which cultivated links with Slovakia and both Eastern and Western Germany, but Tázlár is nowadays an exclusively Hungarian settlement. Children do, of course, learn when they are still very young that the Magyars are themselves migrants who arrived gloriously in their present homeland in the Carpathian Basin little more than 1000 years ago. But they are not brought up to pay any heed to later migration histories or to the non-Magyar origins of a high proportion of local inhabitants. Even the few Roma households of the village communicate only in Hungarian. Neighbouring Kiskunhalas has a much larger Roma population, which the Hungarian majority of the town was prone to invoke when discussing the *migránsok*: "if there is still so much to be done in terms of integrating these fellow-citizens, how can we be expected to accept Muslim foreigners?" Viktor Orbán has himself made this point in arguing against EU proposals to impose a mandatory quota on all member states. His approval ratings in the opinion polls increased significantly as a result of his handling of the crisis in 2015. Orbán may be a pariah in the liberal West, but his aggressive posturing on behalf of the civilization of Christian Europe goes down well at home, especially in the countryside.

Conclusion

Hungary is an instructive setting in which to examine the post-Cold War world from the "overheating perspective". I have argued that the more familiar patterns of "acceleration" and "overheating" identified by Eriksen (this Special Issue) have only limited relevance here. The international mobility of labour and capital has increased since 1991, but the asymmetries of migration and direct foreign investment reflect the country's new peripheral status within a civilization with its centre to the West. In some respects, the present marginality is a return to that of the pre-socialist era rather than a "shift to a higher gear". The main cause of contemporary rural overheating in the dimension of "identity" is the collapse of the socialist civilization which enabled poor peasants to transform their collective infrastructure and narrow the gap separating them from urban elites. Peasants such as those who settled the *tanya* world of the Danube-Tisza interfluve in the late nineteenth century came to internalize expectations of further improvement, but these were shattered in the 1990s. The dissolution of collective farms and the privatization of their assets, including the land itself, brought wealth to a few. But for the majority, it brought uncertainty and, if not absolute impoverishment, then a stagnation and vegetation that contrasted with the forward-looking trajectories of socialist days. The disillusionment is strongest in the rural sector because, relatively, this sector was the biggest winner in the Hungarian variant of socialism; so the fall from grace is greater. But inequalities have widened within the urban as well as within the rural population. They have also widened between regions (with eastern and northern districts losing out most completely and the interfluve roughly in the middle in this respect). The ensuing tensions create fertile terrain for politicians adept at playing the nationalist card. The anti-*migráns* rhetoric of 2015 is a continuation of the trends which have seen internal minorities stigmatized (that is Roma and Jews) and Brussels pilloried for every action or statement that is not in keeping with the actions and statements of the true guardians of European values by the Danube.

Hungary is not alone in this regard. It was the most visible scapegoat for the obscenities of summer 2015, but it is well known that public opinion in Slovakia, the Czech Republic and Poland is roughly congruent with opinion in Hungary. This is not surprising. When German Chancellor Angela Merkel decided that Syrian refugees would be welcome in Germany, but then very soon afterwards began to insist on quotas to distribute the influx throughout the European Union, one does not have to be a strident nationalist to feel that one's country is being treated in a high-handed manner. Many Western commentators have criticized Eastern Europeans who do not understand what it means to belong to a solidary community such as the European Union. If Hungarian farmers benefit from the subsidies distributed by Brussels agricultural policies (so the argument goes), then they must also be ready to share the costs of accommodating refugees. Eastern Europeans might have had multi-cultural empires in the distant past, but they morphed into selfish nation-states under socialism and are now accused of a "compassion deficit".

Criticisms of this kind are echoed within the countries of the Visegrád Group by liberal elites in the capitals who deplore the growing xenophobia of the masses. It is true that some villagers in places like Tázlár utter the most shameful things about *migránsok* (and repeat them in the social media). They have never encountered a *migráns* in their lives. I know them as decent people, caring parents and helpful neighbours, not crypto-Fascists. Hannah Arendt might not be convinced, but those who rush to condemn Eastern Europeans as backward and reactionary should bear at least three points in mind. First, during and even after the decades of socialism, most East Europeans (even those in the larger cities; in fact everywhere outside the capital) had little opportunity to encounter foreigners. This ignorance is no excuse for outrageous posturing of the kind that is common today, but it is well established that fear and negative stereotypes are seldom broken down until there is more concrete interaction with the groups in question. The second factor is the unambiguous evidence of increased poverty in rural society. Finally, in the context of economic decline it is important to note the new westwards migration of Hungarians themselves, especially since EU accession opened up western labour markets. Millions of Eastern European families now have one or more members working abroad (most often young people, most often in Britain). Given this background, is it surprising that the sight of millions of non-EU citizens being given assisted passage to enter the region's most prosperous country gives rise to anger and resentment? It is rather hard to learn German or English in Hungary to a level at which one could enter a prestigious segment of those foreign labour markets. Most Hungarian emigrants, including well-qualified college graduates, therefore end up in hotels and catering, or in some form of care work. Perhaps some of these mobile Hungarians will, following their experiences abroad, become more sympathetic to the region's new *migránsok* than their parents. But for many, both those who stay and those who leave, the dearth of opportunities within Hungary itself is the proof that the EU has failed, that their country, and in particular the large rural sector, is back in the "underdog position" from which it ephemerally escaped thanks to the socialist economic synthesis.

In some circles (at least in Western academia) it has become politically incorrect to make any distinction between those fleeing oppression and those migrating in the hope of improving their lives (and the lives of family members, who they hope will join them in due course). It is obvious that the categories and sub-categories are fluid. All of the victims and losers of unequal global forces deserve the sympathy of rich Europeans. Hungarians are undeniably prosperous compared with many, perhaps most, of those on the migration trail to Western Europe in 2015. But cosmopolitan liberal elites need to understand the realities of relative deprivation in their own backyards. They need also to recognize that the complete abolition of border controls (the logical recommendation of those who despair of drawing any distinction between economic migrants and those with an immediately compelling case for humanitarian support) is good for business, because it drives down the price of labour and boosts the rate of profit. There are some unlikely coincidences in some countries, including Germany, between the demands made by human rights activists and the recommendations of employers' lobby groups. But this response to some of the most conspicuous symptoms of contemporary "overheating" is hardly compatible with social democracy and the kinds of solidary community that European states – both in the West and in the East – have created over generations to domesticate international capital.

Notes

1. Shanin (1987, 3–4). The author specifies as an additional general characteristic "specific cultural patterns linked to the way of life of a small rural community" (Shanin 1987). He has in mind the social controls exercised in a nuclear settlement. Scattered resettlement of the *puszta* obviously produced conditions very different from those found in traditional villages; but immigrants brought their normative and "cognitive" dispositions with them and Shanin's general type retains its basic validity for the colonists of the interfluve in the pre-socialist generations.

2. Ironically, this Park was initiated in the socialist era, the brainchild of leftist populist Ferenc Erdei (see Hann 2015b).
3. Orbán regularly gives interviews to the mass media in Germany, well aware that his views concerning migrants and Christian Europe command widespread support in German society. In one particularly inflammatory contribution at the height of the crisis he spoke of civilizational competition and alleged that, unless corrective action was taken, Muslims would threaten the *kulturelle Identität* of Europe. See "Am Ende werden die Muslime mehr sein als wir", *Die Welt*, 16th September 2015 (interview with Boris Kálnoky).

Disclosure statement

No potential conflict of interest was reported by the author.

Funding

This paper represents the confluence of two research projects supported by the European Research Council [Grant No. 295843] (Overheating, directed by Thomas Hylland Eriksen) and [Grant No 340854] (Realeurasia, directed by Chris Hann).

References

Arnason, Johann P. 2003. *Civilizations in Dispute: Historical Questions and Theoretical Traditions*. Leiden: Brill.
Creed, Gerald W. 2011. *Masquerade and Postsocialism. Ritual and Cultural Dispossession in Bulgaria*. Bloomington: Indiana University Press.
Den Hollander, Arie. 1960–1961. "The Great Hungarian Plain: A European Frontier Area." *Comparative Studies in Society and History* 3: 74–88, 155–169.
Geertz, Clifford. 1963. *Agricultural Involution: The Process of Ecological Change in Indonesia*. Berkeley: University of California Press.
Hann, Chris. 1980. *Tázlár. A Village in Hungary*. Cambridge: Cambridge University Press.
Hann, Chris. 1990. "Second Economy and Civil Society." *Journal of Communist Studies* 6 (2): 21–44.
Hann, Chris. 1993. "Property Relations in the New Eastern Europe: The Case of Specialist Cooperatives in Hungary." In *The Curtain Rises: Rethinking Culture, Ideology and the State in Eastern Europe*, edited by Minka Desoto, and David G. Anderson, 99–119. New York: Humanities Press.
Hann, Chris. 2014. "The Economistic Fallacy and Forms of Integration During and After Socialism." *Economy and Society* 43 (4): 626–649. doi:10.1080/03085147.2014.898824.
Hann, Chris. 2015a. "Backwardness Revisited: Time, Space and Civilization in Rural Eastern Europe." *Comparative Studies in Society and History* 57 (4): 881–911. doi:10.1017/S0010417515000389
Hann, Chris. 2015b. "Why Postimperial Trumps Postsocialist: Crying Back the National Past in Hungary." In *Anthropology and Nostalgia. Ethnographic Studies*, edited by Olivia Angé, and David Berliner, 96–122. New York: Berghahn.
Hann, Chris. 2015c. "The New *Völkerwanderungen*: Hungary and Germany, Europe and Eurasia." *FocaalBlog*. Accessed September 11. http://www.focaalblog.com/2015/09/11/chris-hann-the-new-volkerwanderungen-hungary-and-germany-europe-and-eurasia/.
Hann, Chris, and László Kürti. 2015. "Agrarian Ideology and Local Governance: Continuities in Postsocialist Hungary." In *Rytíř z Komárova—K 70. narozeninám Petra Skalníka* [Knight from Komárov—To Petr Skalník for his 70th Birthday], edited by Adam Bedřich, and Tomáš Retka, 83–106. Praha: AntropoWeb.
Harmes, Adam. 2012. "The Rise of Neoliberal Nationalism." *Review of International Political Economy* 19 (1): 59–86.
Kalb, Don, and Gábor Halmai, eds. 2011. *Headlines of Nation Subtexts of Class: Working-Class Populism and the Return of the Repressed in Neoliberal Europe*. New York: Berghahn.

Keller, Judit, Katalin Kovács, Katalin Rácz, Nigel Swain, and Monika Váradi. Forthcoming. "Workfare Schemes as a Tool for Preventing the Further Impoverishment of the Rural Poor." *Eastern European Countryside* 22.
Kürti, László. 2015. "Neoshamanism, National Identity and the Holy Crown of Hungary." *Journal of Religion in Europe* 8: 1–26.
Magyar, Bálint. 2016. *Post-Communist Mafia State. The Hungarian Case.* Budapest: Central European University Press & Noran Libro.
Schlanger, Nathan, ed. 2006. *Techniques, Technology and Civilisation/Marcel Mauss.* New York: Berghahn.
Shanin, Teodor. 1987. "Introduction: Peasantry as a Concept." In *Peasants and Peasant Societies*, edited by Teodor Shanin, 2nd ed., 1–11. Oxford: Blackwell.
Swain, Nigel. 1985. *Collective Farms Which Work?* Cambridge: Cambridge University Press.
Swain, Nigel. 1993. *Hungary: The Rise and Fall of Feasible Socialism.* London: Verso.
Swain, Nigel. 2011. "A Post-Socialist Capitalism." *Europe-Asia Studies* 63 (9): 1671–1695.
Vidacs, Bea. 2015. "From Pig-Sticking to Festival: Changes in Pig-Sticking Practices in the Hungarian Countryside." In *Economy and Ritual: Studies of Postsocialist Transformations*, 79–106. New York: Berghahn.
Wacquant, Loïc. 2012. "Three Steps to a Historical Anthropology of Actually Existing Neoliberalism." *Social Anthropology* 20 (1): 66–79.

Index

Note: **Boldface** page numbers refer to figures, page numbers followed by "n" denote endnotes.

accelerated growth 6–8
"Agenda for Prosperity: the road to a middle-income country" 39
"agrarian developmentalism" 108
Alliance of Young Democrats (Fidesz) 141
"alterglobalization movement" 4
Angé, Olivia 22
Anglo-Saxon political principles 23
Angostura Dam 101, 102, 113
Angostura-Siguas consortium 102, 110
anthropological research 10–12
Arendt, Hannah 145
Are there Social Groups in the New Guinea Highlands? (Wagner) 118
Argonauts of the Western Pacific (Malinowski) 10
Aston, Guy 96–7
"asylum shopping" 75
AUTODEMA 105, 111, 113

Barclays Bank 126–8
Bear, Laura 63
Belaúnde Terry, Fernando 108
Bendixsen, Synnøve 16
Berliner, David 22
Bermúdez, Morales 108
"blind pool transactions" 127
"borderless world" 69, 81
Borderless World, The (Ohmae) 81
boundaries, destabilization and restabilization of 16; *see also* European border policies
Bourdieu, Pierre 61–2
Broughton, Martin 124, 125

Cabatit, Reynato An 24
Carson, Rachel 13
Castells, Manuel 4
CEAS *see* Common European Asylum System
Checkpoint Charlie 69
Chilean Water Code 110
Chinese Labour in a Korean factory (Kim) 33n14
Clark Air Base 24, 25, 33
clashing scales 13–15
Coalfield Communities Campaign 89
Common European Asylum System (CEAS) 72, 75
Common Security and Defence Policy 74
Company, The (Micklethwait and Wooldridge) 117
Congo, mining coltan ore 56
Cooper, Elizabeth 32
crossing of state borders 73–6
"culture of fear" 5

Danube-Tisza interfluve 135; civilizational encounters and migrations 135–9; collapse and migration westwards 139–41; "migrant crisis" of 2015 143–4
DELCO *see* Sierra Leone Development Company
disenchantment and modernity 9–10
Dodd Frank Wall Street Reform Act 128–9
Doncaster 88, 98–9; coal and mining industry 88–9; cosmopolitan, discontents of 94–6; council campaign 93; museum exhibition 93; neoliberal policy agenda 89; nostalgia and social reconnection 91–2; precarization of labour 90–1; tourism strategy 93–4; United Kingdom Independence Party *see* United Kingdom Independence Party
Doncopolitan 94–5
Draper, Warren 94
Dublin Convention (1990) 75–6, 83n16

EDCA *see* Enhanced Defense Cooperation Agreement
EEC *see* European Economic Community
el Monumento al Colono 107
Emergency Coordination Committee 103

149

INDEX

Enhanced Defense Cooperation Agreement (EDCA) 26–7
Epstein, A.L. 130
Erdei, Ferenc 139
Eriksen, Thomas Hylland 135
Essay on the Principle of Population (Malthus) 8
Estonian oil shale mine 53–4, 64; accident rate in 65n1; cyclical time of production 60–1; health and safety rules 63; labour in 60; machines and men 57–8; national and regional time 56–7; *novaia tekhnika* (new technology) 58–60; production process and pay system 61; time–space compression 54–5; time wage 62
ethnographic method, strengths and limitations of 12–13
European border policies 6, 69; borders vs. boundaries, conceptualization of 71, 73, 82; Common European Asylum System 72; "compensatory measures" 72; Dublin regulations and 75–6, 83n16; EURODAC registration system 72; Europeanization, Norway's role in 72; "illegality industry" 70; regionalization process 71; Schengen Agreement 69, 71–2, 83n7; temporal and spatial experience 70
European Economic Community (EEC) 108
"Ever-Changing Face of Doncaster, The" 93
Expectations of Modernity (Ferguson) 42

Farage, Nigel 96, 97
"Farewell Brodsworth Pit" (Gray) 88, 89
First Estonian Republic 56, 57
fixed social groups 122
Free Trade Agreement 110
Friedman, Milton 108
Fujimori, Alberto 109–10
"Fuji-shock" 104, 109
Furedi, Frank 5

García, Alan 110
Gazelle Peninsula of East New Britain Province 122
Geertz, Clifford 10
Gillett, George 123, 124
globalization, contradictions of 2–5
Gloria Group 110–11
Goody, Jack 9
Gordon, Richard 26
Gray, Brian 88, 89
Gray, John 6
growth pole, notion of 38–9
Growth Poles programme, in Sierra Leone 38

Hann, Chris 15
Hatfield Colliery 90
Helmer, Roger 87, 97–8
Hicks, Tom 123, 124, 126

Holmes, Douglas 96
Humala, Ollanta 103, 111
Hungary: agricultural production 137–9; Hungarian Democratic Forum 142; Hungarian Socialist Workers' Party 139, 141; impact of capitalism 137; "internal frontier" 136; market socialism 137, 139; National Historical Memorial Park 142; "overheating" phenomenon 135, 139, 143; Treaty of Trianon (1920) 137; workfare schemes 140, 142

ILGs *see* incorporated land groups
"imagined communities" 119
incorporated land groups (ILGs) 121, 129
Independent Smallholders' Party 141, 142
Information Society, The (Castells) 4
International Organization for Migration (IOM) 79

Jinkyung, Lee 27
Juntas de Usuarios 109

"Keeping the lights on" report 98
Kesküla, Eeva 15
Kim, Jaesok 33n14
Kop Investment LLC 123–6
Kwon, Heonik 4, 23, 31, 32n7

Le Pen, Marine 96
Lévi-Strauss, Claude 9
Liverpool football club (LFC) 123–6, **125**
Liverpool Football Club and Athletic Ground 124
"London Interbank Offered Rate" 131n3
London Mining, re-opening of iron ore mines *see* Marampa Chiefdom, Sierra Leone
Lovelock, James 8

Majes-Siguas Irrigation Project 101–4, 114; debt, loss and vulnerability 108–12; expectations of growth and modernity 104–6; "extractivism" 102; hard work and sacrifice 106–8; struggles for land rights and water justice 112–13
Making of Olongapo, The (Cabatit) 24
Malinowski, Bronislaw 10
Malthus, Thomas 8
Marampa Chiefdom, Sierra Leone 36–8; 'Agenda for Change' 39; expectations of change 39–43; financial compensation 46–7; growth pole, notion of 38–9; inside/outside of concession 43–4; Lunsar 39, 45; mining operations and workforces 45–6; 'overheating' 47–9; period of darkness 40; re-opening of iron ore mines 38, 39; Sierra Leone Development Company 38, 41; spatial and social divisions of change 43–7; time and temporality 41–2

INDEX

Martínez, Nelson 111
McArthur, Douglas 32n8
"Melanesian heavy industry" 121
"Men, Stone and Machines" (Pärtel) 62
Mercedes car factory 140
Merkel, Angela 143
"migrant crisis" of 2015 143–4
Miliband, Ed 97
monoline insurance company 131n5
Moores, David 123

National Historical Memorial Park, Ópusztaszer 142
natural disasters 25, 33n11
"new dangerous class" 6
New Economic Mechanism (1968) 138
New England Sports Ventures 125–6
New Guinea highlands, social groups in 121–3
Norway: asylum policy 76–9, 83n17; in Europeanization 72; return agreements 80–1
novaia tekhnika (new technology) 58–60

Ohmae, Kenichi 81
Orbán, Viktor 141–4, 147n3
Ostrom, Elinor 8
Other Cold War, The (Kwon) 4, 32n7

Papua New Guinea (PNG): customary land 122; social groups in 121–3; Tolai people 130, 131
Pärtel, Aksel 58, 62
Paulino, Mayor Rolen 20
People Power Revolution 25
Peru, Majes Irrigation Project *see* Majes-Siguas Irrigation Project
Philippines: economic growth 23; US colonial rule 23, 31; Visiting Forces Agreement 26
Pijpers, Robert 15
post-Cold War world 4, 15, 16, 71–3
Poverty Reduction Strategy Papers (PRSPs) 39, 49n4
Protium Hedge Fund 126–8
PRSPs *see* Poverty Reduction Strategy Papers

Reseña histórica del Distrito de Majes (Zamalloa) 104
Revenge of Gaia (Lovelock) 8
Ringel, Felix 61–2
"Rio Tinto Zinc" 119
Rolling Stone Magazine 21
Romány, Pál 139
Rushdie, Salman 6

Sahlins, Marshall 10
Sao Tome and Principe 42, 55
Sarkozy, Nicolas 9
Satanic Verses, The (Rushdie) 6
scalar clashes 13–15

Schengen Agreement 69, 71–2, 83n7
Schober, Elisabeth 15
Sex Among Allies (Moon) 24
Shanin, Teodor 136, 146n1
"shock therapy" 56
Sierra Leone: Marampa Chiefdom *see* Marampa Chiefdom, Sierra Leone; political administration 49n2; surface rights 49n7; unemployment 50n10
Sierra Leone Development Company (DELCO) 38, 41
SIV 128–9, 131n7
social groups: *Are there Social Groups in the New Guinea Highlands?* (Wagner) 118; elicitations 120, 130; fixed 122; fuzziness of 122–3; limits and boundaries of 131; in Melanesia 118, 119; in New Guinea highlands 121–3; time-discipline, Thompson's version of 120; Wagner's description 118–19; in Western world 119–21
"socialist civilization" 137
Soros, George 6
South Korea: 'capitalism of barracks' 27–8; submilitarism in Vietnam 27
Spanish–American War (1898) 24
"Special Agricultural and Business Leases" 122
Special Economic Zone 26
"specialist cooperative" 137
Standing, Guy 6
Stensrud, Astrid 16
Stiglitz, Joseph 6
Story, Tony 94
Subic Bay Freeport Zone 22, 26, 29
Subic Bay, US naval base in 15; nostalgia in 22–3, 28–30; "overheated" economic in 20–3; and US Navy 23–5; "We rose from the ashes of Mt. Pinatubo" 30–1
Sutton, Charles W. 105
Syrian refugee crisis 68–70; asylum seeking in Norway 76–9, 83n17; crossing nation-state borders 73–6; European border policies 71–3; return to Afghanistan 79–81; voluntary return programme 83n19

Taft, William Howard 23
"*tanya* world" 136
tekhnika besopasnosti 63
Thompson, E. P. 60
Thorleifsson, Cathrine 15
time-discipline, notion of 120
Tolai people, in Papua New Guinea 130, 131
Treaty of Trianon (1920) 137
Tristes Tropiques (Lévi-Strauss) 9
Trump, Donald 96
turguvuai 130

INDEX

"ubiquity of borders" 69
United Kingdom Independence Party (Ukip) 87, 95, 96–8
Urry, John 4
US Armed Forces 26, 27
"U.S. military-industrial complex" 31

Vásquez, Absalón 109–10
Velasco Alvarado, Juan 105, 106
Vietnam War 21, 27

Visiting Forces Agreement 26
voluntary return programme 83n19
vunatarai 130

Wagner, R. 118–22, 131n1
"Water for everyone" 110
Western world, social groups in 119–21
World Bank's Growth Poles programme 38

Zamalloa, Edgar 104, 107